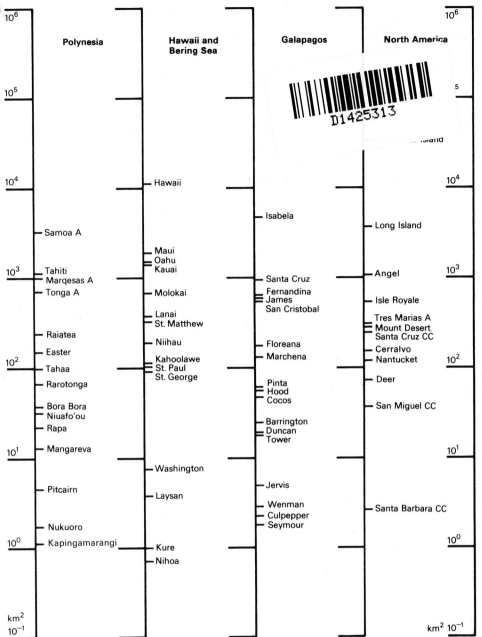

while Jersey and Herm are the largest and smallest Channel Islands. Other islands in these two archipelagos are not shown. The North American set includes three from the California Channel Islands, marked CC. The six main islands range in size from Santa Cruz to San Miguel, Santa Barbara being the smallest individual island. In the British and French set, two inland areas discussed in Chapter 5, Eastern Wood of Bookham Common and the Cockermouth area studied for geological types, are included for reference.

Island populations

Island
populations

MARK WILLIAMSON

OXFORD UNIVERSITY PRESS

Oxford University Press, Walton Street, Oxford, OX2 6DP

OXFORD LONDON GLASGOW
NEW YORK TORONTO MELBOURNE AUCKLAND
KUALA LUMPUR SINGAPORE HONG KONG TOKYO
DELHI BOMBAY CALCUTTA MADRAS KARACHI
NAIROBI DAR ES SALAAM CAPE TOWN
and associated companies in
BEIRUT BERLIN IBADAN MEXICO CITY NICOSIA

OXFORD is a trade mark of Oxford University Press

British Library Cataloguing in Publication Data

Williamson, Mark Herbert
  Island populations.
  1. Island ecology
  I. Title
  574.5'0914'2   QH541.5.18   80-41507

ISBN 0-19-854139-2

First published 1981
First issued in paperback 1983

Set by Western Printing Services Ltd.
Printed in Hong Kong

Preface

Islands and island life have fascinated biologists for a long time. Part of the interest of islands is the light they shed on the process of evolution. The importance of the fauna of the Galapagos Islands in forming Darwin's views is well known. To Wallace the theory of evolution by natural selection came as a sudden idea while he was on the island of Ternate (in Indonesia) and he went on to publish *Island life or the phenomena and causes of insular faunas and floras including a revision and attempted solution to the problem of geological climates* in 1880. So the study of islands has been important right from the start of the study of evolution and natural selection.

Islands are also important to ecologists. The delimitation of the area, and the restriction of the numbers of species found on islands, should make some ecological problems more tractable than on mainlands. In the last decade, the relevance of islands to the study of the composition and variability of ecological communities has been widely appreciated. The islands studied have been not only islands in the sea, but also islands in inland waters, and island-like habitats such as mountain tops, lakes, and even patches of vegetation, and individual plants.

The origin of this book lies in a series of lectures given to undergraduates in which I discussed island biota in order to give, reasonably succinctly, some indications of the interplay between evolution and ecology. A very great deal has been published on this, but rather little of it is readily accessible either to students in universities, or to scientifically-inclined amateur naturalists. Both groups will, I hope, find topics here of interest to them and relevant to their own particular specialist interests. This book can be no more than an introduction, but I hope a reasonably balanced one, to modern studies of island biota. Many recent ecological studies have arisen from MacArthur and Wilson's *The theory of island biogeography*. Their theory has led to some surprisingly bitter arguments, and so in this book I have tried to give an account of that dispute, and of the strengths and weaknesses of MacArthur and Wilson's theory.

The main reason, though, both for giving the lectures, and for expanding them into this book, is that I find islands fascinating and fun, and the study of their flora and fauna a never-ending source of delight.

The book is divided into four sections. The first section sets the scene.

All studies of natural populations require some knowledge of sciences besides biology: of geology, geography, and climatology. I have tried to include enough of these to make the rest of the book intelligible, but not to distract from its prime purpose of being a biological book. The biological background also finds a place in the first section. The second section deals with basic facts and theories of the number of species on islands. This number is a major variable in the comparison of islands, and an understanding of how it varies is essential for all the succeeding topics. Evolution is the theme of the third section, from microevolutionary changes up to speciation. The fourth section indicates what we know about the structure of island communities, and considers the ecological processes involved and their relation to the evolutionary processes considered before. Work on this aspect of island biota is only starting to come together to make a coherent story, but there is no doubt that the study of island communities will be important in our understanding of the structure of other communities.

York M.H.W.
January 1980

Acknowledgements

In preparing this book I have been helped by very many people, who have been generous with their advice, comment, and information. John Currey, Ed Connor, Andy Higgs, and Charlotte Williamson read all of the book; Alastair Fitter, John Lawton, and Michael Usher parts of it. I have tried to take their advice, but they are in no way responsible for the faults that remain. Fran James, Ian Galbraith, Raymond O'Connor, and Geoff Oxford have been generous with information; Malc Storey helpfully supplied some computer-drawn maps; and Hugh and Sophia Williamson helped with the bibliography. Margaret Britton, Linda Partridge, Lorna Skiera, and Emma Williamson have all helped. Isobel Devane typed almost all the book; Sue Sparrow drew almost all the figures. To all of these I am most grateful, and to the many others with whom I have discussed points.

I am grateful for permission to reproduce diagrams and figures: to the editors of *Evolution* for Fig. 7.4; to Dr W. Junk B.V. Publishers for Figs. 2.6 and 3.2; and to the University Press of Hawaii for Fig. 8.1.

April 1982: The preparation of a paperback edition has allowed some minor points to be corrected. I am grateful to Dr Hampton Carson and Mr Richard Rafe for their comments.

Contents

PART 1

Background

1 Geophysical and biogeographical patterns

The properties of the populations of plants and animals on islands depend to a large extent on the nature and history of the islands on which they are found. So as a preliminary to considering populations, this chapter deals with the major geological processes that are now known to affect the earth's surface, and the results of these processes both in the types and variety of island that exist and in the major distributional patterns of life on earth. Geophysical processes move land both horizontally and vertically, and affect the climate and sea level: some understanding of these is necessary for the understanding of the biological processes on islands, and for understanding the distribution of biota on the continental masses, which are the sources from which islands have been colonized.

Most of the island populations which will be discussed in this book occur on islands in the sea: hence the emphasis on geological processes producing and affecting such islands. Populations that can be treated as insular also occur on islands in lakes, or, inverting land and water, lake populations themselves can be regarded as insular. Sometimes populations in reasonably well-isolated habitats, isolated mountain ranges, for example, can also be treated as island populations. The biological principles and processes affecting these island populations on non-marine islands are much the same as those for marine islands.

Geology and geological history of islands

Plate tectonics

It is only during the last decade or so that it has become clear that the major surface features of the earth result from the processes of plate tectonics: the movements of large slabs of the earth's surface relative to one another. At present the earth's surface is made up of half a dozen major plates, each larger than a continent, and at least as many smaller ones, more or less completely separated along mappable geological lines. The nature of the zone separating two plates depends on whether the plates are moving apart, moving towards each other, or moving past each other. There may be active movement in the zone, as down the mid-Atlantic, or movement may have ceased many millions of years ago, as in the Tasman Sea between Australia and New Zealand. These contact zones occur both under the oceans and under the continents, but in general are more easily studied and clearly delineated under the oceans. Figure 1.1 is a map of the major and some of the minor plates.

The plates themselves are made up typically of two parts: an oceanic part, in which the major rock is basalt, and a continental part, in which the major rock is granite, though some plates, such as the Pacific, Nazca, and Cocos plates, have no continental part. About two-thirds of the earth's surface is covered by basaltic, oceanic areas and the other third by the continental granitic areas. The granitic rocks are lighter, i.e. have a lower density, so that there are two major levels in relation to sea level found round the world. The basaltic parts of the plate lie mostly within 1000 metres of 4000 metres below sea level, while the average height of the granitic parts is only a few hundred metres above sea level. As a first-order generalization, islands on the oceanic parts of the plates may be termed oceanic, those on the other parts, continental.

The outer edges of the granitic part of a plate generally extend down to about 200 metres below sea level, this zone being known as the continental shelf. Then there is a very sharp transition zone, the continental slope, down to 2000 metres or more, to the abyssal plane, which is the basaltic part of the plate. The continental shelf in some parts of the world is very wide, with many islands. The British Isles are a good example, and Fig. 1.2 shows a cross-section across the British Isles from the deep Atlantic to the North Sea, showing the two major levels of the Eurasian plate.

Although the predominant parent rock of the continental parts of the plates is granite, the rocks found at the surface of the earth's plates are very varied. This is because the relative motion of the plates, both horizontally over the earth's surface and vertically in relation to sea level, during the hundreds of millions of years of the earth's history has resulted in a great variety of geological processes, and especially in the production of sedimentary rocks under the sea at various times. A great variety of sandstones, limestones, shales, and clays now found on dry land has been laid down under the sea, and those that persist essentially unchanged, though more or less folded, are known as sedimentary rocks. Thrusting through the sediments are the remains of volcanic eruptions and other violent acts: the igneous rocks. The events leading to igneous rocks change the sediments through which they thrust, forming metamorphic rocks.

Islands on the continental shelf reflect all these geological processes,

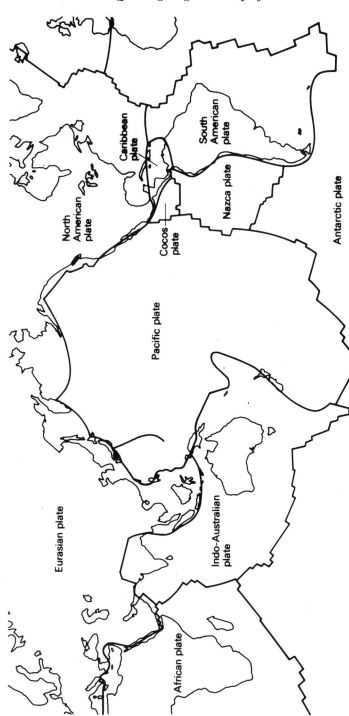

FIG. 1.1. A map showing the major tectonic plates and some minor ones.

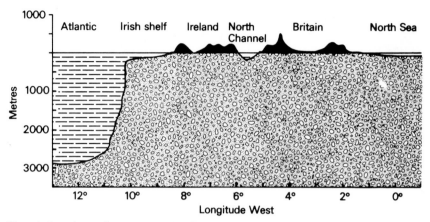

F IG. 1.2.   A section across the British Isles at 55° N. The section passes through Londonderry in Northern Ireland, Cairnsmore of Fleet in Scotland and Newcastle-upon-Tyne in England.

and so may be made up of sedimentary, metamorphic, or igneous rocks, or any combination of these. About the only generalization that can be made is that the geological structure of continental islands is usually similar to that of parts of the main continent near by.

Continental islands are usually easily recognizable from any map that shows the edge of the continental shelf. Most of the larger islands of the world such as Australia (an island continent), Java, Borneo, Ceylon, Britain, and Newfoundland are continental. Figure 1.3 shows a small island off Britain, Skokholm, which for some purposes can be treated as a typical small continental island. It is made of sedimentary sandstones, rocks which also occur four kilometres away on the neighbouring mainland.

In some places, the continental part of a plate may be found at depths of considerably more than 200 metres below sea level, and can be referred to as sunken continental shelf. Examples include the area round the California Channel Islands (Shepard 1977), various parts of the Arctic and Antarctic, and a large area in the south-west Pacific, including parts of the Coral and Tasman seas (Fig. 1.4) (Molnar, Atwater, Mammerickx, and Smith 1975; Raven and Axelrod 1972). Consequently, islands like Fiji and New Zealand, which because of their isolation and other features discussed below would be regarded as oceanic on biological grounds, in fact contain continental rocks. There are also minor fragments of continental plates with islands: an example is the Seychelles archipelago which, as small islands in the middle of the Indian Ocean, looks non-continental on a small-scale map. However, the islands are based on a minor fragment of continental plate

(Fig. 1.5) left stranded during the evolution of the present Indian Ocean, and the larger islands in the Seychelles have granitic rocks. The largest island in the group, Mahé, is a mere 145 km².

Types of oceanic islands

The size, shape, and rocks of continental islands reflect the processes of uplift and erosion which are the bases of the study of the geology of the major land masses. Oceanic islands formed in the deep, basaltic parts of the earth's plates are formed by a different set of processes, associated primarily with the relative movements of the plates.

At least three types of islands can be distinguished, resulting from different tectonic processes: these are oceanic ridge islands, hot-spot islands, and the islands of island arcs. The first two types are islands formed from volcanoes arising from the depths of the ocean floor, and so, when young, are of a simple conical form. Figure 1.6 shows Tristan da Cunha in the South Atlantic, 2060 metres high and less than a million years old. The other, older islands in the Tristan group are

F IG. 1.3.   An aerial photograph of a continental island, Skokholm, Wales. The strata of the sedimentary Old Red Sandstone can be seen. The cliffs at the lighthouse are about 55 m high (*Aerofilms Ltd.*).

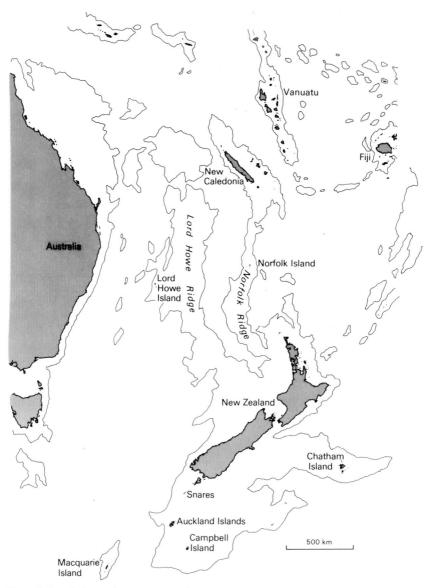

F IG. 1.4.   Submarine topography in the Tasman Sea area. Contour at
2000 m. The Norfolk and Lord Howe ridges, and the areas within the contour
east and south of New Zealand, are made largely of continental rocks.

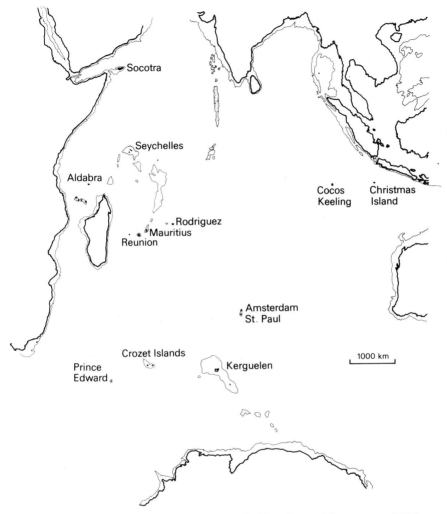

FIG. 1.5 Submarine topography in the Indian Ocean. Contour at 1000 m. The Seychelles bank and the nearby banks are made largely of continental rocks.

worn-down volcanoes and so are lower and more irregular in shape (see the map Fig. 2.3).

When two plates are moving apart, molten rocks well up from the interior of the earth and accrete at the edge of each plate. Some of this upwelling is violent, resulting in the formation of volcanoes which, if tall enough, rise through thousands of metres of sea to form islands. These volcanoes are added to one or other of the plates, and with the

Fɪɢ. 1.6.   A photograph of Tristan da Cunha, a volcanic, oceanic island. The peak is 2060 m and the settlement is on the low peninsula in the foreground.

formation of ever newer plate, the volcanic island is carried away from the contact zone. Consequently, old mid-ocean ridge islands may be found at considerable distances, hundreds of kilometres, away from the present plate boundary. Tristan da Cunha and other islands of the mid-Atlantic ridge are one example; the Galapagos, near the boundary of the Nazca and Cocos plates, are another.

Hot-spot islands are different in that they are formed in the middle of a plate, and not at the edge. The hypothesis is that there is a fixed hot-spot in the depths of the earth which gives rise to a linear series of volcanic islands as the plate moves across it. The Hawaiian islands were the first and are still the best example known. The present chain of islands seems to have been formed by the steady movement of the Pacific plate in one direction for the last forty million years. Before that the plate appeared to have moved linearly, but in a different direction, and that phase has left behind the Emperor Seamounts, strung out from the edge of the Hawaiian chain up to Kamchatka (Fig. 1.7). Many other islands in the middle of the Pacific occur in more or less linear groups (Clague and Jarrard 1973) and could have been formed by hot-spots.

When two plates collide, islands are formed in yet another way, though again the first structure to result is often a simple volcano built on the ocean floor. Quite commonly, one of the plates is driven down under the other, and is consumed in the depths of the earth. This descending plate gives rise to volcanic eruptions which produce a series

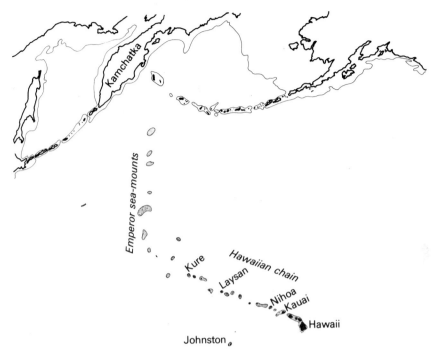

F IG. 1.7.   A map showing the relationship of the Hawaiian and Emperor chains of islands and seamounts. Depths less than 3000 m in the regions of these chains shown stippled.

of volcanoes at the surface of the upper of the two plates. The overriding plate frequently forms an arc with its convex side facing the descending plate, which can result in an arc of volcanic islands, as shown diagrammatically in Fig. 1.8. Many more complicated things can happen when two plates collide. The variations have been discussed by many geologists, for instance Uyeda (1978). The most important of these modifications is when the plate forming the island arc has its continental areas near the edges. In that case an arc of large islands with continental rocks can be formed, as for instance, in parts of Indonesia facing the Indian Ocean. So island-arc islands, while frequently simple volcanic and oceanic, can also be complex and continental.

All these volcanic processes can lead to very high islands. Figure 1.9 shows all islands that have a peak of 2000 metres or more. All the small islands which have such peaks have been formed by one of the three processes just mentioned, though large islands with such peaks have a more varied history.

Darwin (1842) was perhaps the first to point out that oceanic islands

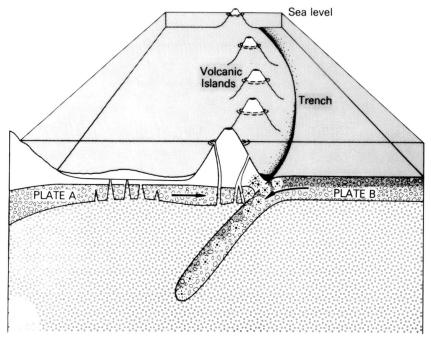

F I G. 1.8.   A diagram of the formation of an island arc, by the subduction of one plate under another.

are frequently made up either of volcanic rocks or of limestones. He noted this on the voyage of the *Beagle*, and it was on this voyage that he developed his theory of the origin of barrier reefs and atolls. Coral reefs may be fringing reefs with no lagoon between them and the land, or barrier reefs in which there is a considerable lagoon, or may occur as atolls which consist just of a circlet of reef with the only dry land derived from reef material. The islands of atolls are thus low limestone islands.

The development of volcanic oceanic islands was described above. When such an island is first formed in tropical seas where reef-building (hermatypic) corals occur, a fringing reef will be formed. Darwin's theory of reefs was that if the volcano, which is roughly conical, then subsided, the reef would grow upwards and retain the same diameter, but the cross-section area of the volcano at sea level would decrease, and so a lagoon would develop between the volcanic part of the island and the reef, creating a barrier reef. If this process continues until all the volcanic rocks sink beneath the sea, then an atoll is formed. In this theory it is the relative level of volcano and ocean that is important, so a rise in sea level will be equivalent to subsidence to the same extent of a volcano. However, sea-level changes are measured in hundreds of

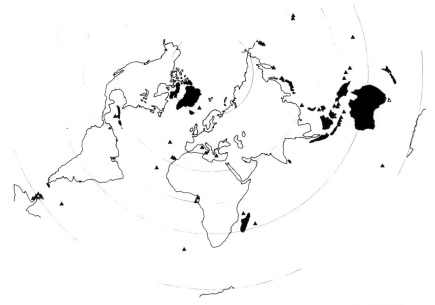

F IG. 1.9.   A map showing the location of all islands with a peak of 2000 m or more. Large such islands are shaded, small such islands are indicated by ▲.

metres at most, while volcanic islands can stand a couple of thousand metres above sea level (Fig. 1.9), and the volcanic base below some atolls is several thousand metres below sea level. Consequently, sub-sidence must be the major process in the formation of atolls. Modern research, and in particular deep borings in atolls, have shown that Darwin's explanation is essentially correct for oceanic islands (Steers and Stoddart 1977). Figure 1.10 shows the appearance of an atoll; the great difference between this and both the volcanic high islands (Fig. 1.6) and continental islands (Fig. 1.3) can be seen.

Many of the islands in the tropics are either high islands, obviously volcanic, with fringing or barrier reefs when in the region of hermatypic corals, or atolls, low islands. Another important, but less common, type is raised atolls. These islands are somewhat higher limestone islands, in some cases a hundred metres or more above sea level at their highest part. While in theory these could be atolls formed at a time of higher sea level and left stranded, the known history of sea levels in the last 100 000 years, discussed below, fits with other evidence that these moderately high limestone islands have generally been formed by earth movement pushing the atolls above the sea.

The common high volcanic islands and low islands of atolls, and the less usual raised reefs and continental fragments, account for almost all

FIG. 1.10.   An aerial photograph showing the appearance of an atoll. The island with trees in the foreground, Akaiami, is about 1 km long, and the distance across the lagoon to the far reef is about 5 km. The reef, its associated islands, and the remnant of a high island in the lagoon are called collectively Aitutaki, which is in the Cook Islands; strictly the reef is a barrier reef (*Aerofilms Ltd.*).

the oceanic islands of the world, though intermediate and mixed types do occur (Thomas 1963). Atolls are particularly characteristic of the Pacific, which on Thomas's list number 309. The Indian Ocean has 73, the Caribbean 26, and the Atlantic only one, Rocas off the coast of Brazil (Fig. 2.2), or two, if Bermuda (Fig. 2.1) is counted as an atoll.

When considering biological distributions, the type of an island, or more generally the available body of different types of islands in a region, is clearly important. So, too, is the climate of an island. High islands usually, by their effect on air movement, have heavy rainfall though they can also have extensive dry areas in the rain shadows. Low islands are drier; and for that reason, as well as their isolation, have impoverished biota (Fosberg 1976). The past history of climate and sea level is also important in determining the biota that are found today.

Climatic history and sea-level changes

The period of geological history that has to be considered when study-ing an island varies enormously with different islands. At one extreme, for all islands in the Arctic and for many islands in more favourable climatic regions, the entire flora and fauna has been derived since the last glaciation or during periods when the climate and sea level were not very greatly different from those at present. At the other extreme, ancient, large islands like Madagascar, New Zealand, and New Cale-donia have species on them whose ancestors first arrived back in the Miocene period or earlier, tens of millions of years ago. These ancient elements in the modern biota have survived two major types of change. The first is changes in their physical surroundings: particularly the climatic changes of the Pleistocene, but also other climatic shifts, and changes in many cases in the size and shape of the island. The second is the changing nature of the biotic community, as new species become established and old ones become extinct. This turnover of species in geological time is indisputable: the importance of turnover in very much shorter periods will be examined in detail in Chapters 4 and 5.

The importance of climatic and sea-level change in determining what kinds of species are found on islands has been, and continues to be, a source of much dispute. However, there are some singular ex-amples showing the importance of considering past conditions. One such will be found in Chapter 9, where the distribution of species of *Anolis*, which are small arboreal lizards, is related not to modern islands, but to the submarine banks on which the islands stand. Each bank has one to many islands on it (Fig. 9.2). About 7000 years ago, the sea level was lower (Fig. 1.11), so that each bank formed an island, and the modern islands were merely the higher parts of those ancient islands. The distribution of *Anolis* suggests that the major phase of dispersal was at this time of lowered sea level.

For the last two million years, from the beginning of the Pleistocene period, changes in climate and in sea level have gone together as ice caps have waxed and waned. During glacial periods, when the north-ern-hemisphere ice caps spread over vast areas of North America and Europe, not only was the general climate very cold, but because of the water locked up in the ice caps, the sea level fell to about 100 metres below the present level. Conversely, in interglacial periods, the climate and sea level were much as now. It is now known that there were up to 20 glacial periods (the exact number depending to some extent on how they are defined) in contrast to the four glacial periods that were thought only 20 years ago to encompass the Pleistocene. The evidence for this multiplicity of glacial periods comes particularly from deep-sea cores, and the periodicity in these cores matches the periodicity of various perturbations in the earth's orbit (Imbrie and Imbrie 1979). While these astronomical variations may indeed be 'the pacemaker of the ice ages', there is still a great deal to be understood about the course of events during any particular ice age, and the nature of the coupling between the earth's orbital variations and the earth's climate.

One common, but not universal feature of the record in the deep-sea cores is that a glacial period usually ends abruptly, changing rapidly into an interglacial one. However, the change from interglacial to glacial has usually been much more gradual. The end of the last glaciation, which reached its peak about 18 000 years ago, is an example of such an abrupt termination. The consequences for sea-level changes are shown in Fig. 1.11. The records from different places are in good agreement, showing a rapid rise from about 100 metres below the present level, with the most rapid change of sea level about 10 000 years ago.

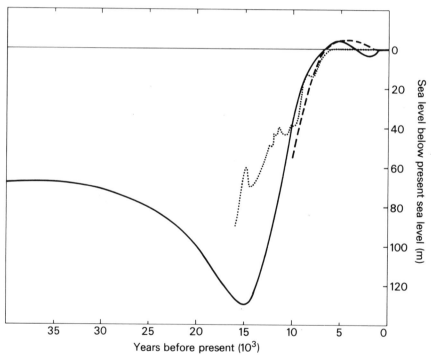

FIG. 1.11.   A diagram of interpretations of the change in sea level since the height of the last glaciation.
——— Mitchell's eustatic curve (Mitchell 1977);
‒ ‒ ‒ Sea levels in the Strait of Malacca (Geyh, Kudrass, and Streif, 1979);
...... Mörner's eustatic curve (after Synge 1977).

Since the sea attained roughly its present level, records from different places show minor differences: some show the sea level as more or less constant, others as higher than now, yet others as undergoing complex oscillations. In part, these differences are caused because, superimposed on the general global rise in sea level, there are local adjustments in the continental masses, particularly in areas which have been under the ice sheets, leading to a complex series of rises, falls, and tilts as the rocks reach a new equilibrium in relation to each other, different from that which they had found under the ice sheets.

As a generalization then, in the temperate and Arctic zones many islands would have been connected to the neighbouring mainland within the last 20 000 years, but with a climate appreciably colder than that at present. The unravelling of the movements of plants and animals northwards as the ice retreated, and a determination of whether any particular species could reach certain islands before the sea level cut them off, is difficult and controversial. Even if there were good fossil evidence of the time at which a particular species had reached what is now an island, it would still be difficult to know whether it had reached there across the sea or over a land bridge when the climate was colder than at present. The importance of dispersal, and the difficulty of studying it, will be a recurring theme throughout this book.

In a shorter time span, considering intervals of tens and hundreds of years rather than thousands, quite a lot is now known about the variation of the climate in the past. The ability of a species to exist on an island depends not only on its relation to other species, but also on its ability to survive periods of less favourable climate. One important generalization that can be made about climatic history can be summarized in an important phrase: climatic variation has a reddened spectrum. This means that short-term variations in climate (the blue end of the spectrum) have a lower amplitude than long-term variation (the red end of the spectrum). It means that the variance of climate within decades is less than the variance within centuries, which is again less than the variance over millennia. Over periods ranging from one year up to 10 000 years, the tendency for long-term variations to be more marked than short ones is remarkably consistent in different records (US Committee GARP 1975). Explanations for this phenomenon are starting to appear (Hasselman 1976). The importance of such climatic variation for the persistence of species on islands is that species have to be adaptable if they are to survive. Almost the only statement that can be made about climatic changes covering a few hundred generations is that they will be of a type that has not been experienced in quite that pattern before.

Biogeography of land masses and islands

The processes that lead to the particular mixtures of species found on islands can be understood only in relation to those species that occur on the major land masses, which are the continents and the island continent of Australia. The basic data of biogeography, both for islands and for continents, are tables of the occurrence of species in areas. A full understanding of such a two-way table needs an analysis of the variation both by rows (species) and by columns (areas), with the ultimate aim of drawing these analyses together to a full understanding of the data matrix. In practice, in most studies the emphasis is either on an analysis by species or on an analysis by areas. An analysis of biogeographical data by species leads naturally to an analysis of the origins of the different species in time and space. For continental areas this implies a more sophisticated analysis than the traditional analysis by areas (Mayr 1976; Holloway 1977).

In the analysis of distribution by areas there have been two traditional approaches. The more important one for the study of islands is the division of the world into various biogeographical zones. The major zones, their relationships with plate tectonics and with each other, are discussed below. Further subdivisions into minor zones in hierarchical schemes have been popular with some biogeographers, for instance van Balgooy (1971) and Udvardy (1975), but this practice has been attacked by Mayr for leading to no further generalizations. No doubt it has its uses for keeping data in order. The second approach is to distinguish areas by biomes, such as rain forest, desert, taiga, and tundra. This approach leads to the formulation of general biogeographical rules, which will be discussed in Chapter 2, and it certainly brings in the necessary background for understanding the distribution of species on islands. It is, for instance, well known that there are rather few species in deserts; as Olson (1975) says 'it takes no deep figuring to realise that a desert island will have rather few species on it'. The obvious and general point that the biota of an island will reflect its climatic type is often overlooked in theoretical discussions. Nevertheless, it is interesting to ask whether a desert island has fewer species than would be expected in the same area of continental desert; where the species on it come from; whether they show different adaptations and interactions from being on a desert island rather than on a continental desert, and so forth. The answers to these questions are far from obvious, but must be made in the context of the island being a desert one.

The first approach to understanding distributions of plants and animals on continents can usually be made most easily by an analysis by area. For oceanic islands, this approach is much less useful, and a direct study of species and their origin is more profitable. This will be done for Hawaii and the Galapagos in Chapter 9. Continental islands fall in between. The major features of their biota are determined by the continents near by. The detailed origins of the taxa on a continental island, and the distribution of these taxa on a nearby continent, can be known. So the study of the species found on continental islands offers one of the best prospects for integration in biogeography, the simultaneous analysis of tables of distributions by species and by area.

It is perhaps important at this point to emphasize how little is known of the biota of many islands, and for that matter of many continental areas. Birds are as well a known group as any, but a new species of Hawaiian honeycreeper, in the important and well-known family Drepanididae, was found only in 1973 (Casey and Jacobi 1974) and placed in a new genus under the name *Melamprosops phaeosoma*. There have been several new records for birds on the Cook Islands in the South Pacific (Holyoak 1974). Clarke (1971) spent a year studying the microlepidoptera of Rapa Island, the southernmost of the Polynesian Islands in the Central Pacific (Figs. 2.9, 6.4) and 77 out of his 130 species records are new. No such intensive study has been made of the microlepidoptera of any other of the Austral islands, or for that matter most of the Pacific islands. Because of these uncertainties about the distribution of many species, much biogeographical work has been confined to well-worked groups such as birds, mammals, and angiosperms. In the last group there are many genera in which the concept of the species as a Mendelian population cannot hold, and much uncertainty about the taxonomic limits of species in some groups where it does hold. For this sort of reason, van Balgooy (1969) discusses plant distribution in terms of genera. Outside the vascular plants and the vertebrates, the taxonomic status and the distribution and limits of most species are as yet known only approximately. A particularly fascinating example of a group in which species are still being discovered rapidly is the Hawaiian Drosophilidae, considered in detail in Chapter 8.

Biogeography and plate tectonics
During the nineteenth century, when reliable data on the geographical distribution of life became abundant, it also became clear that the world could be divided quite reasonably into a number of regions, each with its characteristic forms. Basing their generalizations largely on birds and mammals, Sclater, Wallace, and others divided the world into six major zoogeographical regions. One version is shown in Fig. 1.12. The major divisions for plants and for insects differ somewhat,

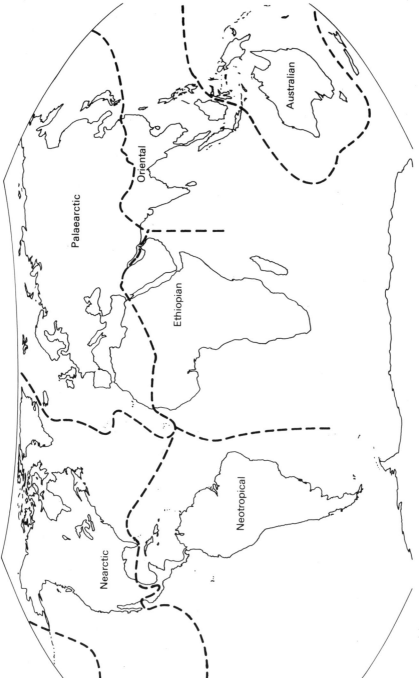

FIG. 1.12. A map showing one version of the zoogeographical regions distinguished by Sclater and by Wallace. In this version the Philippines are in the Oriental region (cf. Fig. 1.13).

and this will be discussed in the next section (see Fig. 1.14). The fact that the world can be divided satisfactorily into biogeographical zones emphasizes two points: the importance of geological history, and in particular plate tectonics, in determining the distribution of life, and, secondly, that the distribution of species is not in equilibrium in the world as a whole. The second point will be discussed in the last section of this chapter.

The importance of plate tectonics in determining distributions is readily seen by comparing Figs. 1.1 and 1.12. Nevertheless, the match is not exact, and the reasons for the differences are worth considering in detail.

The closest match between a zoogeographic region and a plate is in South America. However, the South American fauna extends northwards into Central America and on to the Caribbean plate, and some South American forms are found in North America. For much of the Tertiary there was a large sea gap between South America and North America, and the interchange between these two continents as the gap closed is a classic story in zoogeography (Simpson 1950). The details of the timing, and the relation of these flows to change in species number are still in dispute (Marshall and Hecht 1978), but that South American forms such as opposums and armadillos migrated into North America, while North American forms—horses, lions, and llamas for instance—migrated into South America, in both cases accompanied by extinctions of native species, is not in dispute. The disentangling of the story is certainly not helped by the extinction of many species of large mammals in the last 20 000 years or so. A very plausible theory of the last massive extinction ascribes it to a wave of human population moving across the Bering Strait, through Alaska, down to the tip of South America (Martin and Wright 1967; Martin 1973).

The Nearctic region also corresponds very closely to a plate, the North American plate. The distinction between the Nearctic region and the Palaearctic region is not very great (numbers demonstrating this are given below) and the two regions are sometimes combined into one, the Holarctic. Hulten (1974) shows the connection between these two across the Bering Strait, as well as many maps of the distributions of Arctic plants. The distinction between the North American plate and Eurasian plate is very well marked in the North Atlantic up through Iceland, Jan Mayen (Fig. 2.1), and across the Arctic Ocean, but the course of this boundary becomes obscure in Siberia and is still disputed. So in this case the obscurity of the division between the two plates matches the obscurity of the division between the two faunas.

Coming to the Palaearctic region, although the bulk of the region corresponds with the bulk of the Eurasian plate, the boundaries of the region and those of the plate are really quite distinct. South of Europe, the plate boundary runs through the centre of the Mediterranean, while zoogeographically Africa north of the Sahara is part of the Palaearctic region, and the faunal distinction runs through the middle of the desert. Although a small number of desert species are found on either side of this boundary, it seems that the Sahara Desert, the largest in the world, forms a much greater barrier to the distribution than the Mediterranean Sea, which many species can cross by hopping islands. However, the distinction between the European and the African faunas has been exaggerated by extinction; many characteristically African forms such as lions, elephants, hyaenas, and rhinoceroses lived in the Palaearctic during the Pleistocene and some died out in historical times. Deserts are less important as boundaries farther east, where all the great Asiatic deserts are by their faunal composition clearly part of the Palaearctic zone, though a distinct subregion of it (Vaurie 1972). The boundary in Tibet is indeed the plate-tectonic boundary of the high mountains formed by the collision between the Indian plate and the Eurasian plate. But farther east the boundaries again diverge. South-east Asia and southern China, which geologically are part of the Eurasian plate, form with India the Oriental zoogeographical region. The boundary between the Oriental and the Palaearctic region in China is diffuse, and different authors put it in different places.

As has been seen, the Ethiopian region corresponds to only part of the African plate, and that plate also includes the island of Madagascar which is frequently classified as a separate region, so distinct is its fauna and flora (Carlquist 1965).

The final zoogeographical region, the Australian, occurs on the same tectonic plate as India, which is in part of the Oriental zoogeographical region. A study of the relative movement of the Indo-Australian plate and the Eurasian plate is one of the great successes of plate tectonics. From the biogeographical point of view, the important point is that the Australian region has been approaching Asia, and so the separation between the two regions has been much greater in the past. The boundary between the Oriental region and the Australian region is therefore one of the most interesting, for various reasons.

It was the distinction between the faunas of the islands of Bali and Lombok in Indonesia that led Wallace to draw his line which marks the edge of the Oriental region. There are several variants of this line, but the most common follows the edge of the continental shelf of Asia (Fig. 1.13). There is another continental shelf joining Australia and New Guinea, and there are numerous islands in the gap between the two shelves.

Wallace's line is a major but not complete barrier to the dispersal of mammals from the continent. Table 1.1 lists mammal groups which are not found east of Wallace's line and those in which some species have managed to cross the line. In other groups, the effect of Wallace's line is much less drastic. For birds and reptiles, the island arc from Java to the Aru Islands is better described as a filter than a barrier, and the effect is shown in a figure in Carlquist (1965) [reproduced in Wilson, Eisner, Briggs, Dickerson, Metzenberg, O'Brien, Susman, and Boggs (1973)].

For plants and insects, Wallace's line is even less important. Figure 1.14 shows a map of regions that may be recognized by the study of insect faunas. Plants show a similar pattern (Good 1974; van Balgooy 1971). For these groups, New Guinea is an extension of the Oriental region, and there is a zone of overlap in the Queensland rain forests of Australia between the typical Australian biota and the Oriental. The oceanic islands of the Pacific derive both their insects and their plants primarily from Asia rather than from Australia.

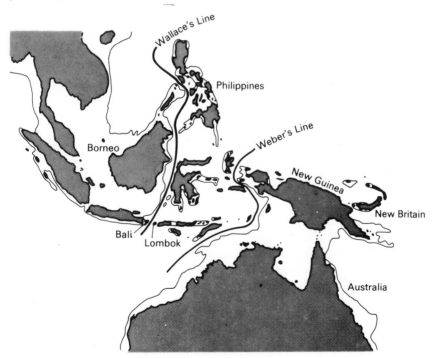

FIG. 1.13.   A map showing Wallace's line and how it runs along the edge of the Asian continental shelf. Weber's line is the main limit of the Australian fauna, and follows the Australian continental shelf. The islands between the lines, including Lombok and the Philippines, have relatively impoverished vertebrate faunas. The contour at 200 m defines the continental shelf.

Table 1.1. *Distribution of some families and subfamilies of mammals,
found on islands of the Oriental region, in relation to
Wallace's Line*

Order	Only west of the Line	Some species east of the Line
Insectivora	Erinaceidae, hedgehogs	Soricidae, shrews
Dermoptera	Cynocephalidae, flying lemurs	
Primates	Tupaiidae, tree shrews	Lorisidae, lorises
	Pongidae, gibbons and	Tarsiidae, tarsiers
	orang-outang	Cercopithecidae, monkeys
Pholidota	Manidae, pangolins	
Lagomorpha	Leporidae, hares	
Rodentia	Rhizomyidae, bamboo rats	Sciuridae, squirrels
		Hystricidae, porcupines
Carnivora	Canidae, dogs	Viverridae, civets
	Ursidae, bears	Felidae, cats
	Mustelidae, weasels	
	Hyaenidae, hyaenas*	
Proboscidea	Elephantinae, elephants	Stegodontinae*
Perissodactyla	Tapiridae, tapirs	
	Rhinocerotidae, rhinoceroses	
Artiodactyla	Hippopotamidae,	Suidae, pigs
	hippopotamuses*	Tragulidae, chevrotains
	Giraffidae, giraffes*	Cervidae, deer
	Caprinae, goats	Bovinae, cows

* Fossil only, on the Oriental islands.
Data from Carlquist 1965 and Hooijer 1970.

The relationship between zoogeographic areas

The distinctiveness of the various areas is best shown by using quantitative measures. There are several ways in which this can be done;
two simple ones are a calculation of similarity coefficients between the
areas, and counts of the faunal elements in the different areas. Both of
these need to take into account the different sizes of each region, and the
different biomes found in them. As will be seen in Chapter 3, it is an
almost universal rule that there are more species in larger areas, and
there are also, against almost universally, more species in equitable
climates than in harsh ones.

Of all the numerous similarity indices that have been put forward,
only one is specifically designed to take account of the variations in the
total numbers of species in the two regions being compared. Preston's
(1962) index is derived mathematically from the rule (discussed more
fully in Chapter 3) that the logarithm of a number of species increases
linearly with the logarithm of the area,

$$\ln (\text{species}) = c + z.\ln (\text{area}).$$

His index is *s*, defined by the equation

$$s = 1 - 1/x,$$

where *x* is the solution of the equation

$$t^x = a^x + b^x,$$

where *t* is the total number of forms found in the two areas being compared, *a* the number of forms in one of the areas, and *b* the number in the other; *s* can vary only from 0 to 1. The logarithmic relationship of species to area results in *x* appearing as an exponent, and this relationship also means that area is allowed for, indirectly, in Preston's *s*. Preston compared the six classical areas using families of birds and families of mammals and his results are shown in Table 1.2.

Amongst the points that arise from Table 1.2 are that all regions show some relationship to others, and that the relationship between the regions as measured by the similarity of birds is appreciably greater than the relationship as measured by mammals. The greater ability of birds to disperse is one important cause of that. In both birds and

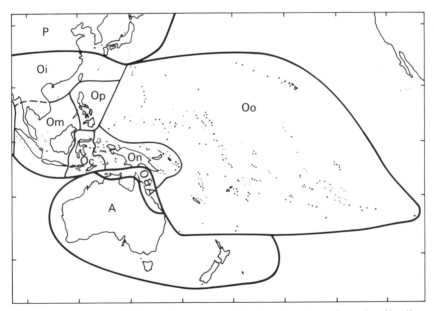

FIG. 1.14.   A map of the major geographical regions based on the distribution of insects.
P Palaearctic; O Oriental with subregions—Oi Indo-Chinese, Om Malayan, Op Philippines, Oc Celebes, On New Guinea and Oo Oceanic; A Australian. O & A marks the area of overlap of Oriental (New Guinea) and Australian. (After Gressitt 1961.)

Table 1.2. Comparisons of faunas using Preston's similarity index

	Birds						Mammals					
	Neo-tropical	Nearctic	Palae-arctic	Ethiopian	Oriental	Australian	Neo-tropical	Nearctic	Palae-arctic	Ethiopian	Oriental	Australian
Total number of families in the regions	95	67	67	84	74	73	43	31	27	50	43	21
Preston's similarity index												
Neotropical		0.62	0.42	0.42	0.44	0.40		0.54	0.29	0.20	0.26	0.13
Nearctic			0.71	0.52	0.53	0.44			0.50	0.26	0.31	0.14
Palaearctic				0.71	0.68	0.66				0.45	0.35	0.16
Ethiopian					0.85	0.58					0.60	0.20
Oriental						0.73						0.25

After Preston 1962.

mammals the Australian region has low similarities with other regions, as does, in birds, the Neotropical. Perhaps more surprising is that the Oriental and Ethiopian show the highest similarities with each other, reflecting the present similarities in their range of climates.

Preston's index allows for the difference in richness in the different regions, and these differences are also of interest in themselves. In Table 1.2, the richness of the three tropical areas, the Neotropical, Ethiopian, and Oriental, compared with the two northern ones, the Nearctic and Palaearctic, is striking and emphasizes the importance of the climate in affecting diversity. The Australian region is, on the whole, a warm one, but it is also a small region and includes a large amount of desert. For birds, it is possible to estimate the number of species in each region. This is given in Table 1.3, confirming and emphasizing the figures for families given by Preston.

Table 1.3. Estimates of numbers of all bird species in different biogeographic regions

Neotropical	3000
Ethiopian	1600
Oriental	1400
Palaearctic	1050
Australian	950
Nearctic	800

From various sources.

Similar quantitative studies have not yet been made on insects or plants. The results would probably be rather different. The major shift in the boundary between the Oriental and Australian regions has already been noted in Fig. 1.14. The contrast between plants and insects on the one hand and birds on the other is shown most sharply in the Southern Hemisphere. The birds common to the Neotropical and the Australasian regions are almost all cosmopolitan species: there is no group confined to these two areas. In contrast there are many species of plants which show a link across the Pacific, deriving from the ancient connection between South America and Australia via the Antarctic before the break-up of Gondwanaland. Examples of such southern distributions can be found in the weevils (Coleoptera Curculionidae) of Tristan da Cunha, an oceanic archipelago in the middle of the South Atlantic (Fig. 2.2), which will be discussed in more detail in the next chapter. The genus *Pentathrum* is found, as well as on the Tristan da Cunha archipelago, in South America in Chile, and in the South-West Pacific in New Zealand, New Caledonia, and Tasmania. The tribe Listroderini, with 15 species in the Tristan archipelago, is more widespread and has been found in the whole of the southern half of South America, extending north along the Andes, and also in Central and North America, while on the other side of the Pacific it is found in New Zealand, Australia, and Tasmania. No birds show this type of distribution. Amongst the mammals only the marsupials do, and they are not found naturally even on large isolated islands such as New Zealand, let alone on small isolated islands. Detailed comparisons of the southern biomes are given by Keast (1972*b*) and Meggers, Ayensu, and Duckworth (1973).

The other way of looking at the similarity of the regions is to list the faunal elements in each region. This approach is particularly helpful for oceanic islands, and will be pursued in Chapter 9. As an example of their use in continental areas, the following data are taken from Voous (1960). Of the 419 species of European breeding birds, including sea birds, 265 can be called Palaearctic species. Most of the rest are categories which are Palaearctic and wider. The commonest are the Holarctic species, that is to say Palaearctic and Nearctic, and they constitute 95. Other wide groupings, involving the Oriental/Ethiopian region and cosmopolitan species, account for 46 more. Very few species belong to groups with centres of distributions in other zoogeographic realms. There are a mere three Nearctic species, and only four Ethiopian ones. That leaves six species, five which fit no clear category, and one, a sea bird, with Antarctic connections. Another way of looking at European birds, still using the data of Voous, is to classify them by the biome in which they occur. This is done in Table 1.4, from which it can be seen that there is no marked difference in the abundance of birds in different habitats, except for the tundra being poor. However, there is no desert area in Europe.

Table 1.4. Distribution of species of European birds by biomes

Biomes	Found in biome	Confined to biome
Tundra	91	17
Boreal	304	35
Temperate	280	1
Mediterranean	248	7
Steppe	246	4

From Voous 1960.

Ideally, as Mayr and Short (1970) stress, the unit for biogeographical comparisons should be the superspecies, that is sets of closely related, more or less allopatric species. The data for such studies are as yet readily available only for birds north of Mexico (Mayr and Short

1970) and birds in Africa (Hall and Moreau 1970; Snow 1978). The last two are particularly useful for the study of birds on islands around Africa.

The lack of equilibrium in geological time

One major question about island biogeography is to what extent the number of species found on an island is in equilibrium. The answer to this question depends primarily on the time-span considered. Given sufficient time, hundreds of millions of years, almost all species become extinct and on that time scale no living species are in equilibrium. The biotic distinctions between the major biogeographic zones show differences on a somewhat shorter time scale from hundreds of thousands of years up to millions of years and a lack of equilibrium again. The

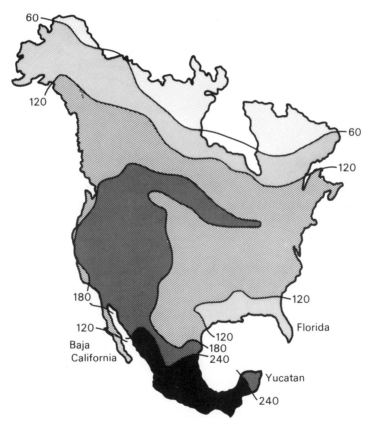

FIG. 1.15.   A map indicating the number of species of land and freshwater breeding birds in quadrats of 60 000 km². Contours at 60, 120, 180 and 240 species. (After Cook 1969.)

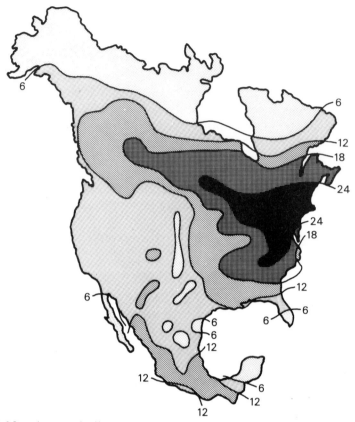

FIG. 1.16. A map indicating the number of species of Parulidae (wood warblers) in quadrats of 60 000 km². Contours at 6, 12, 18 and 24 species. (After Cook 1969.)

isolation of the regions from each other, the variation in the earth's climate, combined with the limitation on species' dispersal, has produced the distinction between regions. That this distinction is a disequilibrium can be seen both in the details of present distributions and in man-induced changes in distributions.

The relation of species' distribution to climate and topographical factors, and the effects of evolutionary history, both involved in the disequilibrium between regions, can be shown in North American birds. It is well known that the number of bird species decreases from the Tropics to the Poles, and that the number of bird species is usually larger in areas of varied topography, particularly mountainous country, than in the more monotonous plains. These generalizations are shown in Fig. 1.15, where both the north–south gradient, and the importance of the western mountainous region, can be seen. Figure 1.16, on the other hand, indicates, perhaps more arguably, the importance of evolutionary history. The wood-warblers, Parulidae, are particularly characteristic of the eastern deciduous forest, and their evolution has been associated with this biome. Their species density is related to the distribution of this biome.

Clear evidence for the lack of equilibrium between zoogeographical regions comes from the effect of the introductions of species by man into various regions. The success of many introduced species in New Zealand, including European birds and Australian marsupials, is too well known to need recounting here. So is the invasion of North America by starlings, *Sturnus vulgaris*, and sparrows, *Passer domesticus*, following deliberate introduction. An interesting example of a species which, having been deliberately introduced to a mainland has spread successfully to isolated islands, is a finch, the redpoll *Acanthis flammea*. This species was introduced into New Zealand from Europe in the nineteenth century, and has spread to a variety of sub-Antarctic islands, including Chatham, Snares, Auckland, and Macquarie Island (Watson 1975). Such an example emphasizes the importance of geographical and climatic limitations on the occurrence of species on islands: it was the origin of the redpoll in the Palaearctic region that kept it from the sub-Antarctic islands, and not its ability to live on them. It is now time to consider the biological constraints affecting the mix of species to be found on islands.

2 Features of island life

The fauna and flora of islands have several features that distinguish them from the flora and fauna of continents. Many of these features are related to difficulties of dispersal. Organisms that can disperse well are more likely to be found on islands than those that cannot. Once on an island, particularly an oceanic island, a species may evolve so as to lose its ability to disperse far, with many interesting effects on both morphology and reproduction. These changes will be introduced with what Sir Joseph Hooker said, a century ago, about the flora of oceanic islands. The biota of the Tristan da Cunha archipelago will then be examined to serve as an illustration.

After these two introductory topics, some features of island life will be discussed in more detail. The variation in dispersal ability and the subsequent evolution on islands produces a disharmonic biota in many cases, disharmonic in the relative proportions of different taxa compared with those on the mainland. Forms on islands are often bigger than their mainland relatives, they are prone to extinction, and interesting relict and endemic species are found.

The climate of an island is usually more temperate than that of the nearest mainland, i.e. less subject to extremes of temperature. It is also, usually, more humid and much windier. These features, the limited area, and the limited range of habitat types, are all more marked for oceanic islands than continental ones. The geological nature of oceanic islands was discussed in the first chapter. In the nineteenth century Wallace drew attention to the biological distinctiveness of oceanic islands: in general, they lack mammals (other than bats), amphibia, and freshwater fish. On some oceanic islands, marine groups of fish have evolved new freshwater forms, not closely related to the freshwater groups of continents.

Some of the features of island biota result simply from the maritime climate of islands. There are a number of well-known rules of geographical variation, summarized by Mayr (1963) and James (1970), which apply particularly to birds, but also to other animals. Bergmann's rule says that body size is larger in cooler climates. Allen's rule says that extremities tend to be proportionately shorter in cooler climates, though that rule does not hold for wings and tails of birds, which of course, do not have a blood supply in the feathers. The third general rule is Gloger's, which is that colouring tends to be darker in warmer or humid climates or both. More specifically, warm, dry climates lead to browns, while cold, humid climates lead to blacks. All these rules can be exemplified by island races.

In a famous lecture to the British Association in 1866, J. D. Hooker discussed the characteristics and origins of island floras. The lecture was published in parts and in several places, and a convenient survey, with a discussion of some of the points made and their relation to the history of biology, is given by Turrill (1964). Hooker noted that the flora, as well as the climate, tended to be more polar than the island's position. Thus, the Canaries, off the coast of Africa (Fig. 2.1), have a generally Mediterranean flora, and Kerguelen (Fig. 1.5), in the Indian Ocean, is distinctly bleak and Antarctic for its latitude.

Hooker's other points can be grouped under the headings used later in this chapter. He noted that there were few species compared with continental areas of the same size, and that genera were represented by few species and families by few genera. These are both parts of 'Impoverishment'. In relation to 'Disharmony', Hooker noted many evergreens, few herbaceous plants, few if any indigenous annuals, alpines and sub-alpines rare or absent from island mountains, and that the floras were rich in cryptogams, especially ferns. These last two points relate to 'Dispersal'. Ferns, by virtue of their light spores, are good dispersers; alpines, whether good dispersers or not, are generally not well placed geographically to disperse to oceanic islands.

Other points in the lecture refer to the taxonomical peculiarities of island floras. Hooker, indeed, raised points about the relative abundance of species which are still poorly understood. Most of the species on an oceanic island are related to species on one particular continent. For the Canaries, Madeira, and the Azores, this is Europe; for Kerguelen, surprisingly, it is South America. Many are endemic, and Hooker stated that the more distantly related to the continental forms the rarer, i.e., the lower the population density, so that species in endemic genera are rarer than species in continental genera. But there is an exception. Those endemic species that are so distinct that they have no known continental relations, are often abundant on the oceanic islands on which they are found. An example is the Kerguelen cabbage, *Pringlea antiscorbutica*, which, like other cabbages, is a member of the Cruciferae, but is placed by taxonomists in a tribe of its own, Pringleeae.

Hooker also discussed another effect with taxonomic consequences: the extinction of species. He ascribed it both to the loss of island area through subsidence, and to the hand of man. On Madeira (Fig. 2.1),

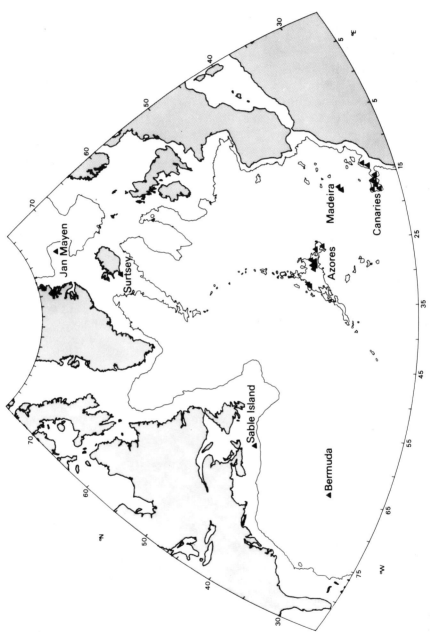

FIG. 2.1. Islands in the north Atlantic. Contour at 1000 fathoms (1800 m).

the native forest was set on fire by the first settlers; on St. Helena (Fig. 2.2) cutting of the forests and the introduction both of goats and of foreign plants led to extinction of endemic species. All Hooker's points are shown in the biota of Tristan da Cunha.

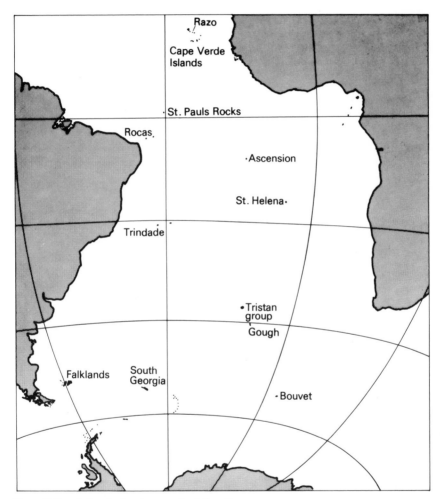

FIG. 2.2. Islands in the south Atlantic.

The biota of Tristan da Cunha

The archipelago of Tristan da Cunha lies in the South Atlantic, and the islands are typical mid-oceanic ridge volcanic islands (Figs. 1.6, 2.2, and 2.3). Although in the latitude of the Cape of Good Hope and slightly less than 3000 km from it, most close relatives of Tristan species are found in Southern Patagonia, the tip of South America and the Falkland Islands, over 4000 km away, but to windward.

The archipelago consists of the Tristan group of three islands in sight of each other, Tristan da Cunha, Inaccessible, and Nightingale, and of isolated Gough Island, about 350 km south-east. The features of the biota can be brought out by contrasting them with the continental island of Skokholm (Fig. 1.3), which will be considered again in Chapters 5 and 6. Table 2.1 shows, for the individual islands and for the natural groupings, the areas and the numbers of breeding land birds, angiosperms, and pteridophyte species. Extensive accounts of the environment and biology of the archipelago can be found in Baird, Dickson, Holdgate, and Wace (1965), and there are geographical and ornithological details in Watson (1975). For Skokholm, Lockley (1947)

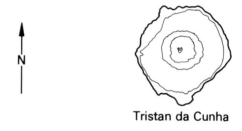

Tristan da Cunha

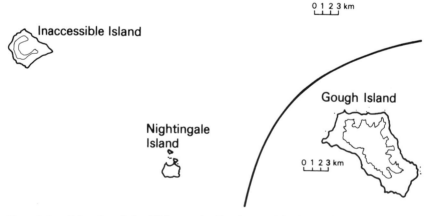

F I G. 2.3.   Islands of the Tristan da Cunha archipelago. See also Fig. 2.2. Contours at 500 m.

gives a general account with details of many aspects, while Goodman and Gillham (1954) describe the vegetation.

Two of Hooker's points are immediately clear in Table 2.1. The birds and the flowering plants are impoverished compared with the continental island, but there is an abundance of fern species. The birds are given in detail in Table 2.2; all are endemic. The thrushes and buntings are probably most closely related to South American species; *Rowettia* is definitely close taxonomically to the Patagonian *Melanodera*. The rails are all flightless, a common feature of island rails. The *Gallinula* are close relatives of the cosmopolitan moorhen, *G. chloropus*, which also has related forms on Hawaii and the Galapagos (see Chapter 9). *Atlantisia* is quite abundant on the one uninhabited island on which it is found. Two fossil species in the genus have been described, one from St. Helena and one from Ascension (Olson 1973*a*, 1975, 1977) (Fig. 2.2), and the genus may be derived from Africa. Both extinctions may have occurred during the last few centuries.

Table 2.1. Data for the islands of the Tristan da Cunha archipelago and for Skokholm, Wales

Island	Area in km²	Breeding land bird species	Angiosperm species	Pteridophyte species
Tristan da Cunha	86	3	32	29
Inaccessible	12	4	26	27
Nightingale	4	3	17	14
Tristan da Cunha group	102	5	36	31
Gough	57	2	31	26
Tristan–Gough archipelago	159	7	41	33
Skokholm	1	10	208	8

Data from Baird *et al.* 1965, Gillham 1953*a*, and Lack 1969*b*.

There is no evidence as to whether *Atlantisia* ever occurred on the larger and newer island of Tristan, and if so, whether it died out after the invasion of *Gallinula*. The archipelago as a whole has suffered less from extinction than most oceanic islands, partly no doubt because the only permanent settlement, which is on the main island and dates from 1816, is small. Nevertheless, cats, rats, and goats have been introduced, and at least one island subspecies of bird, the island 'canary', is extinct, and an introduced northern hemisphere plant, *Rumex acetosella*, has become dominant in a zone just below 1000 m on Tristan.

The general relationship of Tristan biota to South American emphasizes the importance of wind in dispersal. Birds, too, are important, and carry propagules in various ways (Falla 1960). All the islands in Table

Table 2.2. The land birds of the Tristan da Cunha archipelago

Family of birds	Species	Tristan da Cunha	Inaccessible	Nightingale	Gough
Turdidae, thrush	*Nesocichla eremita*	*N.e. eremita*	*N.e. gordoni*	*N.e. procax*	—
Emberizidae, buntings	*Neospiza acunhae*	*(N.a. acunhae)**	*N.a. acunhae*	*N.a. questi*	—
	Neospiza wilkinsi	—	*N.w. dunnei*	*N.w. wilkinsi*	—
	Rowettia goughensis	—	—	—	*R. goughensis*
Rallidae, rails	*Gallinula*	*G. nesiotis*	—	—	*G. comeri*
	Atlantisia rogersi	—	*A. rogersi*	—	—

* Extinct

2.1 have huge colonies of sea birds (for Skokholm, see Cramp, Bourne, and Saunders 1974). Holdgate (1960*b*) has suggested that the distribution of the rhamnaceous shrub *Phylica arborea* and the tussock grass *Spartina arundinacea*, which dominate parts of the vegetation on Tristan and Gough, may be related to the distribution of the yellow-nosed albatross *Diomedea chlororhynchos*. All three occur not only on all four islands of the Tristan archipelago, but also on Amsterdam Island in the Indian Ocean (Fig. 1.5). *Phylica arborea* also occurs on Mauritius, and is in an African genus. *Spartina arundinacea* occurs on the island of St. Paul, next to Amsterdam Island, and while the genus is widespread in northern temperate regions, it seems to occur as a native in South America only in the southern temperate zone (Baird *et al.* 1965). *Diomedea chlororhynchos* probably breeds occasionally on St. Paul and also breeds on the very bleak and more southerly Indian ocean island of Prince Edward.

Birds may also be important in the dispersal of flightless insects and other animals. For instance, Kuschel (1962) noted identical forms of the flightless beetles *Tristanodes scirpophilus* (Curculionidae (see Table 7.1) and *Bidessonotus involucer* (Dytiscidae) on Tristan and Gough, though both genera have speciated on the Tristan group. The possible importance of bird dispersal to the fly *Trogloscaptomyza* will be mentioned in Chapter 8.

As a result of several expeditions the biota of the Tristan archipelago are known as well as those of any oceanic island, though for many of the invertebrate species only a single specimen has been found (Kuschel 1962). The biota show almost all the characteristics of island forms, which will now be discussed in detail; impoverishment, disharmony, dispersal ability and its loss, extinctions, and the occurrence of relicts and endemics. Changes in size and in reproductive strategy have not been shown for Tristan taxa, nor listed by Hooker, but these, too, are often characteristic of island life.

Impoverishment

As Hooker noted, there are often fewer species on an oceanic island than on the same-sized area of a continent. For Tristan, from the data in Table 2.1 this seems obvious, but the comparison with Skokholm is not only a comparison with a smaller island, but a comparison of southern hemisphere islands with a northern one. There are definitely far fewer species of angiosperm in the temperate zone of South America than in Europe, and so that is a partial cause of the impoverishment of Tristan.

A more exact measurement of the impoverishment resulting from isolation can be obtained from Fig. 2.4. This compares vascular plants, birds, and pteridophytes on the Channel Islands, off the north coast of France (Fig. 10.1), and the Azores, in the Atlantic far to the west of Portugal (Fig. 2.1). As the Azores are to the south of the Channel Islands, and as both archipelagos derive their biota from Europe, the comparison is reasonably free of effects from differences in climate and source area.

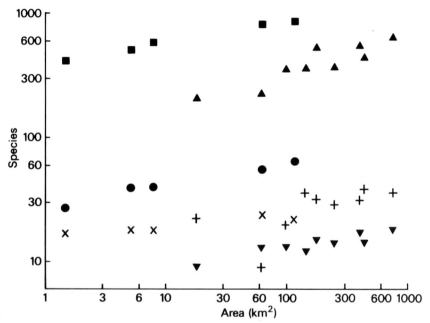

F IG. 2.4.   Species–area relationships in the Azores and the Channel Islands. ■ Channel Island vascular plants, all records. ▲ Azores vascular plants, all records. ● Channel Island land and freshwater breeding birds. ▼ Azores land and freshwater breeding birds. × Channel Island native pteridophytes. + Azores native pteridophytes. (Data from Bannerman and Bannerman 1966, Eriksson *et al*. 1974, Jalas and Suominen 1972, Perring and Walters 1962, and Sharrock 1976.)

All six sets of points in Fig. 2.4 show an increase of species number with area, a phenomenon that will be discussed in the next chapter. All six sets can be fitted by straight lines with slopes not significantly different from 0.2. This allows the statement that on islands of equal area there are two-and-a-half times as many vascular-plant species, four times as many breeding-bird species, but about the same number of pteridophyte species on the Channel Islands as on the Azores. So there is marked impoverishment among the birds, less among the angiosperms, and none in the pteridophytes of the Azores.

Another quantitative study of impoverishment is that by Wyatt-Smith (1953) on the flora of the island of Jarak in the Straits of Malacca. Jarak is a mere 40 ha in area, 64 km from the Malayan mainland (51 km from the next nearest island) and 96 km from Sumatra. Although covered in forest there are no trees of the Dipterocarpaceae, the dominant family in Malaya. On one-acre (0.4-ha) plots, counting plant individuals 10 cm in diameter or more, there were only 33 species on the Jarak plot, compared with 94 and 102 in two mainland plots. Large trees, over 40 cm in diameter, showed no clear impoverishment, the number of species being 16, 23, and 15.

Impoverishment is not a simple phenomenon, but it is of major importance in the study of island populations. It will be considered again in the final chapter.

Disharmony

Disharmony is rather difficult to define. For most authors it seems to mean that the mixture of species found on an island is different from the mixture of species found on the neighbouring mainland. Because of impoverishment, this is bound to be so. Different habitats and ecosystems on the mainland will also have different mixtures and species, and, to some extent, therefore, will be out of harmony with each other. An island is an extreme maritime habitat, and so might be expected to differ on that ground alone.

The small number of species found on oceanic islands is a consequence both of small area and of impoverishment, but these effects are stronger higher up the food chain. For instance, the birds on the Azores are more impoverished than the plants, and this food chain effect leads to disharmony. In Tristan there are, for instance, no birds of prey. However, with so few species of land birds and no land mammals on the islands, and a small land area, it is doubtful if a predator population could maintain itself. This effect on the species in a community will be considered again in Chapter 10. As would be expected for oceanic islands, neither the Azores nor the Tristan islands have land mammals or amphibians, and this disharmony is clearly related to dispersal ability. Disharmony is perhaps a more natural concept in relation to the species found on the Hawaiian islands, because these are derived from a variety of biogeographical regions. (Chapter 9). In none of these ways of looking at disharmony is the community thought to be in any way unstable or unbalanced. Elton (1958) points out that islands seem to be more vulnerable; more easily invaded and their species more liable to extinction than continental species.

Dispersal

The biota of islands tends to come from those taxa that have good dispersal mechanisms, whether active or passive. This is scarcely surprising as the species have to cross the sea, so those species which disperse readily on the wind, by floating, by flying, or by being carried by flying animals are clearly the most likely to reach islands. Ferns and other pteridophytes have light spores, easily carried great distances in the wind. Figure 2.4 shows that the pteridophyte flora of the Azores is not impoverished. Lorence (1978) notes that the pteridophytes of Mauritius (Fig. 1.5) have few endemic species, which he ascribes to their ready dispersal. Of 186 species on the islands, only eight are adventitious or naturalized and eight endemic, leaving 170 naturally-occurring species that are also found elsewhere.

The variation in dispersal ability can be shown in other ways. Figure 2.5 shows the limits of various groups of breeding land-birds in the Pacific. Firth and Davidson (1945) indicate that this pattern applies to most, but not all, groups of land birds. However, the size, type, and density of islands must also be considered, and there is a general thinning out of islands, if somewhat irregularly, from Fiji to Easter Island. So this type of filtering, of thinning out of taxa, must be interpreted cautiously, as stressed by van Balgooy (1971).

Another method of showing which groups are good dispersers has been devised by Holloway (1977). Norfolk Island (Fig. 1.4) is closer to New Caledonia and New Zealand than it is to Australia, but the latter is the larger source. Consequently, relatively good dispersing groups will be represented mostly by species of Australian origin, less good dispersers more by those of New Zealand and New Caledonian origin. As with ferns, it can be argued that good dispersal will lead to low endemism. Figure 2.6 shows these two measures of dispersal applied to the Norfolk Island biota, with the best dispersers top left, the less-good ones bottom right. The sequence across the graph agrees with general biological knowledge of dispersal in the groups.

Indeed, evidence of a common-sense natural history sort, such as was used by Hooker for plants, is available also for animals. Vagvolgyi (1975) points out that most species of land snails on the Pacific islands tend to be small, with their maximum dimension being 10 mm, and frequently very much less. Carlquist (1970) gives pictures and diagrams that substantiate this for the Hawaiian fauna. MacArthur and Wilson (1967) stated that the beetles on St. Helena are mostly wood

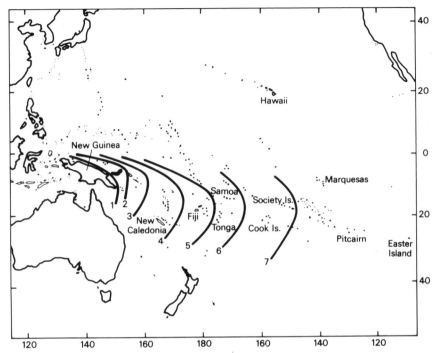

Fɪɢ. 2.5. Eastern limits of families and subfamilies of land and freshwater breeding birds found in New Guinea. The decline in taxa is fairly smooth, and shows both differences in dispersal ability, and that there is a general decline in island size to the east. Not beyond:

1: New Guinea, Pelecanidae pelicans, Anhingidae snakebirds, Ciconiidae storks, Alaudidae larks, Motacillidae pipits, Orthonychinae logrunners, Laniidae shrikes, Oriolidae orioles, Grallinidae mudnesters, Cracticidae butcherbirds, Paradisaeidae birds of paradise, Ptilonorhynchidae bower-birds, Neosittidae Australian nuthatches, Climacteridae Australian tree-creepers.

2: New Britain and Bismark Islands, Casuariidae cassowaries, Phasianidae quails and pheasants.

3: Solomon Islands, Strigidae owls, Podargidae frogmouths, Hemiprocnidae crested swifts, Meropidae bee-eaters, Coraciidae rollers, Bucerotidae horn-bills, Pittidae pittas, Dicruridae drongos, Nectariniidae sunbirds, Dicaeidae flower-pickers.

4: Vanuatu and New Caledonia, Podicepedidae grebes, Phalacrocoracidae cormorants, Pandionidae ospreys, Turnicidae button-quails, Caprimulgidae nightjars, Malurinae wren warblers, Corvidae crows.

5: Fiji and Niuafo'ou, Accipitridae hawks, Falconidae falcons, Megapodiidae brush turkeys, Artamidae wood swallows.

6: Tonga and Samoa, Anatidae ducks, Campephagidae cuckoo-shrikes, Turdinae thrushes, Pachycephalinae whistlers, Meliphagidae honeyeaters, Zosteropidae white-eyes, Estrildidae waxbills.

borers or bark clingers, and so are more likely than other beetles to be
carried across the sea.

Direct evidence of the effects of dispersal can be seen from double
filters, a thinning out in two opposite directions, where a chain of
islands connects two mainland masses. Here again, there are difficulties in interpretation. If the chain is a fairly recent connection between
two ancient land masses, it may well be that the invading species have
problems of competition as well as dispersal. One example that mini-
mizes that effect is shown in Fig. 2.7. This shows a number of species of
Palaearctic, Nearctic, and Holarctic plants found on various Aleutian
islands. As the bulk of the species is Holarctic, competition may be
presumed to be much the same all along the chain, and so the progressive dimunition of the two other components away from their mainland
may reasonably be interpreted as being caused by dispersal difficulties.
Another example of a double filter is shown in Fig. 7.2 (p. 163), with
double gradients of faunal resemblance in the butterflies of the West
Indies.

All these sorts of evidence show the relative variation of dispersal
ability in different groups; none gives any information on the absolute
rates of dispersal. Simpson (1940) distinguished between island hopping, where the distances dispersed are within the ability of the average
number of the species, and sweepstake dispersion, which requires
exceptional and improbable circumstances. The former is shown by
mammals such as hippopotamuses, deer, and elephants across sea gaps
of several kilometres, but dispersal to oceanic islands must, for most
forms, be of the sweepstake sort. Sondaar (1976) develops this theme
for mammals, particularly on Mediterranean islands.

Successful sweepstake dispersal may be very rare, but still has an
important effect on island biota. In Chapter 8, it is estimated that a
successful colonization of one Hawaiian island from another by *Drosophila* species has taken place only every 25 000 years on average.
Wickens (1979) gives some plausible calculations indicating that a
successful establishment of a new plant species by bird dispersal occurs

---

7: Cook and Society islands, Tytonidae barn owls, Hirudinidae swallows,
Sturnidae starlings.
Beyond 7: Marquesas and Pitcairn group, Ardeidae herons, Rallidae rails,
Columbidae pigeons, Psittacidae parrots, Cucuiidae cuckoos, Apodidae
swifts, Alcedinidae kingfishers, Sylviinae warblers, Muscicapinae flycatchers.
Others: Aegothelidae owlet-nightjars, one species (one specimen!) New Cale-
donia, otherwise limit 1. Threskiornithidae ibises, one species Rennell (Solo-
mon Islands), otherwise limit 1. Rhynochetidae kagu, endemic family of one
species, New Caledonia.
(Updated from Firth and Davidson 1945.)

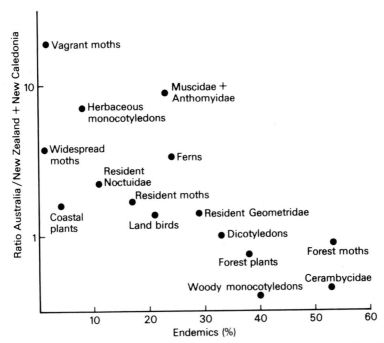

FIG. 2.6. Two indicators of dispersal ability in different groups of the biota of Norfolk Island. Poor-dispersing groups will have a higher proportion of endemics, and are more likely to have reached Norfolk Island from either New Caledonia or New Zealand than from Australia. The converse will hold for good dispersers. (After Holloway 1977.)

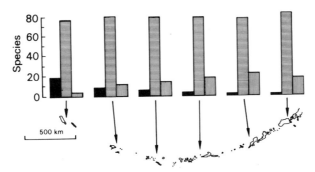

FIG. 2.7. Double-filter effect for plants on the Aleutian islands between Siberia and Alaska. Left-hand columns, palaearctic species; centre columns, holarctic species; right-hand columns, nearctic species. The histograms refer to the groups of islands indicated. The decline of palaearctic species and nearctic species towards the other region is evident. (Modified from Carlquist 1965.)

on the Aldabra atoll (Fig. 1.5) every 650 years, and that two-thirds of the flora probably reached the islands in this way. The remaining species were mostly dispersed by sea, only 5 per cent of the flora being wind dispersed. Wickens also quotes figures that the average interval between the introduction of new plant species by birds may be 8000 years in the Galapagos, 25 000 years in Hawaii.

MacArthur and Wilson (1967) related dispersal ability to their concepts of *r* and *K* selection. This classification is now thought to be oversimplified (Whittaker and Goodman 1979), and it is far from clear if the demographic features on which it is based are closely related to dispersal ability (Stearns 1977; Williams 1969). The distribution of dispersal ability across different taxa remains an important variable in considering island populations.

Loss of dispersal ability

While the occurrence of good dispersers on islands is to be expected, the occurrence also of flightless forms and others that have lost their dispersal ability is more surprising. Perhaps the best-known flightless bird is the dodo of Mauritius, *Raphus cucullatus*, which is one of a group of large flightless birds related to pigeons, once found on Mauritius, Réunion, and Rodriguez in the Indian Ocean and now all extinct. Other well-known examples of flightless birds are the kiwis and moas of New Zealand. Many island rails, such as all three species in the Tristan da Cunha group (Table 2.2), are flightless.

In some flightless birds the wings have become so small that they are kept close to the sides of the body at all times, though in no case has the wing structure disappeared completely. In some other species, such as the Galapagos cormorant, *Nannopterum harrisi*, or the kagu, *Rhynochetos jubatus*, of New Caledonia, the wings are still waved around conspicuously, possibly for cooling or for courtship display. Both these birds are interesting taxonomically. The cormorant is the largest member of its family and the only flightless one known either living or extinct. The kagu is placed in a family of its own, Rhynochetidae, in the order Gruiformes, which includes the rails. There are many examples of flightless insects. On Tristan da Cunha, of the 20 endemic species of beetle, all but two have reduced wings (see also Table 7.1). Another Tristan example is shown in Fig. 2.8, a drosophilid fly. The evolution and dispersal of *Drosophila* and *Scaptomyza* on Hawaii and other islands will be considered in Chapter 8.

Dispersal mechanisms have been lost in plants too. The genus *Fitchia* (Compositae) is endemic in Polynesia; the occurrence and seeds of the known species being shown in Fig. 2.9. The closest continental relatives

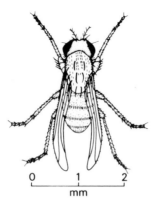

FIG. 2.8. *Scaptomyza frustulifera*, a flightless drosophilid from the Tristan da Cunha archipelago (Nightingale and Gough islands). (Modified from Holdgate 1960*a*.)

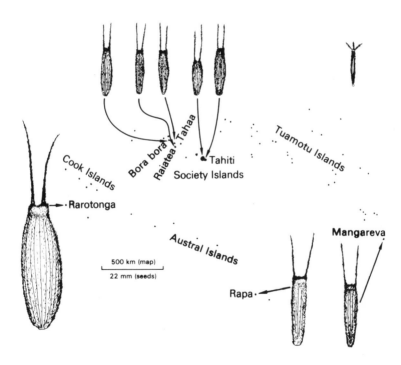

FIG. 2.9. Seeds of the known species of *Fitchia*, a genus of the Compositae endemic to the south Pacific. Inset: a seed of *Bidens*, lighter and more toothed, and so more easily dispersed. (Modified from Carlquist 1974.)

to *Fitchia* are herbs with spiked seeds of the sort also shown in Fig. 2.9, the spikes being an adaptation for dispersal by animals. In *Fitchia* the spikes are relict, the plants are trees, and the fruits can only drop passively to the forest floor.

As in the interpretation of dispersal patterns, the interpretation of loss of dispersal ability should not be hasty. Flightless species of insects occur widely on continents, and flightless birds such as the ostrich, *Struthio camelus*, are continental. Nevertheless, island environments frequently seem to encourage the evolution of the loss of dispersal ability. Two reasons are often put forward for this loss. The first is that with the absence of predators, flying no longer has a selective advantage, and indeed might have a disadvantage in that the energy used in flying could be more usefully put to other purposes. The second explanation is that flying forms are more likely to be swept to sea by high winds, giving a selective advantage to the flightless ones. Both explanations could well be true, but there is a lack of hard evidence.

Reproductive change

In some birds and reptiles, females of island races lay larger and fewer eggs than their close relatives on the mainland. Table 2.3 compiled from Lack (1970) shows the variation of all the subspecies of ducks found on remote islands. The locations of these islands are shown in Fig. 2.10. These data show not only the reproductive shift, but are also examples of the size shifts discussed below; in ducks, island subspecies are normally smaller than the mainland species. On the mainland, and for that matter on large islands such as Britain, there are commonly a number of species of duck in the genus *Anas*, which divide up the resources between them in an interesting way as described and illustrated by Lack (1974). On the small islands shown in Table 2.3 there is only one resident species, even though in most cases some of the other species in the genus pass through on migration. The island subspecies are reported to have more catholic tastes than their mainland counterparts, and even in some cases have become slightly marine. The Laysan duck has become, to some extent, a terrestrial species. There is an aerial, coloured, oblique photograph of Laysan in Eliot and Blair (1978), who give a brief description of the ecological disaster that hit Laysan, also discussed by Schlanger and Gillett (1976). Rabbits were let loose in about 1903; they multiplied and destroyed most of the vegetation. Those rabbits that had not died of starvation were exterminated by an expedition in 1923. The Laysan duck survived this disaster and now has a population of about 250 birds.

Table 2.3. Sub-species of ducks in the genus *Anas*, endemic on remote islands

Name	Place	Male wing length mm	Eggs in clutch	Egg as % body weight
On tropical islands:				
platyrhynchos (Mallard)		265	11	5.4
p. laysanensis	Laysan	201	5	10.9
p. wyvilliana	Hawaii	220	8	8.5
strepera (Gadwall)		271		
s. couesi (extinct)	Washington	199		
bahamensis (Bahama pintail)		214		
b. galapagensis	Galapagos	203		
gibberifrons (Grey teal)		202		
g. remissa	Rennell*	187		
On subantarctic islands:				
acuta (Pintail)		271	8	
a. eatoni	Kerguelen + Crozets	218	4–5	
georgica (Yellow-billed pintail)		245	8	6.0
g. georgica	South Georgia	217	5	8.0
castanea (Chestnut teal)		218	9	8.0
c. chlorotis	New Zealand*	199	6	10.5
c. auklandica	Aucklands* + Campbell	±136 (nearly flightless)	3–4	18.0

* Rennell and Auckland have one other species of *Anas*, New Zealand has four. The remaining islands have no other resident *Anas*.

A. superciliosa (Grey duck) is on Rennell, Auckland, and New Zealand, *A. gibberifrons* (a recent immigrant), *A. platyrhynchos* (introduced), and *A. rhynchotis* (New Zealand shoveler) are also in New Zealand. For comparison there are seven British species: *A. platyrhynchos* (Mallard), *A. acuta* (Pintail), *A. crecca* (Teal), *A. querquedula* (Garganey), *A. strepera* (Gadwall), *A. clypeata* (Shoveler), and *A. penelope* (Wigeon). Data from Lack 1970.

Table 2.3 shows that, as measured by the male wing length, subspecies are smaller. They also tend to have duller and less distinct plumage, which may reflect both Gloger's rule and also the lessened need for the males to be distinct when there are no other species to cause confusion. The weight of the egg is more or less constant, not changed, but on the island forms the body size, where it is known, tends to be less, and consequently, the egg is a percentage of the body weight tends to increase. So there is no consistent change in the total weight of the clutch (clutch size × egg weight) as a percentage of the body weight.

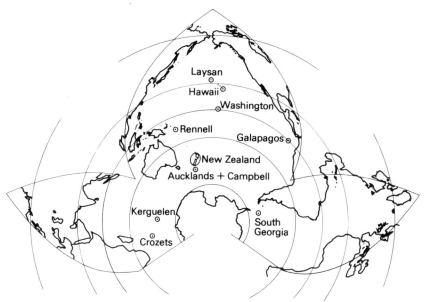

F IG. 2.10.   The location of islands with endemic subspecies of ducks. (See also Table 2.3.)

Size change

Island endemics may be markedly larger, or appreciably smaller, than their mainland relatives. Small ducks and small Pacific snails have been mentioned. There are many striking examples of large forms. The largest earwig (Insecta, Dermaptera) of the world is found on St. Helena; it is a remarkable 78 mm long (Olson 1975). Again, the trees of St. Helena have all been derived from herbs (Carlquist 1965; Wilson *et al.* 1973).

Giant tortoises demonstrate some of the problems of interpreting the occurrence of large forms on islands. All giant tortoises are now put in the genus *Geochelone*, and the modern island forms, up to 130 cm long on Aldabra (*G. gigantea*) and on the Galapagos (*G. elephantopus*, with distinct subspecies on different islands) are well known. As giant-tortoise populations are readily killed off by man, these living forms need to be considered not only with other living forms, but also with those recently extinct. Other species of *Geochelone* occur, or were found, in South America (in the same subgenus, *Chelonoidis*, as the Galapagos species), in *G. (Aldabrachelys)* on Madagascar and the Seychelles, as well as Aldabra, and in other subgenera on the Mascarene Islands (Réunion, Mauritius, Rodriguez), and on the African mainland. An

African species is up to 80 cm long, one Madagascan species up to 122 cm, while one of the two Rodriguez species reached only 42 cm, the other reached 85 cm (Arnold 1979). So island tortoises are not always the biggest. It is not certain that large size was evolved after reaching the island; it might be that it made dispersal to oceanic islands easier. Arnold suggests that large size can come from an absence of large predators, an absence of large competing herbivores, and the simplicity of community structure, and that it could be a buffer against climatic variability. The same factors could be evoked to explain flightlessness or the increase in egg size. All are reasonable; evidence is lacking.

Some evidence about selective forces can be obtained from wider comparative studies. Foster (1964) has compared the size of insular subspecies of mammals with the nearest mainland form; his results are summarized in Table 2.4. Broadly, on islands, small mammals become bigger; large mammals become smaller. Rodent subspecies are larger in 87 per cent of the island races. This might result from the absence of predators, leading to greater intraspecific conflict, and therefore an advantage to large size. On the other hand, carnivores and artiodactyls become smaller in 85 per cent of cases. The simplest explanation for this is that the limited food supply on an island gives an advantage to smaller individuals: possibly either the small individuals eat the same food as the larger ones, but need less of it and so are better able to survive, or, alternatively, smaller individuals eat smaller and commoner food items. The first possibility is more plausible for artiodactyls, the second for carnivores. The second possibility also involves a niche shift and such changes will be considered in Chapter 6.

Table 2.4. The size of mammalian insular subspecies

	Smaller	Same	Larger
Marsupials	0	1	3
Insectivores	4	4	1
Lagomorphs	6	1	1
Rodents	6	3	60
Carnivores	13	1	1
Artiodactyls	9	2	0

After Foster 1964.

Foster's data for his other three orders are much thinner, and so more difficult to interpret. Lagomorphs (hares, etc.), large compared with rats and mice, mostly become smaller, and it may be that their food requirements and social structure lead to them changing in the same way as artiodactyls. Insectivores are carnivorous, but as both their own size and their prey sizes are small, it is perhaps surprising that the insular subspecies also on the whole become small. Two few marsupial species were measured for the numbers to be interpreted.

The data in Table 2.4 all relate to living species and subspecies. There are a number of fossil island races of mammals known, and the most interesting of these are the dwarf forms of large-sized animals. The most striking are the dwarf elephants and hippopotamuses. Pygmy elephant remains have been found on Mediterranean islands such as Sicily, Crete and Cyprus (Sondaar 1976), and on the Californian Channel Islands (Philbrick 1967). Table 2.4 points to the importance of finding numerous examples before drawing any general conclusion, but there seems little doubt that the Probiscoidea were quite commonly small when on relatively small islands, fitting the general rule for large mammals.

Extinction

The rate of extinction on islands is an important aspect of the Mac-Arthur and Wilson theory of island biogeography, discussed in Chapters 4 and 5. There is no doubt that much extinction has occurred on islands, but a very great deal of it has been caused by man, which makes it difficult to obtain estimates of natural rates of extinction. Man's destruction may be direct, as with the dodo, indirect by clearing the habitat as Hooker noted for Madeira and St. Helena, or by the introduction of other mammals such as cats, rats, goats, or pigs. Elton (1958) stressed the vulnerability of island populations to all forms of introduction. Since 1680, on the estimates in Thompson (1964), 127 races or species or birds have become extinct, 11 of them on continents, 29 on large islands, and 87 on small islands. Most of these extinctions are caused by man. In many cases, as on Ascension Island (Fig. 2.2) (Stonehouse 1960), many species of sea birds, and no doubt the other organisms associated with them, survive only on outlying islets.

Natural extinction undoubtedly occurs, and the difficulties in estimating its rate will be considered in Chapters 4 and 5. An example is the song thrush, *Turdus philomelos*, which now occurs all over the British Isles including Orkney, except in Shetland (Sharrock 1976). The thrush was absent from Shetland in the nineteenth century, and established itself on the islands in about 1906. It usually bred near trees, of which there were very few in Shetland, the largest groups of trees, at Kergord, being planted in 1909. By the 1940s there were about 24 pairs of thrushes breeding. The winter of 1946–7 was very severe, and the population dropped to three to four pairs from then until 1953 (Venables and Venables 1955). It became extinct between 1953 and

1969. This example demonstrates the importance of climatic extremes in determining the survival of island populations. Winters as severe as 1946–7 have occurred in the British Isles in this century about once every 15 years.

Relicts

In contrast to the occurrence of extinction on islands, relicts are species that have survived on certain islands but have become extinct elsewhere. Many of the best examples are on the island continents or near-continents such as Australia and Madagascar. There is no need here to discuss marsupials or lemurs; they are described in many books. Carlquist (1965) gives an account of the birds and plants on Madagascar as well as the mammals, while Moreau (1966) gives a more systematic account of the birds. *Sphenodon*, a lizard-like reptile in New Zealand is another well-known relict (Kuschel 1975). Relicts are, of course, endemics at the same time. A relict represents the remains of a group formerly widespread, whereas an endemic is merely a form special to a particular area. It may, indeed, sometimes be a relict, but is more frequently merely different.

It is a common observation that evolution generally progresses more rapidly in larger continental areas than in smaller ones. As a result, forms evolve on the major continents then migrate and suppress those on the islands. A classic case is the superiority of placental mammals over marsupial mammals. The effects of the placentals introduced in Australia are well-known. Less familiar is the extinction of the Borhyaenids, a family of carnivorous marsupials, in South America, following the invasion of placentals from North America. But whether marsupials, on the whole, are legitimately regarded as a relict group is perhaps more disputable. For instance, the opossum, *Didelphis virginiana*, is a successful marsupial in North America. On a smaller scale, Mayr (1969) documents the repeated invasion of small islands from New Guinea, and the rarity of reinvasion of the large island. Such processes, which create relic species, will be discussed more in Chapter 7 on the taxon cycle. The existence of relicts and endemics on islands is a spur to their exploration and conservation, and an important feature to bear in mind when considering theories of population turnover.

Endemics

Endemic forms, that is to say those found nowhere else, are particularly characteristic of oceanic islands. For instance, on Tristan all the species of land birds are endemic. Hawaiian Drepanidids and the Galapagos

Geospizines (honeycreepers and Darwin's finches) are justly famous cases of endemics. Major features of these two groups are dealt with extensively in many books; some special features of their evolution and ecology will be considered in Chapter 9. Two other cases illustrate the spasmodic occurrence of endemics. The chat *Saxicola dacotiae* is endemic in the Canary Islands, and seems to lie taxonomically between the whinchat, *S. rubetra*, and the stonechat, *S. torquata* (both common Palaearctic birds), though possibly closer to the latter (Hall and Moreau 1970). Another taxonomically-isolated island bird is the lark, *Alauda razae*, which is found only on one very small member of the Cape Verde Islands, the island of Razo of about five km². The species is confined to less than 100 ha, and the population may be as small as 50 pairs (Bannerman and Bannerman 1968).

Treating endemics more quantitatively, Lack (1969a) gives the following list for the percentage of the total avifauna that are represented by endemic subspecies in the North Atlantic: Ireland 3, Iceland 21, Azores 30, Canaries 45. The Canaries are at the southern limit of the Palaearctic, while Iceland is towards the northern edge; so those data show latitudinal effects, fairly readily ascribable to the vicissitudes of the Pleistocene, as well as a distinction between the continental fauna on Ireland and the oceanic faunas on the others. Looking at endemicity along a different dimension, on the Azores there are, appropriately for an oceanic island, no indigenous land mammals, while the beetles and snails frequently belong to endemic species. The birds, in contrast, have no endemic species at all, and 70 per cent are placed in the same subspecies as those on the continent of Europe. There is one species of bat, Leisler's *Nyctalus leisleri*.

Readers may like to know about endemics on the British Isles. For many groups it is not possible to say which species are endemic and which are not, because sometimes when the British taxa have been well studied, the European have not. Certainly, plenty of invertebrate species and lower plants will prove to be endemic. Some cases are well established, like the common, large, and readily identifiable centipede, *Lithobius variegatus*, which is generally more abundant in the north and west than the non-endemic *L. forficatus*, similar in size and general appearance (Eason 1964).

Speciation in plants, as is well known, can take place through polyploidy quite apart from the complications produced by apomixis. Walters (1978) has listed and discussed British endemic plants. (He overlooks *Cochlearia scotica*.) Most of these plants tell us nothing in particular about islands, the phenomena producing them being the same whether or not the plant occurs on the island. There are, however, some which form good geographical segregates. *Rhynchosinapis wrightii* occurs only on the island of Lundy (Fig. 10.1). *R. monensis*, the Isle of Man cabbage, occurs only in and near the Irish Sea (on the Isle of Man, the English coast and the Solway), in the Clyde, and with two outlying records from Iona in the North and the Gower Peninsula in the South (Perring and Walters 1962). *Primula scotica*, found only in the extreme north of Scotland and in Orkney, is a polyploid member of the *P. farinosa* group. The distribution of these two species and the related *P. scandinavica* in north-west Europe is shown by Fitter (1977). *P. farinosa* has a diploid chromosome number of 18 (and occasionally 36), *scotica* of 54, *scandinavica* of 72.

Among birds and mammals, British forms are nowadays regarded as only subspecies, the Irish forms being often the more distinct. The one possible exception is the Scottish cross-bill, *Loxia scotica*, which may be breeding sympatrically with the spruce cross-bill, *L. curvirostra*, but could be a subspecies of either *curvirostra* or of the pine cross-bill, *L. pytyopsittacus*, which is otherwise not found in Britain (Sharrock 1976; Voous 1960). The red grouse, *Lagopus lagopus scoticus*, is probably the most distinct subspecies. It is rufous brown all the year round, and readily distinguished from the closely-related species, the ptarmigan, *L. mutus*, which has white wings in summer and is almost all white in winter. However, the red grouse is only a geographic form of the willow grouse, which is very difficult to distinguish from the ptarmigan either in winter or summer. (In North America the willow grouse is called the willow ptarmigan; the European ptarmigan is known as the rock ptarmigan.)

The time likely to be taken for endemic species or even subspecies to become distinct is largely unknown and has been disputed. Nevertheless, one thing is clear: island endemics have maintained a population continuously on their islands long enough for their distinct races to be formed.

PART 2

The Numbers of Species on Islands

3 Species–area relationships

One of the features of islands is that they have rather few species on them. But in mainland areas smaller plots have fewer species than larger ones. So an important question to be asked about an island is: does it have fewer species than a comparable area on the mainland? And if the answer to that is 'yes', another question follows: can any quantitative statement be made about the degree of the impoverishment of the island? The first of those questions presumes that an area of mainland can be found for which a comparison may legitimately be made.

Both questions relate only to the total number of species. Modern studies of communities, summarized for instance by Pielou (1975), attempt to measure their diversity by more sophisticated measures than just the species numbers. The total diversity of a community can be divided approximately into a richness component and an evenness component. The total number of species is a measure of the richness, while the distribution of individuals over these species is a measure of evenness. Diversity measures seldom allow for the types of species involved, such as predators or herbivores, annuals or perennials, but it would seem that a shift in type of species is also characteristic of island biota. Unfortunately, for many islands the total number of species is the only measure of diversity available for study.

The central topic in this chapter is the observed relationship between the numbers of species and the area. This is followed by a consideration of the effects of isolation and of distance on species numbers, and of a possible peninsular effect. Before dealing with any of these observations, some background theory is needed.

Theories of the distribution of species abundance

Two main theories of community composition have been much discussed. Both arise from the common observation that, in any community, there are few species represented by many individuals, while there are many more species represented by fewer individuals. Where the predictions of the theories differ is on the commonness of very rare species. In the first theory, which originates with Fisher, Corbet, and Williams (1943), it is thought that the most numerous class of species are those that are individually, rarest. This gives rise to the logarithmic series of abundance, which has been discussed in detail by Williams (1964). The alternative theory states that the most numerous species are those of middling abundance, while species with very few individuals are as rare as species with a very large number of individuals. This gives rise to the log-normal curve, which was introduced by Preston (1948). Preston pointed out that if the whole community followed a log-normal curve, and only a sample of it were taken, then only the right-hand portion of the log-normal curve would be observed. He drew a veil line, as shown in Fig. 3.1, and its position is such that species to the left of it would be represented by less than one individual in the sample, that is to say, in general, would not be observed. If the sampling intensity is increased, the veil line is pushed to the left. In the limit, when the whole community has been censused, a whole normal curve would be seen.

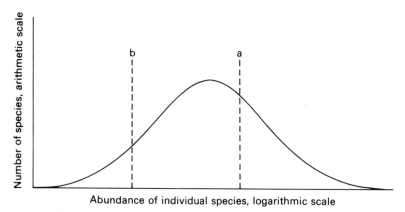

F i g. 3.1.   Preston's log-normal relationship with veil lines (a and b). In a small sample, only species more abundant than a will be observed, in a larger one, species more abundant (to the right of) b.

For quite simple theoretical reasons, neither theory can be exactly true. The logarithmic series was derived as the limiting case of the negative binomial distribution, setting a parameter to zero. This has the impossible implication that the total number of species in a community is infinite. The log-normal theory also has problems with infinity. A normal curve goes to infinity in both directions. In practice, on a finite surface, and even the whole earth is still a finite surface, species cannot be of more than finite commonness or finite rareness. The difference between species is discrete, and so cannot be matched exactly by a continuous distribution such as the log-normal.

As Taylor (1978) shows, in small samples both the logarithmic series and the right-hand part of the log-normal fit equally well, and have, in effect, the same number of parameters, two. This is because two of the three parameters of the log-normal cannot be separated numerically in such a case. In larger samples, there is now general agreement that there are fewer rare species than middlingly common ones. In this situation, the logarithmic series can be generalized to the gamma distribution, which has one more parameter, three, the same number as the log-normal distribution. For the log-normal these are the total area under the curve, its mean, and its standard deviation; the gamma distribution has a parameter k in place of the standard deviation. The total area under the curve is the total number of species in the set being sampled, and so has to be estimated in these cases. The log-series can be regarded as the small sample condition of the gamma distribution.

The log-normal distribution predicts a symmetrical S-shaped curve if the logarithm of the abundance of a species is plotted against the rank of its abundance. Such a plot is shown in Fig. 3.2 for the Lepidoptera of Norfolk Island. Holloway (1977) shows that this curve is slightly skew, not symmetrical about the inflection point. Curves of this sort can be

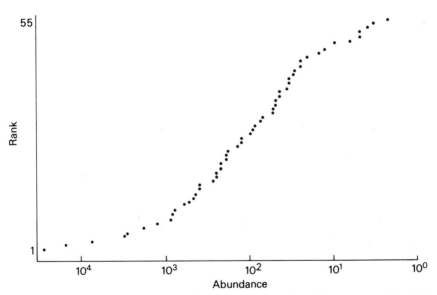

F ɪ ɢ. 3.2.   Species–abundance plot for resident Lepidoptera on Norfolk Island. Each dot represents the count of a distinct species. Plotted this way, a Preston log-normal relationship would be a symmetrical S-shaped curve, the curve of the cumulative normal distribution. Note that the abundance scale runs contrary to the usual convention, so that extra species will occur at the right. (Modified from Holloway 1977.)

fitted well by both the log-normal or the gamma distributions, though sophisticated computer algorithms should be used (Kempton and Taylor 1974, 1978). Similar plots for plants can be found in Whittaker (1969), and the mathematics of the distributions is discussed by Pielou (1975) and Engen (1978).

Both theories in their original form refer to the number of individuals per species. There is obviously something to be said, if the size of individuals in the different species differ widely, for using a measure of biomass or productivity. In practice, studies have been restricted to single taxonomic groups such as vascular plants, or birds, or Lepidoptera. Empirical plots for the distribution over all species in the community are not available, though it seems reasonable to expect the different trophic levels to behave fairly independently. If so, the whole community would not follow either curve, because neither curve is additive over independent samples. This lack of additivity is, indeed, another reason for supposing that neither curve will fit exactly even to one taxonomic group in one place. For instance, if one group of birds, such as the Passeriformes (perching birds), follows a log-normal distribution, and another group of birds such as the Charadriiformes (gulls, waders, etc.) follows another log-normal distribution, with different parameters, then the total of the two groups cannot follow a log-normal distribution.

Both these theories lead to a definite expectation for the shape of the species–area curve, the best-fitting line to the plot of a number of species in different areas. This is reviewed by May (1974, 1975). He also reviews the assumptions that would lead to these two distributions and of some others. For the logarithmic series, the plot of the number of species against the logarithm of the area would be a straight line. For the log-normal distribution, a straight line would be expected from the logarithm of the number of species plotted against the logarithm of the area, though there would be a perceptible steepening of the curve at small areas. For some rather general assumptions about the log-normal curve, May showed that the slope of the log species against log area, often given the symbol z, would be between 0.16 and 0.39, steepening to as much as 0.5 for small areas. For one particular variant of the log-normal theory, that in fact first proposed by Preston and named by him the canonical log-normal, the slope would be about 0.25. (Different authors have given slightly different values for the slope of the canonical log-normal: as it is not, in fact, exactly a straight line, a small range of values is acceptable. This figure is one given by May.) Engen (1977, 1979) has shown that the gamma model also leads to a straight line for the logarithm of the species against the logarithm of the area, and that the line has a slope of $-k$.

From these results one would expect that large samples, or samples from large areas, would produce straight lines on the double logarithmic plot, and that small samples, or those from small areas, would be linear for species number against the logarithm of the area. In view of the close relationship of the logarithmic series and the gamma model, both plots might well be satisfactory in some cases.

Observations on species–area relationships

For island data, Darlington (1957) suggested the rule, based on observation, that an increase in the area of tenfold led to a doubling of the number of species. This is equivalent to saying that there is a linear relationship between the log-species and log-area with a slope of 0.301 (i.e. $\log_{10} 2$). As a rule of thumb, not to be taken too seriously, this works quite well. For instance, Lack (1969*a*) pointed out that Ireland has 60 per cent of the breeding birds on the British list. The total area of the British Isles is 6.4 times the area of Ireland, and this would lead to an expectation in Ireland of 57 per cent of the total.

In Fig. 3.3 the validity of Darlington's rule can be seen. This shows, on a double logarithmic plot, the number of breeding land-bird species (excluding water birds) on a wide selection of individual islands in warm climates, tropical and sub-tropical. The general trend is slightly steeper than Darlington's rule, about 0.33, and there is quite a lot of scatter about it. Individual islands more than 300 km from the next

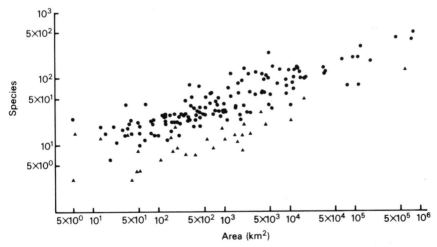

FIG. 3.3. Species–area plot for the land birds of individual islands in the warmer seas. ▲ Islands more than 300 km from the next largest land mass, or in the Hawaiian or Galapagos archipelagos. (Modified from Slud 1976).

largest, and those in the very isolated archipelagos of Hawaii and Galapagos, are shown with a different symbol. Clearly, some of the scatter can be related to isolation, and this will be discussed more fully below.

The slope of plots such as this varies considerably in different surveys. Examples of flatter slopes, about 0.2, can be seen in Fig. 2.4 for various groups in the Azores and the Channel Islands and in Fig. 5.12 for arthropods on mangrove islands; of steeper slopes in Fig. 8.5 for Hawaii; and of both a middling slope and no relationship at all in Fig. 9.3 of the lizard *Anolis* on different island groups in the Caribbean. This variability in slope is, indeed, present in Fig. 3.3. Included in the 162 points shown, 47 are from the West Indies. Slud (1976) shows them separately, along with some data from groups of West Indian islands, and the slope for that region is only 0.17. The larger West Indian islands fall under the main cluster of Fig. 3.3, at the right-hand side, while the smaller ones tend to the top of the cluster at the left-hand side. Cuba is about 200 km from both Yucatan and Florida.

The double logarithmic plot is frequently linear, but its slope, and the scatter about the slope, and its position in relation to the axes (the intercept) vary considerably from study to study. How often is it satisfactorily linear?

For samples within communities, as opposed to the comparison of islands and mainlands, there has been a dispute since the 1920s amongst botanists about the shape of the species-area curve. Early in the nineteenth century, H. C. Watson, the first man to try to map the distribution of British plants systematically, suggested a relationship that implied that the log number of species was a linear function of the log area (see Connor and McCoy 1979). This point of view was championed by Arrhenius (1921). Gleason (1922) disagreed, and thought that the plot of species against log area gave the best straight line. There was at least agreement that the plot of species against the area directly was curved, with the number of species increasing more slowly at larger areas. All this is shown diagramatically in Fig. 3.4. These botanical surveys were based on nested quadrats. The observer starts at a point, and places a quadrat over it. The sample for his next larger area includes his first sample, and so on up to the largest area sampled. This is unsatisfactory statistically, and also not directly comparable to the studies made of different islands. Gleason claimed that the plot he favoured, of species against log area, gives the best extrapolation to the observed number of species in much larger areas. All the published botanical data were studied by Dony (1970), and his main conclusions were noted by Williamson (1973). Dony calculated regression lines using the logarithm of the area as the independent variable, and both

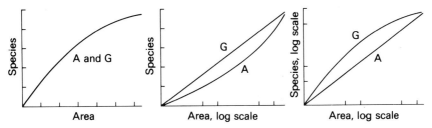

FIG. 3.4. Differing views of the species–area relationship. Arrhenius and Gleason held that various transformations of the axes produced plots like those marked A and G respectively.

the number of species and the logarithm of the number of species as a dependent variable. Statistically this is not entirely satisfactory, as it is evident that some species will occasionally have been overlooked, so the species number is a minimum, while, conversely, not every bit of the area can have been searched for plants, particularly when the area is more than a few square metres, so the area is a maximum of the area that has genuinely been searched. However, applying his procedure systematically gives a fairly unambiguous result, one that would only be changed slightly by using more sophisticated statistics.

Dony found that 47 of the surveys fitted pretty well to Arrhenius' scheme, of a linear relationship between log species and log area, whereas only 12 fitted Gleason's scheme best. For seven, Dony suggested that the best fit could be obtained by two straight lines, with different slopes, on the Arrhenius' plot. Ten schemes fitted neither of these. Dony also tested his fit by extrapolation both upwards to the total British flora, and in some cases also downwards to small areas. The studies he used included bryophytes and lichens as well as vascular plants, and with these the total British flora is of the order of 3000 species. He found six studies of shingle and grass communities led to expectations of 2000 to 5000 species, while the one woodland study led to 22 250. At the other end, 10 studies of bog, salt marsh, dune, and moor, all relatively impoverished in species, led to predictions of a median of only 350. Those extrapolations are all based on the nested quadrat type of survey in quite small areas. From wider surveys using the national grid as quadrats, with units of 1 km², he found that the log–log plot led to reasonable predictions both for the British Isles and for 1 m² plots, while the arithmetic log plot led to rather too low a figure for the total British Isles, and absurd figures for 1 m². His results from one very detailed survey of national grid square SP02 in the Cotswolds are shown in Table 3.1. SP02 is 100 km²; each individual square kilometre was surveyed.

Table 3.1. Predicted number of plant species in areas of different
         sizes from calculated relationships

	Area			
	1 m²	1 km²	4 km²	British Isles
From log/log relationship	18	269	353	3210
From arith./log relationship	−1410	145	300	1600

From Dony 1970.

Dony's figures have been given here in some detail, as his report is
unpublished and the results not readily available. Schoener (1976),
using a great variety of data from islands, observed that the log–log
(Arrhenius) plot generally worked quite well with plant data, while
with birds the untransformed species against log area plot (Gleason)
was more frequently linear. Dony observed a wide range of slopes (zs)
in his studies (though he did not comment on it) from 0.08 to 0.55.
Flessa and Sepkoski (1978) compiled 54 studies from the literature, and
again found a wide range of slopes, from 0.05 to 0.72 (the slopes they
recorded as steeper than this were not strictly comparable). Connor
and McCoy (1979) examined 100 studies, several of which had been
included by Flessa and Sepkoski, several based on their own calculations. They found slopes varying from slightly negative up to 1.13, but
of five slopes steeper than 0.70, only the steepest, for insects on Hawaii,
is a standard set of species on islands (see also Fig. 8.5). Gross (1975)
gives four slopes for lepidopteran studies centred on the south-west
Pacific, all about 0.70. Slopes from this value down to not significantly
different from zero can all be regarded as not unusual, though the
majority do indeed lie in the range indicated by May, from 0.16 to 0.39.
Connor and McCoy examined the goodness of fit not only of species
and the logarithm of species against the logarithm of the area, but also
of species and the logarithm of species against area untransformed.
Taking them in that order, they found best fits for 27, 43, 35 and 14
cases, and satisfactory fits for 38, 75, 47 and 22 cases. As before, the
Arrhenius (log–log) plot is the commonest satisfactory and good fit, but
there are plenty of data sets not linearized by it.
    It has often been said, following Preston (1962), that species–area
curves are steeper on islands than on continents. A common view is
that islands have slopes of about 0.35 and continental areas around
0.20. If there is such an effect, the surveys quoted above indicate that it
is a weak one. Two other systematic variations in the slope may be

mentioned at this point, one confirmed, the other not thoroughly examined. The first is that on archipelagos, the slope is flatter the more isolated the archipelago (Schoener 1976; Connor and McCoy 1979). Figure 3.5 shows this for the Solomon islands, but Fig. 8.5, for Hawaii, is an exception. The other effect concerns islands that have derived their present biota from a larger one, either by submergence or by extinction not balanced by immigration. It has been said that such a biotic decline would steepen the species–area curve (Brown 1971). This implies that the relative rate of extinction is higher on small islands, which might be true, but too few cases have been studied for it to be accepted without further evidence.

Most work on the species–area relationship has concentrated on variations in the slope, in z. Gould (1979) points out that variation in

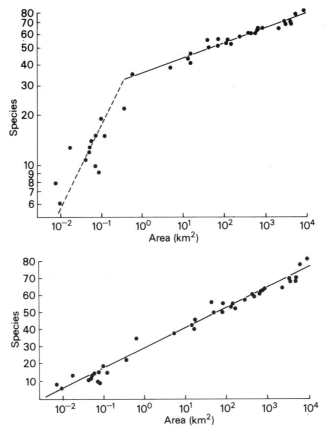

F IG. 3.5. Species–area plots for birds in the Solomon Islands, using Arrhenius and Gleason plots. (Modified from Diamond and Mayr 1976.)

the intercept is also of interest. Figures 2.4 and 3.3 show that the intercept varies between groups and with isolation. Legg (1978) suggests that the difference in intercept is the major difference between lepidopteran assemblages in different parts of the world.

There are three more difficult issues concerning species–area relationships. These are the question of what happens in very small areas, the effects of habitat heterogeneity, and the differences observed in different taxa. Habitat heterogeneity is itself a complicated phenomenon, and it will be discussed further towards the end of Chapter 5. In a sense, what happens on very small islands is part of the same phenomenon.

Some islands are so small and so exposed that they cannot support populations of some taxa. To take an extreme case, St. Paul's Rocks (Fig. 2.2) in the mid-Atlantic have a land area of about 1 ha. However, they are continually washed by waves, and support neither vascular plants nor, more obviously, land bird populations (Smith, Hardy, Leith, Spaull, and Twelves 1974). Indeed, even the smallest species of bird in temperate climates, such as wrens, *Troglodytes troglodytes*, discussed in Chapter 6, would have only two or three pairs per hectare in favourable habitats, too small a population to be permanent. [Schoener (1968) gives a useful table of the sizes of territories in different species of birds.] Figure 3.5 shows species counts on islands in the Solomons down to areas a little less than a hectare. Indeed, any island smaller than about a hectare is likely to have no land-bird species breeding on it, and zeros cannot be plotted on a log–log plot. Including such data by, say, adding one species to each observed count will distort, and frequently steepen, the observed curve. This is a quite different effect from the steepening at small areas predicted by May (1975) for the log–normal distribution.

Islands with no breeding land-birds are not invariably very small. Many Arctic and Antarctic islands only support sea birds, an obvious consequence of climate. In rather warmer regions the oceanic islands of Easter in the Pacific, Trindade in the Atlantic (Fig. 2.2) and St. Paul and Amsterdam in the Indian Ocean (Fig. 1.5) are all without known land breeding birds. Their areas are 165, 10, 8 and 54 km², a comparable range of sizes to those of the Tristan archipelago (Table 2.1, endpapers). Habitats on Easter Island have probably been much degraded by over-population by Polynesians in the past (Bellwood 1978), so the absence of the land birds might or might not be the result of extinction. The other three islands are uninhabited and well vegetated (Nicoll 1909; Watson 1975).

Another effect of small areas on the species–area plot is shown by Diamond and Mayr (1975). Their results for resident birds on individual islands in the Solomon group are shown in Fig. 3.5. From the log–log plot one might think there was an important ecological break at 0.3 km². Above this the slope is 0.08. The species against log area plot, though, appears to be linear throughout. Dony (1970) also found some data sets in which there appeared to be two straight lines on the log–log plot, but none of his examples gave single straight lines on the species against log area plot. Schoener (1976) gives other cases where the plot for birds on archipelagos appears curved on the log–log plot, though none of his data looks like the two straight lines found in Diamond and Mayr's data. The point here is that, if islands of less than 0.3 km² had not been studied, this phenomenon would have been overlooked. Such islands are still quite large in relation to the territories of many species of birds. Rusterholz and Howe (1979) also found a break in the log–log plot of birds on islands in Minnesota. They think the break is a consequence of species reaching the lower limit of territory size.

The importance of habitat heterogeneity will be discussed in Chapter 5, but one consequence of an island being small is that its habitats will be less diverse than those of a larger island. Whitehead and Jones (1969), re-examining Niering's (1963) data on plant species on islands in the Kapingamarangi Atoll (a Polynesian outlier, see Fig. 6.4), pointed out that some breaks would be expected in the species–area curve on biological grounds. Very small islands consist only of the strand habitat, saturated in salt water; rather few plant species can grow on such islands. Once the diameter of the island becomes sufficiently large, more than about 100 m, a lens of fresh water can accumulate under the island, thereby allowing an increase in the number of plant species. As there are relatively few species that can tolerate the strand conditions, the species–area curve on islands of this sort will suddenly steepen at an area of about a hectare, which is what is observed.

What is a very small island for land birds is quite a respectably sized one for vascular plants. There are, however, less obvious taxonomic effects on species–area curves, especially on oceanic islands. Terborgh (1973) studied species–area relationships in different families of birds in the West Indies and found different slopes in different families. One, the Mimidae (thrashers and mocking birds), even had a negative slope, and thus have fewer species on the larger islands. This family has a remarkable number of endemic species in the Lesser Antilles (Lack 1976).

Distance effects

Possible reasons why an increase in area should lead to an increase in species will be considered along with theories of the species composition on islands in the next two chapters. There are, however, a number of other variables besides area which might be thought *a priori* to affect the number of species on islands and which have been tested for. The most important of these is the isolation of the island, the distance of the island either from other islands or from a continental area. The possible effect of isolation on the intercept of the species–area plot has already been noted.

One obvious approach to studying the effect of different variables on the number of species on an island is to use multiple regression. Another approach, through residuals, is considered below. There are some minor difficulties in both. The first problem is to decide not only which variables to include but also how to include them. The distance from the island to the nearest mainland might seem to be a natural variable. But if the probability of a species crossing the gap involves a negative exponential such as

$$pr(g) = k_1 \exp (-k_2 d)$$

where the left-hand side is the probability of crossing the gap, and on the right-hand side d is the distance and k_1 and k_2 are two constants, then it would be sensible to work with the logarithm of the distance. Plausible arguments could be put forward for other transformations, both for the distance and for other variables.

Another problem is that information may not be available on the sort of variables that the investigator would like to include. There has been much discussion on the importance of environmental heterogeneity, but it is difficult to find any satisfactory measure; however, as will be seen, some attempts have been made. For most islands the information that is available tends to be limited to the area, some indication of the elevation, particularly of the highest peak, obvious geographical variables like the latitude and longitude, and distance to various points. Species lists of varying reliability will also be available. The question of how much human interference has affected the number of species will usually be unanswerable.

A third problem is deciding which variables are significant in a multiple regression. Step-wise multiple regression programs are popular, no doubt partly because they are included in some of the standard packages. These programs order the variables on some statistical criterion or other. It is not always realized that the statistical criteria may differ, and that this can produce differing orders (Hocking 1976).

A good example of both what can be done with a multiple regression and its limitations is given by the studies of Johnson and Raven (1970) on plant–species diversity on the California Islands and on the British Isles. Plant species on both these groups are reasonably well-known;

there is no doubt that more intensive study would almost certainly add to the species list of any island. The data for the British Isles were taken from Perring and Walters (1962), in which presence or absence of plants was recorded in 10 km squares of the National Grid. Some squares cover areas both on an island and on the mainland, so for producing island lists this data set has an extra, though fairly small, source of error.

The physical variables Johnson and Raven used were the area of the island, its maximum elevation, its latitude, the distance to the mainland and the distance to the nearest island, and the number of soil types. The last variable is a particularly interesting one, as being some measure of environmental variability. Unfortunately, it was scored on a very small range from 1 to 5. Johnson and Raven solve the problem of what transformation to use on the variables by using two sets of analyses. In one all the variables were taken in the form in which they were recorded. In the other variables were converted to logarithms. This has some slightly odd effects. In the logarithmic analysis the variables include not only log species and log area, but also the logarithm of the latitude and the logarithm of maximum elevation. A relationship that might well be important, namely that of species against log of the area, is not studied. Nevertheless, the results were very interesting and useful. For the British Isles they found that, in the logarithmic transformation, only area and latitude were important variables, and in the arithmetic version the same two variables, but now with soil types added, were important. In neither case did distance appear to have an effect. Area and latitude were again the important variables on the California Islands.

Power (1972), also studying Californian islands, included the number of birds as well as the number of plants, and expressed his results in terms of path regressions, which is a way of expressing partial regression coefficients. Abbott (1974) made a similar study of the plants, birds and insects using 19 sub-Antarctic islands. The results of both studies are shown in Fig. 3.6. Power agrees with Johnson and Raven that area and latitude are the important variables for plants, but finds that both isolation (which is another way of expressing distance) and the number of plant species affect the number of bird species. There is the reasonable assumption that plants affect birds rather than *vice versa*.

Abbott finds that temperature is the most important variable for plants in the sub-Antarctic, although area is still important, but that only plants are important for the birds and the insects. However, in his data there are very few bird species, a maximum of nine on one island and none at all on some others. Power used logarithmic transformations for the variables predicting the plant species, but arithmetic measures of plant species and isolation for predicting bird species.

Several authors have tried to extend this sort of approach to the flora and bird species on the Galapagos. The difficulty here is that the flora is nowhere near as well explored as that on either the Californian islands or the British islands. The result is that different studies tend to come to rather different conclusions. These have been reviewed by Connor and Simberloff (1978) who come to the rather cynical conclusion that the best predictor of plant number is the number of plant-hunting expeditions to any island. The number of expeditions is highly correlated with area, which emphasizes the difficulty of disentangling the importance of correlated variables. Adsersen (1976) in one week on the island of Pinta increased the list of plants recorded from the 102 species in Connor and Simberloff's analysis to 200, and on Fernandina increased the list from 94 to 150. So it would appear that all studies so far have used inadequate data. Nevertheless the conclusions of all of them are the same: area is always important, and distance rather seldom, though other variables like elevation are important in some analyses.

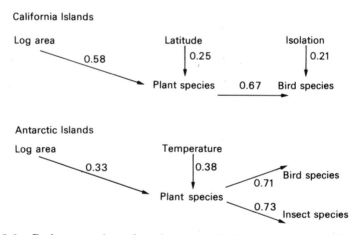

FIG. 3.6. Path regressions for plant and bird species on the California islands and on Antarctic islands. (Derived from Power 1972 and Abbott 1974 respectively.)

From the nineteenth century view of an oceanic island as one with no mammals on it, it might be expected that the effect of distance could be seen in the mammal faunas of continental islands. However, this view is not absolutely correct. There are, for instance, a few endemic species of rice rats on the Galapagos (Thornton 1971). A more serious difficulty is that mammals are readily transported by man. Much of the old literature on the distribution of mammals round the British Isles, which is predicated on the assumption that the mammals arrived there naturally, has had to be reviewed since Corbet (1961) first pointed out that the distributions were much more consistent with accidental transportation by man. The British Isles, with a long history of settlement and considerable variation in the human population-density on different islands, are perhaps unusually prone to such effects. Canadian islands should be almost free from them. A study made by Grant (1970) is therefore interesting. He used rank correlations rather than regressions, which at least overcomes the problem of transformation. He studied the effect of area and isolation and his results are given in Table 3.2. It can be seen that in all three cases isolation appears to be important, and that area is only important in this particular data set, for mammals on the Danish islands. In Denmark, in fact, the effect of area and isolation reinforce each other and the combined effect of two variables is significant to 0.1 per cent.

Table 3.2. Rank correlations for the number of species of mammals

Variable	Canadian Islands	British Islands	Danish Islands
Area	+ 0.16	+ 0.04	+ 0.67*
Isolation	+ 0.43**	+ 0.68***	+ 0.63*

* significant at 5 per cent level; ** significant at 1 per cent level; *** significant at 0.1 per cent level.
From Grant 1970.

Another way of studying the effect of distance is first to fit a relationship of species to area, and then examine the deviations from this relationship, the residuals, against distance. This is a more striking way of comparing the different regressions for the species against area on near islands and on far islands, though conceptually it is essentially the same as a multiple regression. Plots of this sort have been used both by MacArthur and Wilson (1967) and Carlquist (1965). An example of a residual plot, from Diamond (1972), is shown in Fig. 3.7. The relationship is a strong one, despite the variance at any distance. An important point to consider when comparing this result with those discussed above is the very much greater distances involved. The minimum distance in Fig. 3.7 is about 500 km, which is the order of the maximum distance in studies such as that of Johnson and Raven. So another possible cause of this apparent distance effect is that, as the distances are so large, the most distant islands are in an appreciably different climatic zone than the near ones. Diamond's figures relate to islands in the Pacific, and in this same area the number of species of hermatypic corals also decreases monotonically with distance from New Guinea (Stehli and Wells 1971). The corals could indicate a decline in the general favourability of the environment, which could also affect the birds.

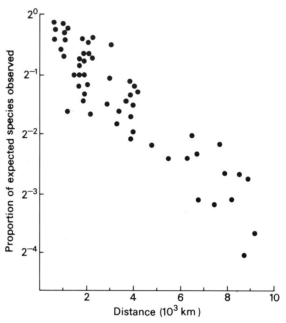

FIG. 3.7. A residual plot of the deviation of species number from that expected for the area of the island, with distance from New Guinea. (Modified from Diamond 1972.)

One slightly different study of the effect of isolation is that of Power (1975), who looked at the similarity of plant species and of bird species on the Galapagos, using Preston's similarity index described above (Chapter 1). Preston's index is designed to remove area effects, so that it is slightly curious that Power includes area as one of his variables. Power's study has also been criticized on other grounds by Connor and Simberloff (1978), but deserves mention as the only one which attempts to study similarity as opposed to diversity by statistical methods. Similarity should be examined in other lists, both by using more sophisticated methods, and by working in areas where the flora is better known. The Galapagos's avifauna is at least well-enough known (Harris 1973a). Power's conclusion was that for both plant similarity and bird similarity isolation was important, and, again, assuming the direction of causation, bird similarity depended on plant similarity.

The peninsular effect

Oceanic islands have fewer species than equivalent-sized continental areas in most groups; continental islands also show a distance effect in some groups. By continuity, peninsulas and other partly-isolated mainland areas might be expected to show their isolation in a reduction in the number of species. Simpson (1964) pointed to an apparent peninsular effect in the mammals of North America. In all the major peninsulas, Baja California, Yucatan, Florida, and the peninsulas of Canada and Alaska, there is a gradient of species in his data. The same effect appears in the three southern peninsulas for birds (see Figs. 1.15 and 1.16).

The strength of the peninsular effect is difficult to measure. The length of the side of the quadrat used by Simpson in his mapping is larger than the width of either Florida or Baja California, and so there would be a reduction in the number of species per quadrat compared with the mainland simply because the land area is less. There is also likely to be a reduction in habitat diversity compared even with a mainland coastal quadrat because of two sea coasts instead of one, and a reduction in the range of land heights. Taylor and Regal (1978) indicated that the peninsular effects in Canada are probably largely latitudinal effects; while some of the Yucatan data is suspect. There is, even allowing for all these effects, a clear peninsular effect in some groups in Baja California, and probably a weaker one in Florida.

As with the distance effect, the peninsular effect is stronger in some groups than others. Taylor and Regal (1978) show a steady decline in the number of heteromyid rodents (kangaroo rats and pocket mice) from twelve species at the north end of Baja California to only two at the tip, 1200 km away. There is also a small reduction in the numbers of birds (Fig. 1.15) and lizards (from 18 to 14) but not in snakes (20 species at both ends). On the mainland opposite, birds and snakes increase markedly in the same latitudes.

For Florida, there is no appropriate mainland for a comparison, and much of the peninsular effect may be a habitat one. Emlen (1978) gives figures for species and individual densities of birds, both permanent residents and winter invaders, and also provides some data on the vegetation and insects. The effect is clearest in the migratory birds, largely Parulids, which points to a habitat effect. As the distance effect is quite difficult to demonstrate convincingly on near islands, it is not surprising that the peninsular effect is even more obscure.

Conclusions

The result of all this computation is disappointingly thin. Larger areas certainly imply more species, but the mathematical form of this relationship varies widely, though Darlington's rule is still a useful starting point. The species–area plot is more usually linear on a log–log plot than in any other transformation, and the slope of that plot, z, is usually between 0.15 and 0.40, though steeper and flatter slopes occur, flatter ones particularly on oceanic archipelagos. The fact that larger areas almost invariably have more species must be allowed for in all population studies on islands; the importance of this for community studies will appear in Chapter 11.

The effect of distance is even harder to pin down. For poorly-dispersing groups, such as mammals, the effect is fairly easily shown. For good dispersers such as birds and angiosperms, the effect is fairly weak, as in Power's study of the birds of the Californian islands, or depends on very great distances, such as Diamond's studies across the Pacific. For pteridophytes the effect is almost, if not completely, absent (Fig. 2.4). That is just considering species number. The effect of distance might show up more clearly if one looks at species composition, the similarity of different communities.

There is other evidence for the effect of distance; two sorts in particular are important. One is the phenomena of double filters, discussed in Chapter 1. The other is the evolutionary phenomena, of the presence of endemics as discussed in Chapter 2, and taxon cycles which will be dealt with in Chapter 7. It is time to see what help theory can give in understanding the possible effects of area and distance, and in explaining how these variables exert their effects.

4 Theories of species composition

The quantitative theory of island biogeography which has dominated discussion during the last decade is that of MacArthur and Wilson (1963, 1967). This chapter and the next are largely concerned with describing that theory and examining its strengths and weaknesses. As a preliminary, it is useful to contrast MacArthur and Wilson's views with those of Lack (1969a, 1976). Lack, like MacAthur, was an ornithologist and ecologist; while Wilson started as an entomologist, and now is perhaps most widely known for his work on sociobiology (Wilson 1975). Lack and MacArthur, unfortunately, both died while still modifying and developing their views on and theories of island biogeography, and so the extent to which they would have agreed, or agreed to differ, can never be known. The contrast between their theories should not be taken too seriously because, as Diamond and May (1976) observe, the two views are to a large extent complementary. Nevertheless, there are points of difference: for example, on the causes of the low numbers of species to be found on small oceanic islands (Diamond in Lack 1976). In this chapter I shall attempt to give a straightforward description of what the authors thought, with some comments on the logical difficulties and limitations in these views. This exposition is made more difficult by the changing accounts in successive papers. In the next chapter some examples will be considered in more detail, to see how well they fit the theories.

The essential difference between the two views is that Lack emphasizes the match between the species occurring on the island and the habitats on the island, the number of species being determined ecologically by the environment of the island. MacArthur and Wilson, on the other hand, emphasize the turnover of species on islands. In their view the number occurring results from a balance between processes increasing the number of species and those tending to decrease them.

Lack's views

Compared with the theory of MacArthur and Wilson, Lack's argument is almost entirely qualitative and much concerned with the ecology of individual species. His views are most clearly put out in his review paper (Lack 1969a). His posthumous book (Lack 1976) restates them, enlarges on them, and makes some comments, but the central argument is rather obscured by the mass of detail. He was concerned only with birds. This is a most important point, because it is obviously necessary that a thoroughly satisfactory theory should cover any group. Lack's views would also no doubt apply to other groups which disperse well, such as ferns with their light spores, and many groups of insects. But an essential part of Lack's argument is that he assumes that the general environment, including the vegetation and no doubt much of the insect life, is established by processes which he does not discuss. From this premise, he argues that the number of species found on an island is that appropriate to the type of the island. That is to say, the number of species reflects the climate, habitats, size, and so on of the island: 'the small numbers of resident bird species on islands are due to ecological limitations'.

Lack is particularly insistent that the failure of birds to establish populations comes from a failure to find the right conditions and not a failure to disperse there. He gives many examples of species that are commonly found on islands but are not native to them and do not breed there. As one example, the purple gallinule, *Porphyrula martinica*, has frequently been recorded from Tristan da Cunha. It is a subtropical marsh bird, a rail, with a range from the southern United States to northern Argentina. Again, there is only one form of duck of the genus *Anas* native to Hawaii, a subspecies of the mallard, *A. platyrhynchos* (Table 2.3), but ducks of eight other species of *Anas* have been seen on Hawaii. So Lack's view of Tristan da Cunha, where there are only three species of land bird, is that this is because there are only 32 species of angiosperms there, leading to a very uniform vegetation (Table 2.2). He would no doubt add that the soil, all volcanic, is also unusually uniform compared with that of continental areas of the same size, and the extreme oceanic climate also makes for uniformity and poverty of species.

The absence of several species of birds found in Britain but not found in Ireland is discussed in some detail by Lack, and we can take his arguments further by considering the data of Sharrock (1976). As Lack says, to the casual visitor Ireland looks remarkably like England. However, it is a much smaller island than Britain and lacks many of the interesting habitats present in Britain. It extends neither so far north nor so far south, and its climate is distinctly more oceanic. Compared with Europe Britain has proportionately fewer forested areas; Ireland has even less forest than Britain, though in both countries large areas of trees have been planted in the last few decades (Mitchell 1976). These differences in climate and habitat are sufficient to account for the absence of some species from Ireland, such as woodpeckers (Picidae, four species in Britain; none in Ireland), the reed warbler, *Acrocephalus scirpaceus*, and the nightingale, *Luscinia megarhynchos*. The absence of the tawny owl, *Strix aluco*, can be ascribed to the absence of voles (microtine rodents). One vole, *Clethrionomys glareolus*, has been introduced into Ireland recently (first recorded in 1964) and is spreading quite rapidly (Crichton 1974). That possibly leaves only the tree pipit, *Anthus trivialis*, a British bird which has been seen occasionally in Ireland but has never been recorded as breeding there, as an unexpected absentee. It is possible that tree pipit is a fairly recent immigrant into Britain and that the breeding population has not yet spread to Ireland (Ferguson-Lees 1978). On the other hand, it is possible that tree pipits used to occur in Ireland, and became extinct with the mass of deforestation in the eighteenth and nineteenth centuries (Sharrock 1979).

This emphasis on the ecology of individual species, and the analysis of faunal lists species by species, is perhaps a little surprising from Lack. He was, after all (Lack 1942), an early expounder of the changes in niche that are sometimes seen among birds on isolated islands, and which will be considered in Chapter 6.

Lack did consider one particular form of niche variation to be important. Essentially his argument is that in small areas, that is on small oceanic islands, a degree of habitat variation which in larger areas would support two species, with different niche specializations, would support only one. This can be thought of either as a refinement of niches in large areas of a habitat, or niche-widening in smaller patches of habitat. Lack (1971) gives many examples of this and only a few need be mentioned here.

The Caroline Islands in the Pacific are mostly low islands, but include five high islands: Ponape, Palau, Yap, Truk, and Kusaie, all very well separated from each other by distances of about 500 km. Yap and Kusaie are single islands; the other three are small archipelagos. Amongst the white-eyes, *Zosterops*, three species are found on Ponape and Palau, two on Yap and Truk, and only one on Kusaie. The areas in square kilometres are respectively 334 and 448, 100 and 100, but Kusaie, which one might expect from its number of *Zosterops* to be the smallest, has an area of 110 km². Other examples are given of *Geospiza* in the Galapagos, humming birds in the West Indies, and sparrows in the Canaries and the Cape Verde Islands. A temperate example is the occurrence of two species of *Regulus* in Europe, but only one of them, *R. regulus* the goldcrest, in the Azores and the other *R. ignicapillus* the firecrest, in the Canaries and Madeira. Lack suggests that which of these occur on a particular island is a matter of chance, but in fact the goldcrest has a generally more northerly distribution, and so it is appropriate that it is found on the more northerly of these three archipelagos.

Apart from its qualitative nature, and its limitation to dispersing groups, what are the main difficulties with Lack's views? Grant (1977) has made a thorough assessment of Lack's case. Here we need be concerned only with those points that are relevant to building a general theory.

The major problem concerns the nature of dispersal; that some birds are good dispersers does not mean that they all are. In particular the dispersal stages may not be breeding stages and so the ability of a species to establish a population may be related to the lack of suitable immigrants as well as to the lack of a suitable ecology. Grant gives examples from the West Indies. Here we may hark back to the purple gallinule on Tristan da Cunha. No doubt its ecology is unsuited to the island but, in fact, most of the recorded specimens are immature and found out of the breeding season. A general theory must take account of the variations in species' abilities to disperse and establish themselves.

Another problem with Lack's views is that although some species can disperse to very isolated islands, not all good dispersers will necessarily reach all isolated islands. The comparative rarity of immigration is shown by the presence of endemics, which were discussed in Chapter 1. Taxonomically-distinct flightless birds, like *Atlantisia rogersi* on Inaccessible in the Tristan group, shows not only dispersal by its ancestors to that island long ago, but also, as it is a relict species, the failure of possible competing species to reach there and establish a population.

The emphasis that Lack places on the suitability of habitat in determining which species become established contrasts strongly with the theory of MacArthur and Wilson.

MacArthur and Wilson's theory

Since their book, *The theory of island biogeography* (1967), was published as the first of the Princeton Monographs in Population Biology, MacArthur and Wilson's views have become very well known. The original title was *An equilibrium theory of island zoogeography* (1963): in four years the theory had become more universal, covering plants as well as animals. The main features of the theory are familiar because it has been used and referred to in a very large number of ecological studies, but it remains controversial. Here I shall review the main properties of the theory, and then attempt to make a balanced assessment of its various components. In the next chapter, various data sets will be considered in the light of the theory.

The essence of the theory is very simple. It is that the number of species on an island is determined by a balance between immigration and extinction. Immigration rates will vary with the distance of the island from the mainland, and extinction rates will vary with the area of the island. All this is shown in the well-known diagram in Fig. 4.1. The theory includes the presumption that there is a pool of species, *P*, from which the species on an island are drawn. The pool is the number of species that could immigrate to the island, and therefore the number that are found on a neighbouring land mass, such as part of a continent. All the immigration, *I*, curves decline to the point, *P*, on the abscissa. All the extinction curves increase monotonically from the origin.

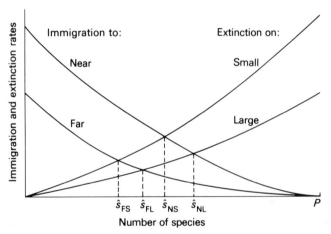

FIG. 4.1. Diagram of the MacArthur and Wilson theory of island biogeography. Equilibria occur at the intersections of the extinction and immigration curves, and are indicated by $\hat{S}$ with subscripts referring to different types of islands. *P* is the total pool of species.

The existence of an equilibrium of this sort is almost a logical necessity. The number of species on an island can only be increased by two processes: immigration, and the evolution of new species on that island. Similarly, the number of species can only decrease by a species disappearing from an island, that is to say, extinction. Putting this into discrete form gives the equation—

$$S_{t+1} = S_t + I + V - E,$$

where S_t is the number of species at time t, and I, V and E are, respectively, the number of immigrants, species evolving on the island, and extinctions. Putting the theory in this discrete form emphasizes that all the numbers involved are integers, and so continuous representations are necessarily approximations. This form also has time as a discrete variable, but that is clearly an approximation itself.

The nature and form of the curves, and the reasons for their variation, are again perhaps most easily followed in the discrete form. Take first the situation when the island is empty, $S = 0$. The unit of time might conveniently be either a day or a year depending on the situation considered. Then of the P species that might immigrate, the probability that any one of them will immigrate in the next unit of time is a number between 0 and 1. These probabilities of immigration in unit time, q_a, will be different for each species, and in particular will vary with the propensity of the species to disperse. The total number of immigrants expected in the first unit of time, I_0, will be given by the expression—

$$I_0 = \sum_{a=1}^{a=P} q_a,$$

so that I_0 is necessarily less than P. After the first species has immigrated, the summation will be over $(P - 1)$ species, and so less. The result is that there will be a series of monotonic curves from I_0 to P giving immigration curves for different faunal sequences. This argument is given by Simberloff (1969) and is set out in detail for two species with different probabilities by MacArthur (1972). MacArthur and Wilson argued that the species with the higher probabilities of immigration would in general arrive first, an almost tautologous statement in fact, so that the I curve will typically decline most steeply at the left-hand end, as is shown in all the curves of Figure 4.1. They appear to have thought of the curves they had drawn as being the most probable curves in some sense. This part of the theory clearly contains a large stochastic element, but the effects of variation around the curve were not discussed.

Distance is the only variable that is shown explicitly as affecting immigration. Other variables, such as area, are thought to be negligible in relation to distance (MacArthur and Wilson 1967, Chapter 6).

For the extinction curve, it is clear that each species is thought to have a finite probability of becoming extinct at all times. If all species had exactly the same probability of going extinct in the next unit of time, f, then the observed number becoming extinct in that unit of time would be Sf. This is a linear function of S which would show on figures like Figure 4.1 as a straight line from the origin to a point Pf units above the point P. MacArthur and Wilson (1963) continue 'more realistically, some species die out more readily than others and the more species there are, the rarer each is, and hence an increased number of species increases the likelihood of any given species dying out'. The probability of each species dying out is clearly thought to be a function of population size, which is certainly correct under stochastic birth and death processes, and the size of each population is thought to be a decreasing function, again no doubt stochastic, of the total number of species present. The effect of these considerations is to produce the hollow curves shown in Figure 4.1.

The argument naturally leads to the conclusion that area will be the prime influence on extinction rates. The argument is, however, not completely direct. There is the assumption that as the numbers of species go up, then, in a probabilistic sense, each and every species population goes down. There is the assumption that the probability of a species becoming extinct will be a monotonically decreasing function of its population size. There is the assumption that as the area increases, the total population of all species also increases monotonically, if not linearly.

In discussion of the shapes of immigration and extinction curves, MacArthur and Wilson (1963) make the point that no extinction curve can reach above point P a height greater than P. That is to say, the extinction curves are constrained within a line from the origin going upwards of 45°. Again, the variance in the E curves is not considered explicitly.

The elaborations of the theory follow quite naturally from the basic theory. Quite a lot of mathematical development depends on the assumption that one transformation of the ordinate will linearize both the I and the E curves. This leads to the following equations—

$$PI = I_0 (P - S),$$
$$PE = E_p S$$

where E_p is the extinction rate when all the pool species are present, that is to say at point P. From this—

$$dS/dt = I - E = (I_0 (P - S) - E_p S)/P.$$

At equilibrium, this differential equals zero, which leads to

$$\widehat{S} = I_0 P/(I_0 + E_P),$$

or in the more general case

$$S = \frac{I_0 P}{I_0 + E_P} [1 - \exp(-(I_0 + E_P) t)]$$

From this last expression, it is easy to see that the increase in number of species is expected to approach the equilibrium species number by a curve of negative exponential form.

Critique of MacArthur–Wilson theory

Laid out like this the theory is very simple and sounds attractive. So much so, that in the wake of the popularity of the theory both Mayr (1976) and Crowell (1973) have been led to claim priority for the concept that the number of species is a consequence of equilibrium. Crowell was, in fact, MacArthur's first research student, and his work then on the birds of Bermuda will be discussed in Chapter 10. The concept can also be found in the work of Preston (1962). All these workers may be given credit for the equilibrium idea; none developed the theory in its mathematical form.

On the other hand, many practising naturalists have reacted adversely to the theory. The major claim has always been that the theory ignores important aspects of the biology of species, and the critics are not mollified by the discussion of immigration given above. Olson's views have already been noted (p. 16), while Berry (1979) says, in relation to the fauna of the Outer Hebrides, 'in the light of these many pressures, simple equilibrium theories of island biogeography are woefully inadequate; every species has to be considered on its merits'. These strong reactions and feelings are unfortunate, because the evident regularity of some features of island life means that there must be theoretical explanations that would help us to understand them. Perhaps one reason for this tension is that some of MacArthur's followers have been over-enthusiastic in pressing the claims of the theory. MacArthur and Wilson themselves wrote in the preface to the book, 'a great deal of faith in the feasibility of a general theory is still required. We do not seriously believe that the particular formulations advanced in the chapters to follow will fit for very long the exacting results of future empirical investigations'. All theories have strengths and limitations; the science of biogeography will best be advanced by taking advantage of the strong points of MacArthur and Wilson's theory, and replacing and restructuring the rest.

Before considering difficulties with each of the component parts of the theory, there are four general points to be made about it. None is controversial; all would be difficult to overcome.

The first point is that the theory deals explicitly only with the number of species, not with the number of individuals in species. It is true that the arguments about extinction, which will be examined in more detail below, do involve some implicit consideration of the population densities. However, the theory does not predict any particular distribution of numbers across species, as for instance does Preston's log-normal theory. If one takes a rather large island, such as Britain, and the breeding birds on it and examines the data in, for example, Sharrock (1976), it is evident that the variation in species number, although it certainly occurs, is only of marginal interest in understanding the population ecology of species in Britain. Most British species have been breeding here for as long as records exist. A lot of the immigrations and extinctions have been of birds like the hoopoe, *Upupa epops*, which breeds in France and to the south-east, but only breeds successfully in Britain as isolated pairs every few years. Again, there have been successful immigrants, such as the collared dove, *Streptopelia decaocto*, which has found a vacant, commensal, niche, and so has not only spread spectacularly but has not affected the populations of other birds (Murton 1971). These changes are of little relevance in the study of bird communities in Britain and those interested in the species themselves are more concerned with their numbers than with their mere presence and absence. This question of immigration and extinction against population numbers will be considered more fully in the next chapter.

The second point is that the theory considers all species together. This may be reasonably satisfactory in studying birds, as MacArthur did, or ants, as Wilson did. It is obviously less satisfactory if one wishes to study the biotic community as a whole. This is a weakness in all present theories of community structure, such as Preston's log–normal, and a major weakness in most studies of diversity.

The third point is that the theory does not allow for historical factors. The presumption is that parameters measured now will be sufficient to explain distributions observed now. In a classic paper, Brown (1971) showed that this is unlikely, at least in one particular case. Mammals found in coniferous woods on the top of mountains in the Great Basin region of Nevada and neighbouring states almost certainly arrived there by walking through coniferous forests which were more continuous when the climate was cooler. These mammals are stranded relicts on these mountaintops and subject only to extinction, not immigration. Historical factors of this sort will frequently be unimportant, but many of the more interesting distributions studied by biogeographers clearly have an historical component.

The fourth point, and one which is perhaps surprising in a theory which was developed in relation to distributions across oceanic islands in the Pacific, is that there was, in its original form, no mention of evolution. The equilibrium part of the theory is a tautology only to the extent that evolution does not take place. For many islands, evolutionary considerations are either unimportant, or if they are important occur nearby rather than on the island under consideration. There are, nevertheless, some instances where evolution is all-important. The most striking of these is the Hawaiian Drosophilidae of which, as will be seen in Chapter 8, the number of species on any particular island is the result, to a very large extent, of the course of recent evolutionary history. Other examples, with less striking effects on the total number of species, are considered in other chapters of Part 3.

It is perhaps unfair to say that evolution is not considered in the theory, both because it is considered in Chapter 7 of *The theory of island biogeography* and because, as an extension of the theory, Wilson (1969) gives the graph reproduced in Fig. 4.2. In this graph Wilson includes evolution as a process likely to increase the number of species on an island, though he gives no detailed model. He also distinguishes between an interactive and a non-interactive equilibrium, the latter being higher. To discover his reasons for doing this, it is necessary to examine the individual components of the theory.

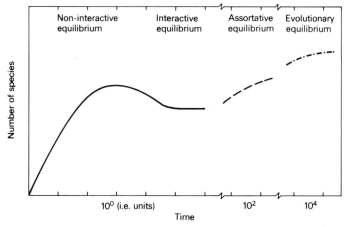

FIG. 4.2.   E. O. Wilson's view of the change of species equilibrium with time. Note the absence of scaling on the ordinate, and that the time scale is in arbitrary units, the length of a unit being a function of the species life history. (Modified from Wilson 1969.)

Immigration and the pool of species

In the simple form of the theory developed above, the probability of a species immigrating remains constant, though it would normally be different from the probability of any other species that might immigrate. The constant probability is intended as a first approximation, but the concept has its difficulties. The simplest of these relates to the pool of species.

For many islands, it is quite difficult to say precisely where immigrants might come from. Even with only one neighbouring land mass, not all of it is necessarily a source of immigrants. This difficulty is mostly removed by automatic adjustments in the probability of immigrating. If the species occurs in the source area but, for any reason would never appear on the island, then its probability of immigrating is zero, and the only consequence of including it in our theoretical considerations is to enlarge P, and drag out the immigration curve to the right. More seriously, the population sizes of potential immigrant species on the mainland will be always varying and so the probabilities of immigration themselves are variable. The effect is to increase the variance around the immigration curve, but as this variance is already not treated in detail under the theory, there are no new difficulties of principle, only of estimation.

Another difficulty with the pool concept comes when there is a number of sources. Again, this can be readily handled in most cases by appropriate adjustments to the probability of immigration. There is one case, that of oceanic archipelagos, which is critical for tests of the theory. The pool for an archipelago as a whole will, in general, be some continental area. The pool for the individual islands on the archipelago will be other islands in the archipelago. So there is a two-stage pool, rather than two distinct pools. This affects the predictions about the species–area relationship. Because the immigration curve for far islands is below that for near islands (Fig. 4.1), the theory predicts a steeper species–area relationship on far than on near island sets. But within a clump of islands, an archipelago, the relationship will become flatter again (MacArthur and Wilson 1967).

In its simplest form, the theory assumes that the probability of the species immigrating is not affected by the other species present, at least not in any mathematical sense. That is, it is non-interactive. Whether species interact depends partly on the definition of immigration, but is mostly a question of biology. As will be seen in the next chapter, the presence of certain species seems to be a necessary prerequisite for the immigration of others. For these others, probabilities of immigration will increase as species numbers go up, at least over part of the range of species numbers. For still other species, it is easy to imagine, though examples are perhaps hard to find, that the presence of a species inhibits the immigration of another. Either way, probabilities of immigration will change with species number and with species composition, and so the variance around the immigration curve will become yet greater. Wilson's view on interactive effects, summarized in Figure 4.2, shows that interaction leads to fewer species, but, as will be seen, he was primarily concerned with the effect of interaction on extinction.

The major problem with immigration, though, is its definition. In their original paper, MacArthur and Wilson (1963) said 'propagules are defined here as the minimum number of individuals of a given species needed to achieve colonization'; and 'a rudimentary account of how many immigrants are required to constitute a propagule may be constructed as follows'. From what follows it is not clear precisely what they meant by colonization, particularly as their theory allows for eventual extinction, but it would seem from their appendix that at that stage they had in mind enough immigrants so that the probability of the colony persisting was 0.5 or greater. By 1967 (on p. 64, under the heading 'Weaknesses of the Equilibrium Model') they say

> the model puts rather too simple an interpretation on the process of making an artificially clear-cut distinction between immigration and extinction. . . . For instance, is a migrating bird, passing through an island, called an immigrant? If so, it goes extinct as it leaves. Suppose we agree to ignore species not 'intending' to stay. . . . We could ignore immigrants that do not colonize with the potential of reproducing. . . . This is what we prefer to call immigration.

Simberloff (1969) was also concerned with this problem of definition, and for that matter with the problem of fuzziness around the immigration curve. His definition was 'Immigration: the arrival of a propagule on an island unoccupied by the species', while propagule is defined as 'the minimum number of individuals of a species capable of breeding and population increase under ideal conditions for that species (unlimited food supply, proper habitat, no predators, etc.'. In 1976 (Simberloff 1976c) he defines immigration as 'a sufficient number of individuals of some species so that reproduction is possible (that is, a propagule)'. He was mostly concerned with arthropods, and some of his experimental observations will be considered in the next chapter.

There seems general agreement that a single individual of a species occurring on an island should not necessarily be counted as an immigrant. The casuals and strays that are found on islands, and made much of by Lack, would not count. On the other hand, a definition that takes into account the probability of colonies surviving has obvious difficulties. Surviving for how long? In sufficient geological time, all colonies will become extinct. An intermediate stage seems to be needed, which is not quite indicated by any of the definitions above, of proved reproduction of a species after it has arrived. In the case of a bird, this would mean the observation of a fertilized egg or of some later stage in development. For a plant, the required observation would be a properly formed seed capable of germination. Even so, naturalists are well aware of many instances of what is usually referred to as casual breeding. That is to say an isolated instance of an organism breeding in a habitat where it does not persist, and where on some good biological ground it would not be expected to persist.

It might be thought that the difficulty of deciding when an immigration has occurred should also have caused difficulty in the discussion of species–area curves in Chapter 3. In practice this seems not to be so. The observations on which the species–area curves are made are normally made at one instant of time. No doubt non-breeding species are occasionally included in lists, but the error from this is surely less than the error of overlooking species present and breeding.

The final difficulty with the concept of immigration in the theory is that it is thought to vary only with distance. Distance is presumably meant in the sense of its effect on dispersal, so that distances downwind would be shorter than the equivalent distances upwind. There are a number of problems. The first is that distance rather seldom has an important effect in multi-regression studies considered in Chapter 3, which suggests that distance is only important over rather large distances, or for rather poor dispersers. The second is that it would seem reasonable, *a priori*, that the size of the island would affect the probability of immigration. One would expect that a bird coming from France, for instance, would find it much easier to find an appropriate nesting site on the island of Britain than on the Isle of Wight (Fig. 10.1), let alone a much smaller island. Indeed, in their 1963 paper, MacArthur and Wilson said 'the immigration rate (M) must be determined by at least two independent values: (1) the rate at which propagules reach the island, which is dependent on the size of the island and its distance from the source of the propagules . . .', and so it is surprising that they did not include in that paper an area effect on immigration. Later, they seem to have convinced themselves that the area effect would be negligible. Not everybody is convinced. For instance, Simberloff (1976b) indicated that there might well be an area effect in immigration. If so, there are rather drastic consequences on the ability of the theory to predict the effect of area. As Simberloff says, 'the higher equilibrium number of species on larger islands could be viewed simply as a consequence of a higher immigration curve rather than a lower extinction curve' and 'if immigration, as well as extinction rates are affected by area, no clear prediction can be made about turnover rates'. The turnover rate is the sum of the extinction and immigration rates. In Figure 4.1 it can be seen that smaller islands and nearer islands are both expected to have higher turnover rates than larger islands and more distant islands. If immigration is affected by area, so that the curves labelled near and far can be relabelled large and small, it can be seen that Simberloff's statement is correct.

Many factors which could affect immigration are not included in the theory: such as the general topography of the area, whether mountainous or an archipelago, the types of habitat on the island, ther other species found there, and so on.

Extinction

In the same way that immigration is difficult to define, so too is extinction. Simberloff (1976*c*) defines extinction as when a species is absent or reduced to non-reproductives (for example, a single male) which fits the view of immigration given above.

MacArthur and Wilson regarded extinction as being affected primarily by area. Brown and Kodric-Brown (1977) have suggested that extinction might be affected by distance too. They point out that a population declining to extinction might be 'rescued' by new immigrants of the same species. Consequently, extinction rates would be lower when immigration rates are high, and that will be particularly so on near islands. If both the suggestion that immigration is affected by area as well as distance, and the Browns' rescue effect on extinction are accepted, the theory still predicts that small islands and far islands will have fewer species than large islands and near islands. These effects, like the original one in the theory of MacArthur and Wilson, are plausible, but are derived more from logic than from observation. The Browns' data are for anthropods visiting thistles, not breeding on them.

The turnover rate defined above, the sum of the extinction and immigration rates, is affected by variations in both those rates. Some authors, including the Browns', use relative turnover rate defined as the absolute turnover rate divided by the number of species present. Williamson (1978) points out that these relative rates, which are given geometrically by the slope of lines through the origin of the MacArthur–Wilson diagram, will depend almost only on the extinction rates.

The definition of extinction, its relation to relative and absolute turnover rates, and the functional relationship of extinction to geographical variables are none of them the major problem in understanding the role of extinction in the MacArthur–Wilson theory. The major problem is to clarify the biological processes that lead to extinction. There has been a lot of uncertainty about precisely what MacArthur and Wilson had in mind. It has been said that they regarded extinction as random; it has also been said that this is mistaken. There is no doubt at all that they regarded extinction as a function of population size. There is a generally accepted proposition, derived from the theory of stochastic processes, that small populations are more likely to become extinct by chance. Indeed, in the theory of stochastic processes, any population has a finite probability of becoming extinct, simply because extinction, the attainment of a zero population, is an absorbing boundary for the population. There are still two uncertainties. The first is how small a population has to be before it is at all likely to go extinct; the second is how does the population come to be small. It is probably the second point which has caused most confusion.

Wilson (1969) thought interactive effects would increase extinction rates. Interactive processes such as competition, for both species concerned, and predation, for at least one, can be expected to lead to smaller population sizes.

One elaboration of the theory which is considered in considerable detail in *The theory of island biogeography* is the effect of population parameters on the probability of extinction. This is one of the more disappointing chapters in the book: it concentrates on a rather limited particular set of conditions and parameters, and the discussion is not related to the very considerable literature on stochastic processes. (For a terse, but comprehensive, review see Bartlett 1973.) Extinction may happen during colonization or after establishment. The critical variable in determining whether a population will go extinct during colonization is, both in the MacArthur and Wilson version and in the elaboration of it by Richter-Dyn and Goel (1972), λ/μ, when λ is the birth rate and μ the death rate. The intrinsic rate of natural increase, r, is $\lambda - \mu$. Armstrong (1978) shows that λ/μ is equivalent to R_0, the net reproductive rate of an individual female. Ignoring density dependence, the probability of avoiding extinction is $(R_0 - 1)/R_0$. This is an interesting and comprehensible first approximation.

After establishment, the probability of a population becoming extinct depends on more variables, including how small it is. However, what constitutes small in the sense of producing an appreciable probability of extinction, varies greatly in different circumstances. Consider two examples. The first is from Leslie (1958). Using Bartlett's formulation, he gives an expression which allows the calculation of the mean time to extinction for a population of the protozoan *Paramecium* growing under very simple conditions in a small volume. This protozoan can divide every eight hours, and in the conditions considered by Leslie, grew logistically to an asymptotic population of a mere 100 individuals. Under these conditions the calculated mean time to extinction was well over a million years. At the other extreme, Bartlett (1957) developed the stochastic theory of measles epidemics. He was able to show that measles could be expected to die out quite quickly, that is to say in the course of a few years, in any single city with a population of less than 200 000. This example will be discussed further in the next chapter (p. 109).

There is no doubt that in geological time almost every species will become extinct. For populations on islands, particularly remembering the short life of islands in geological time, the expectation of extinction is much greater than that expectation for populations on continents. The question at issue is whether a species that has immigrated, in the sense given above, will in general, have a high probability of going extinct in ecological time, that is in a few hundreds of generations or less. In a rather more exact form, the question is what is the distribution of probabilities of going extinct, and how do these probabilities vary? This is a set of questions that can only be answered by observation; it was remarkable that the theory was put forward, and widely accepted, with almost no evidence on this point.

Equilibrium

Although the theory is called an equilibrium theory, it does not, of course, imply that all populations on all islands are in equilibrium. Nevertheless, there is a strong implication that unless most islands are either at or close to equilibrium, the theory would be of limited usefulness.

There is some disagreement among paleontologists about whether the number of species on the earth as a whole has been in equilibrium, or whether it has been increasing. Simpson (1969) gives a graph which suggests, particularly for terrestrial forms, that the numbers of families and presumably the number of species, have been increasing through geological time. The numbers of species do, of course, decrease dramatically at certain geological boundaries, as in the extinction of the dinosaurs, the ammonites, and other groups at the end of the Cretaceous. But these instances do not affect the general shape of Simpson's curves. On the other hand, Sepkoski (1978) gives graphs which, equally convincingly, indicate that the number of marine metazoan orders have been more or less constant since the late Ordivician. He, in fact, suggests that the sudden appearance of metazoan orders at the beginning of the Cambrian is part of a logistic increase in orders starting in the late pre-Cambrian, and reaching an asymptote in the late Ordivician. All the terrestrial fauna and flora have, of course, evolved since then. Whether or not there is an equilibrium in the total number of species, there is a considerable turnover of species by extinction and evolution during geological time.

Does this imply that there is also a considerable turnover of species on islands in ecological time? Ecologists are commonly concerned with processes that take place in tens of generations. Geological time, on the other hand, is more concerned with periods of ten thousand generations and upwards, a difference of several orders of magnitude. Certainly when considering the composition of biota on large and ancient islands, then evolutionary considerations and the turnover of species that that implies are important. Mayr (1976) has argued this convincingly for birds on such islands as Madagascar, New Caledonia, and New Zealand.

There are, however, certain cases where equilibrium has clearly not been reached. Diamond (1974) discusses the birds on various islands affected by volcanic eruptions. These can be viewed as natural experiments, in which the attainment of the appropriate equilibrium can be expected in time, though there might be argument about how much time. However, even for birds, not all islands are in equilibrium. For instance, as was noted in Chapter 3 (p. 66) there are no land birds breeding on the islands of Easter, Trindade, St. Paul, and Amsterdam, though sea birds are quite common. Lack of equilibrium is much more obvious in poor-dispersing groups. There can be no doubt that the absence of voles (microtine rodents) from Ireland was not a state of equilibrium before the introduction of *Clethrionomys* (p. 77). Similarly, the record of introduction of voles and mice on other British islands shows that the habitat is perfectly suitable, but the rate of natural dispersal to them is so low, involving such an improbable event, that they cannot be described as being in equilibrium (Berry 1979): new immigrants in this sort of case will not be balanced by the extinction of species already present.

Consequences of the theory

A good theory should stimulate further work, and should lead to some clear-cut predictions. There is no doubt that MacArthur and Wilson's theory is a winner on the first point; its status on the second is much more doubtful. It makes three important sets of predictions, on turnover, on species–area curves, and on equilibrium.

There is no clear prediction about how fast turnover will be. It depends on absolute immigration and extinction rates. The theory only predicts relative rates on different sorts of islands. Simberloff (1976b) puts forward the reasonable view that experiments are necessary 'to examine whether faunal turnover is significant in sizeable communities or whether it is a quaint, mathematically tractable, but usually minor effect observable only in systems smaller than those of interest to most ecologists'.

The major prediction about species–area curves is that they will be steeper for more isolated islands; the functional form of the relationship is not predicted. It is not clear that this steepness is seen in real data (Connor and McCoy 1979). Figure 3.3 suggests that isolation lowers the intercept, rather than steepening the relationship. The validity of this prediction is still in doubt. Elaborations of the theory that lead to more precise predictions will be considered towards the end of the next chapter (p. 123).

The third prediction, that species numbers represent an equilibrium, has sometimes been taken to mean that each new immigrant is matched by an extinction, and *vice versa*. In general, the connection between immigration and extinction is much weaker than this, as will be seen in the examples in the next chapter.

5 Observations on changes of composition

How well does the theory of MacArthur and Wilson fit real data? Several data sets will now be examined, for their own interest as well as for what they show about the theory. The first examples deal with turnover near equilibrium on islands and in a remarkably informative long-term study of the birds of a small wood. Next the approach to equilibrium on islands made bare either naturally or experimentally will be considered. It is then possible to look again at how area affects species numbers, bringing in incidence curves and a plot of geological variables that mimics the species–area curve. Finally there will be some discussion about how the theory has been and might be refined, and the extent to which MacArthur–Wilson theory is a sufficient description of the processes that affect island populations.

The principal statement of MacArthur–Wilson theory is that the number of species on an island results from an equilibrium between immigration and extinction so that there is a turnover of species at equilibrium. The data below show that immigration and extinction are real and measurable. However, the relationship between these two, and between them and the number of species, is weak. The number of species, as will be seen, varies quite widely over the years, and there is nothing in any of the data sets to suggest, for instance, that a new immigrant is balanced by an extinction, let alone causes one. We shall return to the question of the nature of the equilibrium at the end of the chapter.

An example of a bird community

The emphasis of the MacArthur and Wilson school on turnover, and the way in which a small area can in itself lead to the extinction of a population for which the habitat is otherwise suitable are often misunderstood. An examination of a full data set on the birds of an inland wood will help to clarify these points. The survey is one of the fullest and longest yet made of terrestrial populations, and so is worth discussion for its own sake. It is also particularly suited for setting out the strengths and weaknesses of MacArthur and Wilson's approach to island communities.

The survey was of the breeding birds of an oak wood in Surrey, England (Beven 1976). The habitat, Eastern Wood, Bookham Common, is small for a bird population, only 16 ha. However, it is in an area of dense oak wood, part of the 112 ha that cover the Common as a whole. To produce complete censuses of the breeding population of all birds for 26 seasons is a notable achievement. The survey was carried out by a team of amateur ornithologists, 17 of them in all over the period. Censuses were taken in every year from 1949 to 1975 with the exception of 1957. The full data are given in Table 5.1. Nesting was confirmed in the great majority of species. The reliability of this evidence, collected by an experienced team of watchers on a small area, can perhaps be contrasted with some of the other studies that have been made of turnover, discussed later.

The area, equivalent to a square of sides of 400 m, is small in comparison with most of the islands mentioned in this book. For instance, Skokholm, whose turnover is discussed below, is about six times as large, while most of the islands are very much larger than that (see endpapers). On the other hand, most of the botanical studies of species–area relationships in quadrats, such as those reported by Dony (p. 63), were mostly made on areas appreciably smaller than Eastern Wood, and frequently in simpler and less productive habitats. There is a considerable difference in the minimum area needed to maintain a bird population and a plant population.

The trees of Eastern Wood are *Quercus robur*, pedunculate oak, and the wood is on clay. Oak trees are fully mature at about 100 years old, so the period of 27 years is quite short in the life of an oak tree. No woodland in lowland England can be described as being in a natural state. At Eastern Wood there was an important change of management policy in 1952: up to then, some trees had been felled from time to time, and in the winter of 1951/2 1.6 ha were thinned. After that, felling ceased, and trees and shrubs were allowed to encroach upon the rides. So there has been a continuous, though fairly small, change in the habitat. The most obvious effect is the decline and extinction of *Phylloscopus trochilus*, the willow warbler, which is associated with open woodland. This population change is shown in Fig. 5.1, along with population curves of a selection of other species. A few species show small increasing trends with time, possibly due to the same habitat change. The only species which has immigrated and come to an apparent equilibrium is *Sturnus vulgaris*, the starling.

The only other environmental change that need concern us here is the very hard winter of 1962/3. The population of *Troglodytes troglodytes*, the wren, in particular, was badly affected.

What then do the data show about population changes and island

Table 5.1. The number of territories of singing males of all species in Bookham Common (Eastern Wood) each spring. There was no count in 1957.

Evidence of breeding		Year 49	50	51	52	53	54	55	56	58	59	60	61	62	63	64	65	66	67	68	69	70	71	72	73	74	75
N	Mandarin (*Aix galericulata*)	0	0	0	0	0	0	0	0	0	0	0	0	0	0	0	0	0	0	0	1	2	0	1	0	0	1
N	Sparrowhawk* (*Accipiter nisus*)	1	1	1	0	1	1	1	1	1	1	0̇	0	0	0	0	0	0	0	0	0	0	0	0	1	0	1
N	Pheasant (*Phasianus colchicus*)	0	1	1	1	1	1	0	0	0	0	1	0	1	0	0	0	1	0	1	3	4	4	5	0	1	0
N	Woodcock* (*Scolopax rusticola*)	0	0.	0	1	1	0	0	0	0	0	0	0	1	1	1	1	0	0	0	0	1	0	0	1	0	1
U	Stock dove (*Columba oenas*)	0	0	0	0	0	0	0	0	0	0	0	0	0	0	0	0	0	0	0	0	0	0	1	0	0	1
N	Woodpigeon (*Columba palumbus*)	2	2	5	2	5	4	3	1	3	4	4	3	2	3	5	5	7	8	6	13	15	15	10	12	8	10
P	Turtle dove (*Streptopelia turtur*)	0	0	0	1	1	0	0	2	2	0	0	0	0	2	2	2	1	1	1	1	4	5	1	1	1	0
P	Cuckoo* (*Cuculus canorus*)	0	2	2	2	1	2	1	1	0	1	0	2	1	1	1	2	2	1	2	i	2	2	2	2	2	1
N	Tawny owl* (*Strix aluco*)	0	1	1	1	1	1	1	1	1	1	1	0	1	0	1	1	1	1	1	1	1	1	1	1	1	1
N	Green woodpecker* (*Picus viridis*)	1	2	2	3	2	2	0	0	1	1	1	1	0	1	0	0	1	1	1	1	2	2	2	1	1	1
N	Great spotted woodpecker* (*Dendrocopos major*)	1	2	2	2	3	3	2	2	2	1	2	2	2	2	2	2	2	3	2	3	3	3	3	3	2	3
N	Lesser spotted woodpecker* (*Dendrocopos minor*)	0	0	0	0	0	1	1	0	0	0	0	0	0	1	1	1	0	1	1	1	0	0	1	2	1	1
N	Carrion crow* (*Corvus corone*)	1	1	1	1	1	1	1	1	1	1	1	1	1	1	1	2	2	2	1	1	1	2	3	2	2	2

Table 5.1—*contd.*

Evidence of breeding		Year																									
		49	50	51	52	53	54	55	56	58	59	60	61	62	63	64	65	66	67	68	69	70	71	72	73	74	75
N	Magpie (*Pica pica*)	1	1	1	1	1	1	1	1	1	1	2	1	1	1	1	1	0	0	1	1	3	1	2	3	2	2
N	Jay (*Garrulus glandarius*)	2	5	6	6	5	7	4	3	4	4	4	4	3	4	7	4	5	5	3	4	7	7	8	5	4	5
N	Great tit (*Parus major*)	6	8	8	8.5	11	11	10	12	4.5	11	12	12	11	12	17	17	12	16	19	14	13	13	12	18	19	17
N	Blue tit (*Parus caeruleus*)	NC	6.5	13.5	9.5	13	16	10	14	13	10.5	16	18	16.5	19	19	22	17	16	20	19	20	15	16	19	26	19
N	Coal tit (*Parus ater*)	1	4	3	3	2	2	1	2	2	3	2	3	3	2	5	4	3	8	6	7	5	4	7	9	5	6
N	Marsh tit (*Parus palustris*)	2	2	2	4	5	4	2	4	2	3	4	2	5	3	1	1	3	3	3	3	3	2	2	4	2	1
N	Willow tit (*Parus montanus*)	1	1	0	1	1	1	1	2	1	0	1	1	0	1	0	1	1	1	1	2	1	1	2	2	1	1
N	Long-tailed tit (*Aegithalos caudatus*)	1	1	2	2	1	2	2	2	2	0	1	1	2	0	0	1	2	2	1	1	2	3	2	3	2	2
N	Nuthatch (*Sitta europaea*)	0	1	3	1	2	2	3	4	1	4	4	3	3	2	5	5	5	7	5	3	5	5	4	6	5	4
N	Treecreeper (*Certhia familiaris*)	1	2	0	2	2	1	2	1	1	2	3	1	3	1	1	2	2	2	4	4	3	5	3	1	2	2
N	Wren (*Troglodytes troglodytes*)	17	20	20.5	18	10.5	14	11.5	7	16	13	14.5	17	12	1	5.5	11	17	25	26	24	25	17	26	27	27	30
N	Mistle thrush* (*Turdus viscivorus*)	0	0	0	1	1	2	0	0	0	0	0	2	2	2	2	3	2	1	1	2	2	2	2	2	1	1
N	Song thrush (*Turdus philomelos*)	1	1	7	5	3	5	4	5	4	2	3	6	5	4	7	7	8	10	7	7	7	9	6	6	6	4
N	Blackbird (*Turdus merula*)	5	9	9.5	11.5	8	12.5	8	7.5	11.5	9	7	9	8	8	10	12	11	12	11	13	9	14	12	6	12	12
U	Nightingale (*Luscinia megarhynchos*)	1	0	0	0	1	1	2	0	0	0	0	0	0	0	1	0	0	0	0	0	0	0	1	1	0	0

Evidence	Species	22.5	28	28.5	30.5	33	30.5	23	24	32	29	23.5	27	32	21.5	32	37	37	42	43	44	36	44	37	35	38	33
N	Robin *(Erithacus rubecula)*	3	3	4	3	2	3	2	3	3	4	2	4	3	5	3	4	7	6	3	6	1	3	4	3	2	2
N	Blackcap *(Sylvia atricapilla)*	3	3	4	3	4	2	4	4	7	3	3	2	4	2	2	4	1	1	1	3	4	3	0	0	1	1
N	Garden warbler *(Sylvia borin)*	3	3	3	3	4	2	4	4	7	3	2	2	4	2	2	4	1	1	1	1	1	0	0	0	0	0
N	Whitethroat *(Sylvia communis)*	1	2	1	2	2	2	0	1	1	1	1	0	1	1	1	0	0	1	1	0	0	0	0	0	0	0
U	Lesser whitethroat *(Sylvia curruca)*	0	1	1	0	0	0	0	0	0	0	0	0	0	0	0	0	0	0	0	0	0	0	0	0	0	0
N	Willow warbler *(Phylloscopus trochilus)*	16.5	21	16	15	15	11	8.5	17.5	12	5	2.5	2	1.5	2.5	1.5	4	4	2	6	2	2	0	0	0	0	2
N	Chiffchaff *(Phylloscopus collybita)*	1	2.5	4.5	2.5	2	5.5	4.5	4.5	1.5	2	3	1	1.5	2	5	7	6	6	3	3	4	1	1	4	4	1
U	Goldcrest *(Regulus regulus)*	0	1	0	0	0	0	0	0	0	0	1	0	0	0	0	0	0	0	3	0	1	2	1	3	2	2
N	Spotted flycatcher *(Muscicapa striata)*	0	0	1	1	0	0	1	0	0	0	0	0	0	1	1	1	0	1	0	0	0	0	0	0	0	0
P	Dunnock *(Prunella modularis)*	NC	2	2	2	4	2	2	4	1	2	0	1	4.5	4	5	5	4	8	6	6	3	2	1	0	3	1
N	Starling *(Sturnus vulgaris)*	0	0	0	0	0	0	0	0	0	1	2	3	2	5	5.5	10	6	8	12	7	8	8	6	7	9	9
U	Hawfinch *(Coccothraustes coccothraustes)*	0	0	0	1	0	0	0	0	0	0	0	0	0	0	0	0	0	1	1	0	1	0	0	0	0	0
N	Greenfinch *(Carduelis chloris)*	0	0	0	0	0	0	0	0	0	0	0	0	0	0	0	1	1	0	0	0	0	0	1	0	0	0
U	Redpoll *(Acanthis flammea)*	0	0	0	0	0	0	0	0	0	0	0	0	0	0	0	0	0	0	0	0	0	0	2	0	0	0
N	Bullfinch *(Pyrrhula pyrrhula)*	2	2	2	4	4	3	3	4	2	3	2	2	1	2	2	2	2	2	2	3	4	1	4	2	2	2
N	Chaffinch *(Fringilla coelebs)*	9.5	11	12.5	9.5	9	8	8	6	4.5	2	2.5	4.5	7	5.5	5.5	8	7	6	4	4	3	6	8	3	1	3

* Birds with large territories in which only part may be within the Eastern Wood.
Evidence of breeding: N, evidence of nesting; P, probably nested; U, uncertain.
0.5 = a male with only part of its territory in Eastern Wood. NC = No count.
After Beven 1976.

populations? There are 44 species in Table 5.1, which have bred at
some time in the wood during this period of 27 years. Only 16 of these
have bred every year, and of those two, *Corvus corone*, the crow, and
Dendrocopos major, the great spotted woodpecker, are large birds with
large territories of which only a part may lie within the Eastern Wood.
That leaves a mere 14 bird species nesting every year with territories
entirely within the wood. On the face of it, then, if the wood were
suddenly transformed into an isolated island, though still with the
same habitat if such can be conceived, the species list would be expected to drop in a few years from 44 to 14.

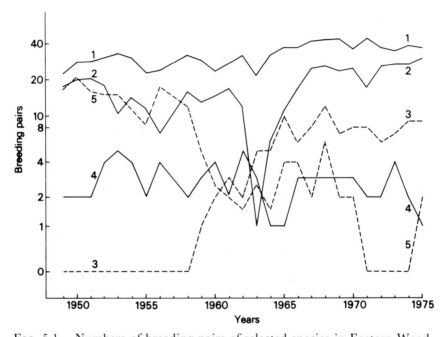

F IG. 5.1.   Numbers of breeding pairs of selected species in Eastern Wood,
Bookham Common. The ordinate is sinh^{-1} (n), which is close to a logarithmic
scale, but allows zeros to be plotted. (Data from Beven 1976.)
1. Robin, *Erithacus rubecula*. 2. Wren, *Troglodytes troglodytes*. 3. Starling, *Sturnus
vulgaris*. 4. Marsh tit, *Parus palustris*. 5. Willow warbler, *Phylloscopus trochilus*.

There are difficulties with both these figures. Of the 44 on the list, 6
have not been proven to breed, which leaves 38. Nine more, including
the two predators *Accipiter nisus*, the sparrow hawk, and *Strix aluco*, the
tawny owl, have never had more than 2 pairs in the wood, and would be
described by most ornithologists as casual species. We shall return to
this below, but removing them leaves 29 species. Of those, 4 take up

territories which extend beyond the wood, leaving 11 species with more than casual populations which have not bred every year, and 14 which have. The very large numbers of immigrations and extinctions would appear to confirm the emphasis in the MacArthur–Wilson theory on the turnover of species. There are, however, two important points. The first is the extreme smallness of the wood; 9 of the 44 species have territories which extend beyond it. The other concerns the population characteristics of those species showing extinction and immigration.

Figure 5.2 shows the number of years that each species has bred. The most common category is, perhaps surprisingly, the species that breed every year. There are several species that have bred in only a few years, usually only once or twice. Casual breeders could be defined as those nesting in fewer than five years, less than 20 per cent of the record. These species all have very few pairs in the wood when they do breed, as is illustrated in Fig. 5.3. This shows the number of breeding pairs of all species that have a zero anywhere in their record. The distribution is very skew, and the right-hand tail, such as it is, consists almost entirely

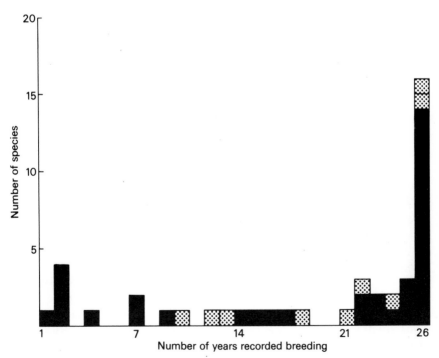

F IG. 5.2. A histogram of the number of years each of 44 species bred in Eastern Wood in 26 years of observations. Stippled squares refer to species with territories extending beyond the Wood.

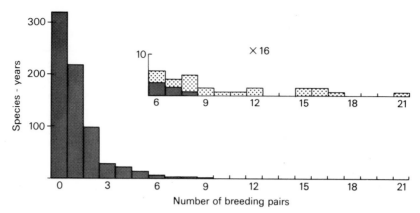

F ɪ ɢ. 5.3.   The number of pairs breeding in Eastern Wood in any one year for all those species failing to breed for one or more years. The inset is the right-hand part of the histogram at a magnification of ×16, and with stipple to show the records for the willow warbler, *Phylloscopus trochilus* and starling, *Sturnus vulgaris*.

of records of willow warblers and starlings, the two species that have undergone marked long-term changes. Species that either immigrate or go extinct scarcely ever have more than five breeding pairs in the wood.

Bird populations are not very variable in size, as can be shown best by the standard deviation of the logarithm of the population size (Williamson 1972). Even so, species with an average population of less than ten breeding pairs, such as the marsh tit in Fig. 5.1, could be expected to reach zero in less than 100 years. The large numbers of immigrations and extinctions in Eastern Wood then reflect the small size of the wood in relation to the average density of bird populations. One disappointing point about both the paper and the book by Mac-Arthur and Wilson (1963, 1967) is that they give no data to match their diagram of extinction and immigration curves against number of species. This can be readily done for the Bookham Common birds (using the convention that 1958 follows immediately after 1956, as no survey was done in 1957). The results are shown in Fig. 5.4.

Although the data all relate to an established bird community, the spread of species numbers is from 27 to 36, a 33 per cent difference, and it can be seen that there is a remarkable degree of scatter about what are normally drawn as definite lines. However, immigration does decline with increasing numbers of species breeding. The regression of immigrants on species number is −0.38, significant at the one per cent level. The extinction data show a weak, statistically insignificant positive correlation. The diagrams emphasize one point which is not usually

mentioned in discussions of MacArthur–Wilson theory, and that is
that all the co-ordinates of the points must be integers. This inevitably
follows from treating annual censuses and counting breeding pairs.
Both the numbers counted and the time intervals are discrete, which
affects the curves that can be fitted.

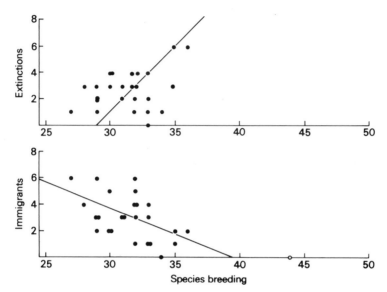

FIG. 5.4.   Immigration and extinction at Eastern Wood. The line in the
extinction diagram is at 45°, indicating one extinction for every species present
over 29. The line in the immigration diagram is the calculated regression line,
with slope −0.38. The open circle is 44 species, the number recorded breeding
at some time in the years 1949–75.

What shaped curves should be drawn through the points in Fig. 5.4?
For the immigration data, a linear regression could be drawn, which
would cut the abscissa, the species axis, at about 40, and the ordinate,
the immigrant axis, at about 16. Such a line would imply that if there
were 40 species breeding in the wood, no more immigrants would be
expected the following year, and conversely, if in some way all the
breeding birds were eliminated in one year, then 16 species would be
expected to start breeding afresh the next year. The latter figure is
perhaps not unreasonable, though a little on the low side, as 27 or more
species have always bred, suggesting that the relationship curves upwards in the way that MacArthur and Wilson expected it would.
Would there be no immigrants had there been 40 species breeding in
the wood?

In the MacArthur and Wilson theory, the immigration curve cuts the species axis at the pool number of species. The pool is more than 40, as 44 breeding species have been recorded. The wood is in National Grid square TQ 15, and roughly twice that number were recorded breeding in that 100 km² between 1968 and 1972, 82 species 'confirmed', 5 'probable', and 4 'possible' (Sharrock 1976). Taking a larger possible area for a pool, the total number of British breeding bird species is slightly over 200, including a number of birds that could not conceivably breed in Eastern Wood, such as those that nest on sea cliffs. No single definite figure can be given for the pool size for this wood, but were the number of the bird species breeding to be 40 or more, the probability of yet another species immigrating to breed the following year would be negligible. So, at least for the stable community, a straight regression line seems an adequate description of the data, and the spread around the line is quite large. At the average number of species, 32, the expected number of immigrants each year is 3 new species. Statistically, anything between 0 and 6, a spread of a further 3 on either side, is perfectly normal.

It is hard to say even as much as that about the extinction curve, though again at the observed average of 32 species, the number expected to go extinct each year is 3. As the relationship of the number of extinctions to number of species is not significant, little can be said about the shape from these data alone. However, it is possible to deduce something about the shape of the underlying relationship. If the wood were crammed with breeding species, say there were 40 or more species present, then any new species could be expected to be an extremely casual one, and breed for only one year with one nest. Each additional species could be expected to lead to one additional extinction but not more, or, in other words, the extinction curve can not rise faster than 45°. A somewhat related point was made by MacArthur and Wilson, as noted in the last chapter. Taking the cluster of points in Fig. 5.4 and extrapolating a line at 45° from the centre shows that a maximum of 15 species could be expected to go extinct if all 44 were present. That would bring the species observed in the following year down to below the average, to 29, so even with very high numbers of species, the rate of extinction would probably be less than one extinction for each species present over equilibrium. The very steep curves for extinction rate shown in some diagrams of the MacArthur and Wilson theory can only apply to continuous time: in discrete time there would seem to be a biological limit to the steepness, barring some biological interaction leading to a collapse of the community to below its equilibrium number of species.

In the other part of the extinction curve, to the left of the observed points, the curve must be much flatter. The expected number of extinctions could scarcely exceed one, and by the time there are only 16 species, the permanent breeders, the probability of an extinction in one year is clearly very small. The extinction curve is effectively on the axis well before it reaches back to the origin. This point has also been made by Diamond and May (1976). The Eastern Wood data cast doubt on MacArthur and Wilson's (1967) assumption that a single transformation would make the extinction curve linear and go through the origin.

What would happen to this bird community if it were on an isolated, oceanic island? The population sizes of even those species that have been found breeding every year are, in general, rather small. On an isolated island, it is likely that any species which could not maintain a population of 10 pairs or more would, allowing for the usual variability of bird populations, go extinct in a few hundreds of generations if not earlier. Even some of those with higher populations might well be expected to go extinct because of changes in the environment. These changes could be in the vegetation, of the sort that led to the extinction of the willow warbler in Eastern Wood; they could be climatic changes, a slight warming or cooling of the sort that is now well known in many climatic records. Taking just the numerical criterion for persistence, then an isolated Eastern Wood island might hold only 5 species, namely *Parus major*, the great tit, *P. caeruleus*, the blue tit, *Troglodytes troglodytes*, the wren, *Turdus merula*, the blackbird, and *Erithacus rubecula*, the robin.

This remarkable survey indicates the severe reduction in the number of species that can be expected on very isolated islands. It also shows that on less isolated islands there will be a considerable turnover of species. The great bulk of this turnover will be of casual breeders, species at very low densities, nesting on the island infrequently. There will be a few species going extinct and others establishing stable populations, and a few previously regular breeders going extinct. Some turnover of species will be easy to relate to environmental changes, like the extinction of the willow warbler. Some turnover will be more difficult to explain. Take the starling population at Eastern Wood as an example.

Starlings often breed in holes in trees. It is possible that the establishment and more or less logistic growth of the starling population from 1959, shown in Fig. 5.1, was a consequence of the change of woodland management in 1952, which may have produced more suitable nesting sites. The establishment of starlings on the island of Skokholm, discussed below, started with a pair nesting in a hole in a rusting corrugated-iron shed (Lockley 1947). While showing the importance of nesting sites in allowing bird populations to establish themselves, both these immigrations may be part of a large-scale population increase in starlings. The British population has apparently been increasing consistently since about 1830 (Sharrock 1976).

What then does the Bookham Common survey tell us of the MacArthur–Wilson theory? In one simple sense the theory is correct. There is a considerable turnover of species, with species immigrating and going extinct in every year. There is apparently a species equilibrium at 32 species, with three new immigrants and three new extinctions each year on average. Is this a sufficient description of the community? Is it even the most important information about the community? The answers to these questions would no doubt depend on one's particular interests, but it is difficult to think that many ecologists would find they could answer both in the affirmative.

The species that most ecologists would regard as making up the bird community in Eastern Wood are those that breed there every year, and probably most ornithologists would also include, bearing in mind the very small size of the wood, those that breed there almost every year, say 21 years or more out of 26. The regular breeders number 16; the almost-regular breeders another 11, making 27 in all. Either figure, and particularly the former, is appreciably less than the MacArthur–Wilson equilibrium of 32. More seriously, an understanding of the bird community requires a knowledge of the population densities of the different species, and also some information on the ecology of the different species. Neither of those comes into the theory.

If the area studied were enlarged, then the proportion of species showing turnover would evidently decrease. Further, population densities of those species showing turnover would be much smaller in relation to the population density of the regular breeders than is found in Eastern Wood. In other words, the information obtained from the studies of the sort emphasized in the MacArthur–Wilson theory will become less important in larger areas, as has already been noted (p. 83).

Turnover on islands

With the establishment of bird observatories for the study of migration, populations of birds on a number of small islands round Britain have also been recorded. Lack (1969*b*) brought together a number of these records, particularly those from Skokholm, where the earliest bird observatory was established by R. M. Lockley in 1928, when he was farming the island of 100 ha (1 km²). There have been habitat changes on Skokholm, particularly in the early years when Lockley was trying to establish a farm, and the turnover of bird species in those years is somewhat greater than later. The island was evacuated during the

Second World War, so there are no records available for the period between 1940 and 1946. After the war, no attempt was made to farm the island, and so there were again progressive changes as the natural vegetation re-established itself, and particularly as *Pteridium aquilinum*, bracken, spread at the expense of *Calluna vulgaris*, heather. In contrast with Eastern Wood, there are no trees on Skokholm; the vegetation comprises heath, with bracken and rabbit-grazed turf. A damp area in the centre, which was a well-established pond at the end of the war, has since become drier. An account of the vegetation is given by Goodman and Gillham (1954).

Even on an island as small as Skokholm, it is difficult for one man living on the island to census all the breeding bird species each year. In fact, in many years after the war no attempt was made to census *Anthus pratensis*, the meadow pipit, of which there are 40 or more pairs. Their numbers are recorded by a question mark in Lack's paper, and interpreted by Abbott and Grant (1976) as meaning possible extinction. Although Lack himself was not clear on this point, all his question marks in fact refer to uncertain population sizes, rather than to possible absences. This is evident in the annual reports of the bird observatory. In addition, Lockley (1947) published records for breeding populations before the war, which not only replace some of the question marks in Lack's table, but also give the populations for 1940 which Lack did not include at all.

For 1928 to 1967 Lack picked out nine species as regular breeding land birds for all or part of this period, and the graphs for these are shown in Fig. 5.5. It will be seen that the populations behaved much as did those in Eastern Wood. Lack considered *Anthus spinoletta*, the rock pipit, to be a sea bird; it has 30 to 40 pairs on the island each year (Lockley 1947).

There is one important extinction, that of *Prunella modularis*, the dunnock, between 1940 and 1946. Another extinction occurred when *Alauda arvensis*, the skylark, failed to breed in 1938 during a period of very low population density on the island, but Skokholm is only 4 km from the mainland of Wales, skylarks fly well and high, and probably the island population of skylarks is scarcely separated from those on the mainland. The population was re-established in 1939.

The dunnock population, though, is a different matter. The species recolonized in 1964 after an absence of about 20 years, following an unusual immigration in the autumn of 1963. There has been one other definite colonization of the island, by the starling, which Lack first records in 1946; however there was one pair in 1940, which is thus the true date of colonization. The increase of starlings on Skokholm, at Eastern Wood, and in Britain as a whole was discussed above.

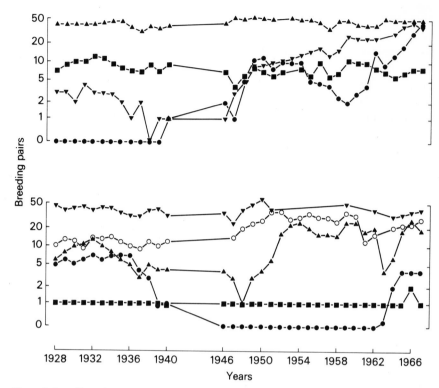

Fɪɢ. 5.5. Population curves for the persistent species of land birds on Skokholm. Ordinate as in Fig. 5.1. Counts not available for rock pipit, *Anthus spinoletta*. Upper graph ▲ oystercatcher, *Haematopus ostralegus*, ■ carrion crow, *Corvus corone*, ▼ sky lark, *Alauda arvensis*, ● starling, *Sturnus vulgaris*. Lower graph ▼ meadow pipit, *Anthus pratensis*, ○ wheatear, *Oenanthe oenanthe*, ▲ lapwing, *Vanellus vanellus*, ● dunnock, *Prunella modularis*, ■ raven, *Corvus corax*. (Data from Lack 1969*b* and Lockley 1947.)

Of the other populations, *Vanellus vanellus*, the lapwing, has shown marked long-term fluctuations, and was almost extinct in the late 1940s. The rest are fairly steady, and in the case of *Corvus corax*, the raven, remarkably so with one pair recorded every year except in 1966 when there were two pairs. For a species like this, with traditional nest sites and very large territories, a stable population is perhaps to be expected. It is worth noting that there are no established populations of bird predators, or for that matter any other vertebrate predators, on Skokholm. Both *Falco peregrinus*, the peregrine and *Buteo buteo*, the buzzard, are on the list of irregular breeders.

From the data published by Lack and Lockley it is again easy to produce immigration and extinction plots, and these are shown in Fig.

5.6. They have the same general appearance as those for Eastern Wood on Bookham Common (Fig. 5.4). The scatter of the points is more impressive than their tendency to lie around a line. In the woodland plots, immigration has a significant negative correlation with species number, extinction an insignificant positive one. At Skokholm, the extinction curve has the significant relationship, again positive, while the correlation of species number with immigration is insignificant (and positive, not negative).

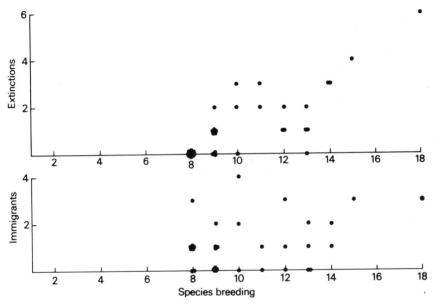

FIG. 5.6.   Immigration and extinction plots for the land and freshwater birds of Skokholm. If rock pipits were included, all points would move one unit to the right.

The plots in Fig. 5.6 again emphasize the discrete nature of changes of this sort, where immigration and extinction are defined by the occurrence, or not, of breeding at an annual breeding season. It is fair to say that during this period of almost 40 years the island had eight or nine regular breeding-species of land birds, including *Hematopus ostralegus*, the oystercatcher, which some would regard as a shore bird, though many of its territories are away from the shore. The MacArthur–Wilson equilibrium, though, is at about 11 species, with an average of one immigration and one extinction per annum, and the difference of two or three reflects the usual number of species found breeding irregularly, typically with only one pair breeding in each species. It is difficult to say anything about the immigration scatter except that it is large. It is not possible, from these data, to suggest where it intersects the ordinate, or what the pool number of species might reasonably be expected to be. It could be argued, for instance, that the number of immigrants would be one species per year irrespective of the number on the island. It is perhaps more reasonable biologically to suggest that four to six species would immigrate if no species were present, suggesting that the immigration curve does indeed bend up sharply as MacArthur and Wilson suggest. There is, however, no evidence for either of these interpretations. Similarly, the extinction curve appears to be going up with the gradient of roughly 1 in 2, a regression coefficient $b = +0.44$, appreciably less than the maximum of 1 in 1 that is the limit for producing a damped return to the equilibrium. The extinction curve would appear to be almost at zero at eight species, and so bends quite sharply at around that value. The natural biological explanation suggests that the extinction curve is not homogeneous. The established populations, generally the population sizes of 10 or more, or with strong traditional territoriality as in the raven, have almost negligible chances of extinction provided there is no marked environmental change. On the other hand, the casual breeders, those that appear as single pairs, frequently breeding in a habitat which is not typical for their species, have a very high probability of extinction. Even among those casual breeders, turnover is low, only about one species per year. This contrasts with the turnover of three species per year in the smaller and much less isolated Eastern Wood.

There is no other set of data which is as complete or as long as the Skokholm data. For some more-isolated islands the data are sufficient to show that turnover is even lower (Abbott and Grant 1976; Slud 1976). Both on Cocos Island (Fig. 9.1) and on the Tres Marias (Fig. 6.5), there appears to be either no turnover at all in about 70 years, or possibly up to two immigrants on the Tres Marias only. These islands are respectively 47 and 300 km². As Abbott and Grant point out, these two are unusual both in that the early censuses were thorough and reliable, and in that the islands have since not been disturbed by man. The same cannot be said of some other island groups of which the Californian Channel Islands have been the most quoted in literature, e.g., by MacArthur (1972). There is a dispute between Johnson and Diamond about the status of various species (Lynch and Johnson 1974; Jones and Diamond 1976). Lynch and Johnson maintain that there had been no turnover that cannot be ascribed to incomplete censuses, human interference, and transient non-breeders. Jones and Diamond disagree, but their disagreement seems to centre on casual breeding species. For instance, they make much of a record of one male humming bird plucking material from a lady's hat during one picnic party. The Californian Channel Islands are quite big, of the order of 100 km² each, and 30–40 km from the Californian coast. One would therefore expect occasional casuals, simply because of the size of the islands, but that, for the same reason, the established populations would show very low turnover. This is indeed also suggested by the number of endemic subspecies recorded. About one-third of the species breeding have been regarded as distinct races, perhaps not always with full justification (Johnson 1972). The time required for these changes would not seem likely to be less than hundreds if not thousands of generations, that is to say an order of magnitude larger than the time usually thought of as ecological time.

All these studies would seem to suggest that for bird populations, any species that can maintain an average density of 10 pairs or more is unlikely to show turnover for stochastic reasons, though it may well show turnover because of environmental changes. The position is quite different with some other organisms. The most extreme case that has been studied quantitatively is the human virus disease, measles. Bartlett (1957) predicted that measles would die out in cities of less than a fifth of a million population, and Black (1966) tabulated the observed survival of measles on islands of different populations, and suggested the critical limit was somewhat higher, perhaps about half a million people. He suggested the reason for the discrepancy might be the more-dispersed populations of islands compared with the dense populations of cities. A graph of his data is shown in Fig. 5.7. It looks as if the present strain of measles can be, at most, only a few thousand years old, as before that the conditions for its persistence, human populations of sufficient size, were lacking.

The figure of a fifth or half a million for a persistent measles population is possibly misleading. Although the number of virus particles in a patient with a disease is very large, the critical population for the persistence of the organism is not the number of viruses, but the number of infected people. Those infected are young children who have not caught the disease before, so the critical population is that of suitably aged, susceptible individuals in the total population, and this is why stochastic effects appear in a total population of hundreds of thousands.

Immigration from scratch

All the examples so far considered are of communities near what could be called the ecological equilibrium. That is to say, at a point which is apparently at equilibrium in ecological time, time measured in tens of

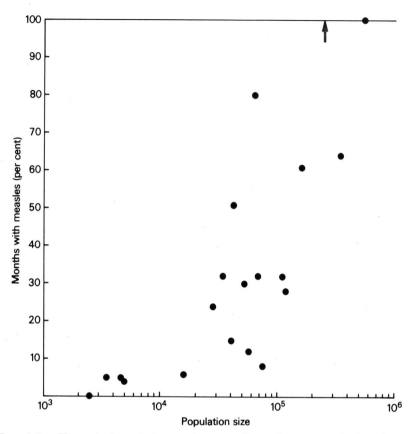

Fɪɢ. 5.7.   The relation of the persistence of measles to population size on various islands. The arrow indicates Bartlett's prediction of the minimum population size for endemic measles, i.e., present in 100 per cent of months. (Data from Black 1966.)

generations, or in the working life-time of an ecologist. They therefore give almost no information about immigration and extinction rates well away from this equilibrium. For that some great disturbance is neces-sary, for instance, by a volcano, or experimentally by a scientist. The best and the best-known experiments have been by Simberloff and Wilson, and these will be discussed below. The best-known biological recolonization after a volcanic explosion is that on Krakatau, between Java and Sumatra, which erupted in 1883. The rather infrequent surveys of this island are discussed by MacArthur and Wilson (1967). For plants, the number of species appears to increase linearly with time, with no indication of a decline in rate between 1883 and 1934. For the birds, on the other hand, they consider an equilibrium was reached as early as 1920. This seems somewhat inconsistent with the continued increase in plants. Somewhat farther east, the islands of Ritter and Long, between New Guinea and New Britain, also suffered volcanic explosions. Ritter disintegrated in 1888 and Long at some time in the eighteenth century. Diamond (1974) compared the avifaunas of these two islands with a set of control islands in the same region overlapping Ritter and Long in size, and concluded that both were still a long way from equilibrium, and that this was primarily because the vegetation was not yet in equilibrium. Ritter, indeed, still has bare areas on its higher parts, and the forest on Long is 'more open and savannah-like than on older volcanic islands'. So it would seem advisable to ignore the three surveys of Krakatau, and note that the re-establishment of the mature community on a tropical island takes several centuries. As that is only a few generations for the dominant trees, the process can still be thought of as taking place in ecological time, even if it is beyond the scope of a single ecologist to study it.

A more recent volcano, which had been studied much more intensively than Krakatau, is Surtsey, which arose out of the sea as the outermost of the Westman Islands off the south-east corner of Iceland in 1963 and is thus the newest island on the mid-Atlantic ridge (Figs. 2.1, 6.3).

The formation of Surtsey by a series of eruptions, and the resulting topography, geology, and climate are given in full detail by Fridriksson (1975). Detailed and careful studies were made of the colonization of Surtsey by mosses and by vascular plants (Fig. 5.8). The standard quadrats were of sides 100 m long, i.e. 1 ha in area. The total area of the island is about 2.2 km^2 though there are rather more than 220 quadrats,

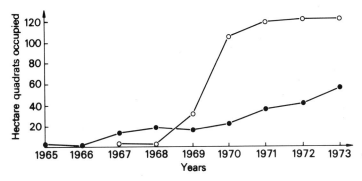

F IG. 5.8. Colonization curves for bryophytes and for vascular plants on Surtsey, as measured by presence in quadrats of 1 ha. The total area is about 220 ha (see Fig. 5.9). ○ Bryophytes, ● vascular plants. (Data from Fridriksson 1975.)

because the ones round the edge of the island each contain less than
1 ha of land. Figure 5.9 shows the quadrat system used for recording
occurrences, and indicates the way the island changed shape.

Within only nine years, the immigration and extinction plots for
vascular plants and mosses, shown in Fig. 5.10, are both rather thin.
They do, however, indicate one phenomenon which is to be expected.
That is that the highest recorded rate of immigration occurs after the
first few plants have become established, rather than at the start of the
process. This is a phenomenon well-known in vegetational successional
studies. A few species are capable of colonizing bare ground, but many

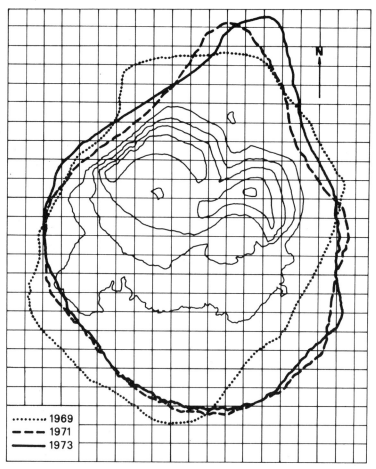

F ɪ ɢ. 5.9.   The shape of Surtsey in three different years, and the hectare grid.
Contours at 30 m intervals (shown for 1971), the highest point over 150 m.
(Compiled from Fridriksson 1975.)

more species require the presence of other vegetation before they can colonize successfully. The same must be true of the animals, though a number of the invertebrates will be influenced by the presence of algae and lichen rather than the mosses and vascular plants shown here.

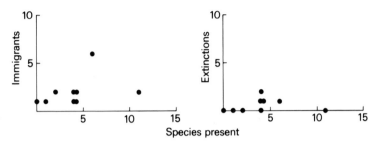

F I G. 5.10.   Immigration and extinction plots for vascular plants on Surtsey. (Data from Fridriksson 1975.)

Experiments in Florida

The experimental defaunation of mangrove trees in the Florida Keys by Simberloff and Wilson is well known, and their recolonization curves have been reproduced in very many places. Nevertheless, a short recapitulation of what was done is necessary before discussing Simberloff's recent results.

The islands studied all consisted of isolated trees at *Rhizophora mangle*, red mangrove, growing in intertidal mud. The trees varied between 11 and 18 m in diameter, and the defaunation was carried out by covering them with sheeting and applying insecticides, mainly methyl bromide. The islands were recensused at frequent intervals during the first year, and again after two years and three years. Figure 5.11 shows the results of the first three years for four of these minute islands, using the additional information in Simberloff (1976c). The richest and poorest islands, both before and after defaunation, were E2 and E1 respectively. E2 is slightly larger, about 12 m in diameter, but only 2 m from the source, the main block of mangroves. On the other hand, E1, 11 m in diameter, is 533 m from the source.

There are a number of special features of this survey which illustrate the practical difficulties of experimental field work. It is clearly impossible in a survey of this sort to draw a firm line between species which are confined to the tree and those that move freely on and off the tree. Accounts were limited to certain arthropod species only, but even studying the arthropods on one species of tree in the subtropics leads to a long list and considerable taxonomic difficulties. The lower plants,

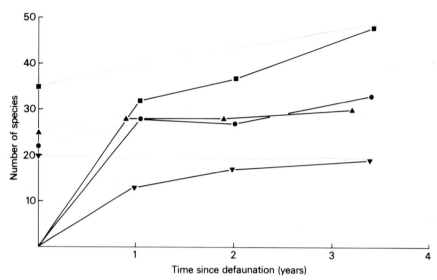

F IG. 5.11.   The first three years of recolonization after defaunation, on man-grove islands off Florida. ▼ E1 island, ■ E2, ● E3, ▲ ST2. (Data from Simberloff 1976*c*.)

the birds and snails that occurred, were not censused. Nor were four groups of insects. The first were foraging insects, that is to say large, vigorous fliers that go from tree to tree, including odonata, cicadas, and bees and wasps that were not found nesting in the trees. The second group were transient butterflies which again fly from tree to tree. The third group was the diptera, except the Hippoboscidae which are bird parasites. The fourth set to be excluded were those arthropods which occur only on the base of the stem and on the mud around the tree. Except for the diptera, which were excluded for practical reasons, excluding the others is clearly an attempt to confine the study to the fauna that treats the tree as an island. However, lepidoptera that breed on trees and are known then to fly to other trees, and bird parasites, were both counted.

In an attempt to restrict the census to reproducing populations, Simberloff and Wilson also adopted the convention that species re-presented only by adult males were not counted. Immature insects were counted and gave clear evidence that the species had bred on the tree since defaunation. But less-good evidence of breeding comes from counting adult females, and rather dubious evidence from counting unsexed adults. All these difficulties led to Simberloff putting forward his definition of immigration and extinction, in the third paper in the series of his work, which has already been quoted above (p. 86).

It can be seen in Fig. 5.11 that the number of species at the end of the first year were near the numbers before defaunation. Nevertheless, on all four the numbers of species continued to increase after that. On E1, which was the slowest to recover, the species at year 3 were within one of the original; on the other three islands the numbers were higher, and in the case of E2 and E3 quite a lot higher. Furthermore, the species found on the islands at subsequent surveys were frequently not those found before defaunation. The details are given by Simberloff (1976c). Although fewer than 50 species were found at any census of one island, the total number of taxa found on the four islands during the four surveys was 118.

Are the sets of species found on a particular island random sets from this 118, or are they in some ways structured sets? Simberloff and Wilson, in their first reports, suggested that the number of species first rose to a non-interactive equilibrium, and then sank slightly to an interactive one (Fig. 4.2). Simberloff (1976c) says 'the figures . . . are consistent with our earlier suggestion that, even after species number equilibrium is reached, an "assortative" equilibriation process occurs as more highly co-adapted species sets find themselves by chance on an island and persist longer as sets'. It is difficult to test this assertion.

The first difficulty is that, despite the strenuous efforts to ensure accurate censuses, it is still far from clear how much of the turnover recorded on the islands was real turnover. Searching a mangrove tree 10 m across and being sure that you have found all the species is clearly extremely difficult. Simberloff (1976b) gives curves for the cumulative number of species found against man hours of searching. These are for island G1, which has an area of 519 m², for the three years 1969–71. The cumulative curve in each successive year is higher, leading to the reasonably assured conclusion that the total number of species in each successive year was indeed still increasing, but Simberloff's assertion that 'a clear asymptote' was reached is distinctly dubious for two of the years. The islands discussed above are all quite a lot smaller than G1, yet in the published tables there are still quite a number of instances where presence of a species has to be assumed at the census even though it was not seen, because it was found at the censuses before and after.

The second difficulty is that the criteria for immigration are very difficult to apply in practice. So, many records of immigration relate to transients, giving rise to quite high apparent extinction rates. Simberloff (1976c) concludes that of 51 extinctions recorded between years 1 and 3, only 12 local extinctions can definitely be described as elimination of breeding non-transient colonists. Thirty nine out of 51 recorded extinctions possibly only show the passage of transients. The rate of about 1.5 definite extinctions per island per year is really quite low when compared with the turnover of breeding birds in the Eastern Wood at Bookham Common. With most of the published turnover data relating to what Simberloff calls 'pseudo turnover', it would obviously be quite difficult to decide whether or not the arthropod communities were moving towards an assortative equilibrium, even if there were clear peaks in Fig. 5.11.

One interesting attempt has been made to see if the islands are in equilibrium. Heatwole and Levins (1972) classified the arthropods into eight functional types, and calculated the proportion of the types before defaunation and at various stages during the recolonization. For their calculations, they grouped all the experimental islands together. The structure of the community at the beginning of the experiment was, by frequency, according to them:

Herbivores	0.359
Ants	0.180
Predators	0.219
Scavengers	0.034
Detritus feeders	0.069
Wood borers	0.046
Parasites	0.069
Unknown	0.020

It will be seen that the first three classes are major classes, but that the other five are all rather minor consistuents. Calling the initial proportions $\hat{p}_i$, with i from 1 to 8, they calculated for each census after defaunation, taken at time t, a deviation of ecological structure, defined as

$$D_t = \Sigma_i \, (p_{i,t} - \hat{p}_i)^2.$$

Using this statistic, and plotting $\log D$ against t, they found a remarkably rapid and linear change from the initial deviation towards the initial structure.

Unfortunately, this demonstration suffers from a very common problem of quantitative studies on island biota. That is, it is very sensitive to the total number of species. Simberloff (1976a) calculated the theoretical curve of $\log D$ against number of species, together with its confidence limits, and showed both a monotonic relationship and that the data points for individual islands scatter in an acceptable way about this theoretical line. It would seem that Heatwole and Levins have merely shown, in a rather sophisticated manner, that the number of species was increasing towards an asymptote during the first year, which is the best-known result from this set of experiments. Simberloff

(1978) discusses these and other data, and concludes that it is not possible yet to say how much of colonization proceeds deterministically, as Heatwole and Levins suggested, and how much stochastically.

Simberloff (1976*b*) also discusses particular cases of interaction between species. He notes an ant-mimicking cockroach, *Latiblattella* sp; an interaction between two species of ants and the availability of different sizes of hollow twigs; a waxy scale insect that seems to be dependent on being tended by a particular species of ant; and an interaction, competitive in effect but possibly brought about by direct attack, between two centipedes. There is still a great deal to be learnt about the ecological requirements of the hundred odd species seen in these experiments. With so many species on but a single species of tree, it is likely that many of the differences in ecological requirements are subtle yet important in determining the balance of a community on any one tree.

Simberloff's later experiments (1976*b*) perhaps exemplify this point. The experiments were again carried out on mangrove islands off Florida, but this time the islands were larger, and included other large plant species. The pool of arthropod species was therefore larger, about 500. The experiment consisted of removing parts of the island. Sometimes more of the island was removed the second year, in other cases it was left, and one island was left as a control for the duration of the whole experiment. The results for all eight islands are shown in Fig. 5.12 as a species–area plot. In all cases the reduction of the island area led to a reduction in number of species, and to a number readily related to the new size of the island. The regression of log species against log area in Fig. 5.12 is rather flat, $b = +0.105$, as would be expected for such homogeneous islands. The slope is between that found by Diamond and Mayr for birds on the Solomon Islands (Fig. 3.5) and those for the Channel Islands and the Azores (Fig. 2.4).

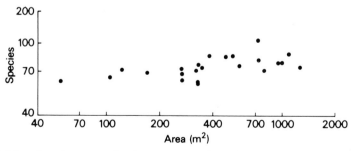

F IG. 5.12. Species–area plot for mangrove islands reduced in size by cutting, including the original surveys. (Data from Simberloff 1976*b*.)

The intention of this experiment was to test a pure area effect. That is to say, removing part of a homogeneous island, so that the only change from the removal was a reduction in the area. In practice this is impossible. The relationship of perimeter to central area changes, and with it a mass of microhabitat factors. As was noted above, the different ecological requirements of the species found are likely to be quite subtle, and so even small environmental factors may be important. Nevertheless, the results may well show the effect of a straight reduction in area. The way in which this is thought to operate is that, by reducing the habitat available to a species below the level on which it can maintain a population, it will become extinct. These experiments are consistent with the idea that a reduction of population size to below a critical level is often important: unfortunately, they are a long way from proving that it is important, or even demonstrating that it is important in any one case. Much more would be needed to be known about the population sizes and population dynamics of individual species. The experiments are also consistent with the view that the number of species reflect the habitat diversity, smaller mangrove islands being somewhat less diverse. The question of how area affects species numbers thus must now be examined again.

How does area affect species number?

The fact that smaller islands have fewer species on them is perhaps the most important quantitative statement that can be made about islands. The subtleties of this statement were discussed in Chapter 3, where it became clear that there was no single relationship that can describe the relation of species to area in all data sets. Further, the variation about the relationship is inconstant. To some extent, the observed species–area curves can be explained as samples from either log-normal distributions or logarithmic distributions, two distributions that do not differ greatly for common species. This only puts the explanation back a step, and as Pielou (1975) in particular notes, explanations for these distributions, for instance in terms of the central limit theory, are at best rather weak. What other explanations can be offered for the species–area curve?

One traditional explanation is that the species–area curve reflects environmental heterogeneity. Some biologists thought that where the species–area curve comes to an asymptote it defines a reasonably homogeneous environment. Many of the claims that the species–area curve does flatten out seem to be based on looking at the direct plot of species against area, and presupposing that the area can be increased indefinitely. As was shown earlier, it is almost always advisable to take the logarithm of the area; and all habitats are of finite size. On such plots, with this limitation in mind, I have yet to see a convincing case that any species–area curve approaches an asymptote.

As well as an upper limit to area, there is also for each species a lower limit. While the upper limit is defined geographically, and is therefore the same for all the species considered, the lower limit will depend on the nature of the species and the nature of the habitat. Turning again to the birds of Eastern Wood at Bookham Common, with an area of 16 ha, there are several species for which this area is too small to maintain a population. These are the species which have territories extending outside the wood, but nevertheless with a breeding pair or two within its confines. Indeed, 16 ha of oak wood is clearly too small a habitat for a permanent population of the majority of the species found there. The remainder can be divided into two groups: those that can maintain a population by remaining part of a larger population in which the wood is embedded, and the small subset of only five species which could maintain a population without exchange across the wood boundary. Bearing all these points in mind, and for convenience of examining published data, it might be suggested that an area of 25 ha, 0.25 km^2, should be the minimal area for studying environmental effects on the species–area curve in breeding land birds. Below that area, the effects of very small population sizes and the edges of the habitat are likely to become all important.

Birds are large and mobile, and equilibrium densities of their populations are low. For most plants and insects the minimal area to be studied would obviously be a very great deal less. For temperate, mesic herbaceous plants, the minimal area might be something between 1 and 0.1 m^2, which differs from the minimal area suggested for birds by about 10^6. It is not surprising, then, that it is difficult to construct ecological theories that relate to plants and birds simultaneously.

The importance of these minimal areas has been stressed in two ways. In a direct, but not very quantitative way, Whitehead and Jones (1969) suggested that the species–area curve for plants on the Kapingamarangi Atoll was markedly affected by the smallest area at which a permanent pocket of fresh water could be established, as we have already seen (p. 67 above). A more quantitative and ingenious method of showing these effects has been developed by Diamond (1975). He has devised incidence curves, which show the sorts of islands, defined by the number of species on them, on which a species may be found. The number of species is closely related to area, so incidence curves may equally well be drawn which relate the probability of a species being found to the area of an island. An example, using British birds on wooded patches of different sizes, is shown in Fig. 5.13.

Many species show incidence curves like that of the wren, with the probability of occurrence increasing monotonically with increasing woodland area. For pseudo-islands, like woodlands, other shapes occur. That for *Passer domesticus*, the sparrow, shows a peak at an area of woodland which is near the minimum for the territory size of a passerine, which merely shows that sparrows are not woodland birds. It is the only species of those shown in Fig. 5.13 that has not been recorded breeding at Eastern Wood, Bookham Common.

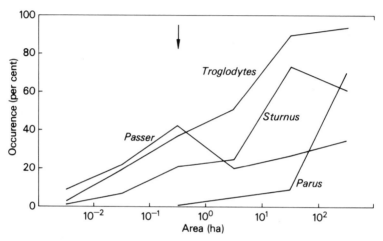

FIG. 5.13.   Examples of incidence curves: birds in British woods of various sizes. Sparrow *Passer domesticus*, wren *Troglodytes troglodytes*, starling *Sturnus vulgaris*, marsh tit *Parus palustris*. The arrow indicates the range of size of a single territory for most British passerines. (Data from Moore and Hooper 1975.)

Species found regularly on islands with a small number of species are referred to by Diamond as tramps. Those species that are only found on islands with very few species and not found on larger islands with more species, that is those with incidence curves which go up and then down again, somewhat like the sparrow in Fig. 5.13, he calls super-tramps. He suggests that such species have to be good at dispersal in order to find their small islands, and so are the earliest species found on islands recovering from volcanic explosions and such like catastrophes.

    Incidence curves as constructed by Diamond for birds on islands give the impression that certain species of birds are only found in species-rich communities. This is by no means necessarily so. They may merely show that certain species can only be found on islands that are big enough to hold a large number of species. The particular habitat requirements of such birds on these large islands may merely be non-maritime and so not found on small islands. So incidence curves, like species–area curves, give no direct information on the relative importance of minimal population size and of environmental heterogeneity on the occurrence of species.

A more direct approach to the importance of environmental heterogeneity is to see how measures of the environment change as the area increases. Remarkably, there seems to be no published attempt to do this directly. For many environmental variables, such as temperature, it is not possible to produce curves corresponding to species–area curves. However, there are other variables, soil types and geological types are examples, which can be used. For the British Isles there is a plethora of information on both of these, and I have made a few preliminary studies of the variation. The situation is remarkably like that in the species–area relationship. The number of types, whether geological or soil, increases monotonically with area. This relationship can be made straight by using the logarithm of the area, and some function of the number of types. The logarithm of the types, the square root of the number of the types, or just the straight number of types give the best apparent straight line in different cases. This variation is interesting in that it mimics the variation found by Dony; these exploratory studies were done in the same way as those reviewed by Dony, namely by starting at one area and nesting larger areas around it.

The results of a rather fuller study are shown in Fig. 5.14, in which a rectangle 16 km by 24 km has been analysed for rectangular sets of 1 km squares within it. The study was of geological types in the Lake District of England, including the geologically famous area of Carrock Fell. The figure shows that the log–log relationship fits these data very well. It shows, too, the considerable variation in slope that would have been found using different individual starting points. The slope of the medians is about 0.35, but the slope from the extreme points varies between 0.2 and 0.45. Should this pattern of environmental variation be found to be common, then at least some of the species–area variation found in plants could be ascribed reasonably directly to the environment in which they are growing, while that of animals might be ascribed either to the environment, or to the plants, or to both.

There have been a few studies in which an attempt has been made to relate statistically the abundance of species to environment heterogeneity. In an important but, unfortunately, unpublished study, Watson (1964) examined the relation between species number, island area, and habitat diversity for birds of the Aegean Islands. His conclusion is that the species–area relationship arises from a correlation between habitat diversity and island size, and he concludes that habitat diversity is more important than area in determining the numbers of birds on an island. Johnson (1975) related the number of birds on coniferous islands in the Great Basin region of the Western United States to habitat variables. His set of islands overlap with those used by Brown (1971) to study non-equilibrium mammal faunas. Birds are not isolated on such islands in the way that mammals are, and Johnson was able to show a satisfactory relationship between bird-species diversity and his measures of environmental heterogeneity.

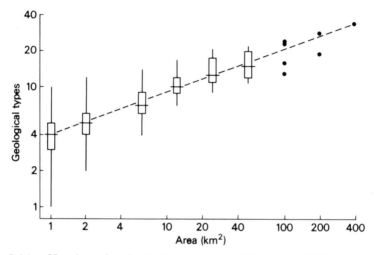

F IG. 5.14.   Number of geological types recorded in areas of different sizes. A box and whisker plot: the ends of the whiskers indicate the extreme observations, the ends of the boxes the quartiles, the centre lines of the boxes the medians. Data from an area 16 by 24 km on sheet 23, Cockermouth, drift edition, of the Geological Survey of Great Britain (England and Wales). The sloping line connects the median for the individual kilometre squares with the point for the total number of geological types recorded in the area.

It seems, then, that area may affect species numbers in two distinct ways, and that both may be important. The first is a direct effect of environmental heterogeneity on species numbers. As the area increases, so does environmental heterogeneity thus allowing more species to occur. At lot of data, including Diamond's incidence curves, are consistent with this view, though it leads to the somewhat uncomfortable conclusion that the regularity in species–area curves is not a reflection of an immediate biological phenomenon, but reflects how environments vary, as measured by their effect on biotic populations.

The other view is that variations in area lead to variations in critical amounts of habitat, leading to the stochastic loss of species. While it is clear from the studies above that there will be such an effect, the importance of it in relation to environmental heterogeneity is not clear. It is, however, a central part of the MacArthur–Wilson theory, and it is now time to re-examine what that theory predicts for species–area relationships.

Theoretical explanations for the species–area effect

One of the few direct predictions from the MacArthur and Wilson's theory is that, because of a distance effect on immigration, the species–area curve for distant islands will be steeper than that for near ones. A major difficulty with this prediction is that many distant islands occur in archipelagos; particularly so in the Pacific, which, as the largest ocean and the best furnished with islands, is a favourite place for study. Schoener (1976) has shown that, on the contrary, within archipelagos species–curves are usually very flat.

Some causes of steepness in species–area plots are the omission of large isolated islands, using the areas of archipelagos rather than of individual islands, the inclusion of islands from different biogeographical regions, and the inclusion of islands with extreme climates. In the Pacific, for instance, the Line Islands are very dry, while the Hawaiian islands derive their avifauna largely from North America (see Chapter 9). In general, Pacific high islands are wet and derive their avifauna from New Guinea. The effect of including a full range of isolated islands in a species–area plot can be seen in Fig. 3.3: the major effect of isolation on individual islands is to lower the intercept.

Schoener explained that flatness of species–area curves within archipelagos by suggesting that for individual islands in an archipelago, other islands in the archipelago are the source of the pool of species for immigration. Between archipelagos the source might be a continental area, but in such cases evolutionary considerations will also become important. He consequently only attempted to model variation within archipelagos. To do this he found it necessary to introduce into the MacArthur–Wilson theory an extra variable, that of average population size.

Both Preston (1962) and MacArthur and Wilson (1963) assumed that equal areas hold approximately equal numbers of individuals. In that case as the number of species goes up, the average population size of each species goes down. This assumption will be met again in Chapter 10. Schoener considered the interdependence of species number, average population size, and area in two extreme models and one that combined them. In his first model each species has limiting factors independent of the other species. This leads to the equation—

$$N = DA,$$

where N is the average number in the species, D is the density of individuals in the average population, and A is the area. This equation contains the additional assumption that the pattern of resources in the area remains the same as the area increases. His second model, an interactive one, is one in which the individuals of the species divide between them some amount of resources that increases directly with area. This leads to—

$$N = D'A/S,$$

where D' is the density of individuals of all species combined and S is number of species. He showed that his first case did not fit his archipelago data, and a good fit could be obtained with the second.

With Schoener's interactive model of species numbers, his slope for log species against log area is not constant, but is convex, curving to an asymptote. Schoener justifies this partly on the grounds that with the ordinary linear log–log function, as the area approaches infinity so does the species number, and he goes on to argue that for an island colonized from a fixed species pool, species number can be no greater than the size of the pool, no matter how large the island's area. This is a somewhat curious argument, in that if the area of the island were larger than the pool source, it is the source that would become the island and the island the source. And in reality no area can go to infinity; we live on a finite planet. Schoener goes on to show that the slope of a log species against log area curve can only vary, on his second model, from 0.5 to 0, and the slope is only dependent on the ratio of the equilibrium number of species on the island to the number of species in the pool. If we let $S/P = R$, then

$$z = (1 - R)/(2 - R),$$

where S is the equilibrium number of species, P is the pool number of species, and z is the slope of the log species–log area curve at S. So islands that draw their species from a large pool will tend to have steeper species–area curves than those that draw them from a small pool; a result in agreement with a difference between the slopes on temperate islands and those on tropical islands that Schoener found.

Schoener's second model shows the power of the interactive form of the equilibrium theory to predict species–area curves. However, to do this it has had to make a number of assumptions about the total biomass on islands and about the way interaction works. More seriously, it allows no variation in environmental heterogeneity, evolution is excluded, and the assumption that immigration and extinction are important and well-defined phenomena appears to be implicit.

Schoener needed to add assumptions about the distribution of population size to produce worthwhile predictions from the Mac-Arthur–Wilson theory. Two other studies may be mentioned to show the difficulty of fitting data with the basic theory. Gilpin and Diamond (1976) tried to predict species–area relationships for birds on the Solomon Islands from known data. Their resulting curves are sigmoid and come to an asymptote, like those of Schoener, which at least show the error in the common assumption that the MacArthur–Wilson theory leads to the Arrhenius relationship, of a linear relation of log species to log area. The other study concerns the peninsular effect (p. 73). Taylor and Regal (1978) tried to fit a colonization and extinction model to the known numbers of species of heteromyid rodents along Baja California. They found that a rather narrow range of parameters would give a satisfactory fit, and they point to alternative possible explanations based on environmental heterogeneity.

Conclusions on observations and on the MacArthur–Wilson theory

All these varied observations have illuminated the strengths and weaknesses of the theory. The major tenet of the theory, that there is a turnover of species producing an equilibrium between immigration and extinction, is clearly correct. This success is, though, a little less satisfactory than it seems at first sight. The turnover, on a time scale measured in generations, consists mostly of casual species, and there seems to be no ecological relationship between the extinction of one and the immigration of another: the equilibrium is a numerical reflection of a variety of ecological processes. From the viewpoint of population dynamics, it seems more sensible to talk about those species which have established populations. The theory does not predict how many will come into this class.

The theory has strength in pointing out the possible importance of stochastic variations in population size, while not predicting explicitly what the distribution of population sizes will be, nor how any particular population will vary. Area, as a variable, only comes into the standard theory through its effect on extinction; there have been suggestions that it should also have an effect on immigration, but the effect of area through variation in environmental heterogeneity is passed over completely. The study of environmental heterogeneity is undoubtedly difficult, but it should not be ignored.

In the basic form of the theory, evolutionary processes are not included. In the next section of the book, some aspects of evolution on islands will be considered, particularly those that bear most closely on the ecology of species on islands. The time scale is now longer, and processes covering anything from tens of generations up to hundreds of thousands of generations will be examined. Even in these periods, extinction is often unimportant. Immigration, genetic change, and interactions between them dominate the scene.

PART 3

Evolution on Islands

6 Microevolution: island subspecies and niche variation

The most important evolutionary event on islands, both from an ecological and from a genetical point of view, is the formation of new species. This section of the book will be concerned with the processes leading to new species and the final section will consider the consequences of speciation in the context of community structure and ecological interactions between species. First, however, it is necessary to deal with the microevolutionary changes, concentrating on those that are seen on islands, so that this type of variation may be subsumed when discussing speciation.

Microevolution involves genetic change, and the first examples in this chapter are of such changes in mice on British islands. Many interesting phenotypes have an unknown genetic basic. The subspecies of wrens on islands in the north-western Atlantic show what can be said in such a case. Dialects of human languages may have no genetic basis at all, but the microevolution of Polynesian dialects demonstrates how the pattern of variation derives from past migrations. The mice and wrens show the earliest stage in adaptive radiation, a small change in ecological niche. The chapter ends with a discussion of niche shifts and of possible changes in niche width found in island populations.

In the early days of genetics, in the period around the First World War, it was commonly thought that species showed little variation other than that produced by mutation. With the development of new techniques, we have now reached a stage in which the genetic variation within species is known to be very large indeed. Much of this variation has been shown up by the techniques of gel electrophoresis, so that to some writers genetical variation has come to mean variation in isozymes (which are proteins), though the inheritance of these variants has not been demonstrated as frequently as is desirable. Nevertheless, many of them are known definitely to be allozymes, that is isozymes determined by alleles at one locus, and with modified techniques the known number of such allozymes has increased dramatically (Throckmorton 1977). The excitement of these discoveries should not obscure the considerable genetic variability in other types of systems. Many species are polymorphic for major genes. Recessive lethals and semi-lethals are common. Polymorphisms involving chromosomes, particularly inversions, are common in some groups, and have frequently been shown to be balanced polymorphisms. There are variations in *B* chromosomes. Various studies have shown linkage disequilibria which, as Carson (1976) points out, emphasize the importance of polygenic variation, and balance in the genome. All this is well known and reviewed in numerous text books. It is, in any case, not specifically related to the island situation. But it is a reminder that a starting point for examining island populations is that all populations appear to contain a considerable amount of genetic variation, and that all populations of all species that have been studied differ from each other to some extent, if only in the proportions of the difference genetic variants present.

Founder principle

Since the earliest days of population genetics, there has been continued dispute about the relative importance of deterministic and stochastic effects in producing the observed variation in gene frequencies from place to place, let alone more major genetic changes. One particular stochastic effect 'founder principle' has been popular, and has been championed particularly by Mayr (1954, 1963) arguing largely from data on birds, and by Carson, whose work will be examined in relation to the Hawaiian Drosophilidae in Chapter 8. The way in which the founder effect is thought to work is this. From an original population, polymorphic at a variety of loci and with an integrated genome, a new population is started by a few founder individuals. By chance, these individuals will be lacking some of the genetic variants in the original population. This will lead to the evolution of a new genetic balance, and so to a genetically-distinct population. This process has been dubbed a genetic revolution (Mayr 1954).

The concept of the founder principle and the genetic revolution is not based on any mathematical theory, but that is not surprising in view of the great difficulties of working with interactions even at two loci. Consequently, its validity depends on the examination of natural populations, where the usual difficulties of distinguishing between stochastic and deterministic effects reappear. If an island population is found with a genome distinctly different from that of a mainland population, the difference can be ascribed either to founder principle or to local selection. That distinction is, perhaps, too starkly drawn. The exponents of founder principle naturally include the local effects of selection in the remodelling of the genome. Nevertheless, it is very difficult in any particular case to be sure whether the remodelling results merely from local selection, or from local selection which started with a different gene pool. The emphasis on the integration of a genome leads advocates of the founder principle to expect continuous continental populations to be more alike than island populations, because the gene flow between the continental populations leads to one particular pattern of genetic integration over all the populations. Before attempting to assess the validity of these views, it is necessary to look at a variety of examples.

Berry's work on mice

One enthusiast for the founder principle is Berry (1977) who studied island populations of two species of mice, *Mus musculus* and *Apodemus sylvaticus*, on islands around the British coast. His work provides a convenient set of examples of the type of evidence involved, and shows the problems in drawing conclusions from such evidence.

The house mouse, *M. musculus*, is in most parts of western Europe a commensal with man. In some places, though, it occurs as feral populations. One such place is the island of Skokholm (Figs. 1.3, 10.1), whose birds were discussed in Chapter 5. Berry gives various anecdotes about the possible origin of the house mouse on Skokholm, from which all that can be said is that its time of introduction is unknown but appears to be around the turn of this century, and that there may have been more than one introduction, each of several mice. The anecdotes add up to the supposition that mice were introduced accidentally in stores taken across to the island by rabbit catchers or farmers or both. There are no other rodents on Skokholm, so competition from voles, or interactions with rats, do not arise.

Two main sets of characters were studied by Berry. These were electrophoretic variants, discussed below, and a major study on what he called 'epigenetic polymorphisms'. These are phenotypic polymorphisms in the skeleton, and particularly the skull, of the mice. Grüneberg had shown that such variants had a multifactorial genetic basis. His group, which included Berry, showed that these variants were common in populations of house mice. From the frequencies of different forms, it is possible to calculate various measures, referred to as distances, of the differences between populations measured over all their characters. The particular measure Berry used was suggested by C. A. B. Smith, and is only one of many possible measures. The mathematics of it, along with two other popular measures of genetic distance, Rogers' and Nei's, are shown in Table 6.1.

Berry's (1964) major conclusion from his study of the epigenetic variants in Skokholm mice was that there had been a marked change in

Table 6.1. Measures of genetic distance

Let there be k loci, with a alles at any one locus (a may be different at different loci) and g alleles (or other distinguishable entities) altogether, i.e. $g = \sum_k a_i$

Let n be the number of entities in a sample: the number of individuals if genotypes are counted, twice the number of individuals if alleles are counted. Let x_i, y_i, be the frequencies of the ith entity (allele or genotype) in two populations X, Y. Then three common measures of the genetic distance of X from Y are:

Nei's measure $\quad -\ln \{[k^{-1}\sum_k (\sum_a x_i y_i)]/[k^{-1}\sum_k (\sum_a x_i^2).k^{-1}\sum_k (\sum_a y_i^2)]^{\frac{1}{2}}\}$

Roger's measure $\quad k^{-1}\sum_k \{\sum_a (x_i - y_i)^2/2\}^{\frac{1}{2}}$

Smith's measure $\quad g^{-1}\sum_g \{\sin^{-1}(2x_i - 1) - \sin^{-1}(2y_i - 1)\}^2 - n_X^{-1} - n_Y^{-1}$

Many other measures have been suggested

From Nei 1972, Rogers 1972, and Smith 1977.

the mice in the period of less than a century that they had been on the island. Expressing Smith's measure of distance as a percentage, Berry found that the genetic distances between nearby populations on the mainland (in the same county) were usually about 5 per cent, while for more distant mainland populations the difference was 10–15 per cent. In contrast, the genetic distances between Skokholm and the populations on the Pembrokeshire mainland were about 30 per cent.

Berry also studied the mice of another small offshore island, the Isle of May in the Firth of Forth (Fig. 6.3). Again he found an appreciable difference, of between about 25 and 30 per cent, between it and the neighbouring populations on the Scottish mainland. The difference between Skokholm and the Isle of May was no less than 63 per cent, and seemed to show that their evolution had been in different directions.

This pattern of change was claimed by Berry as a demonstration of the founder effect. What is clear is that his mainland populations are all much alike, and the two island populations are different both from the mainland populations and from each other.

The major difficulty in ascribing Berry's results to founder principle is this. The founder effect is presumed to rest on a re-balancing of the genome, resulting from the random loss of certain genetic variants. There is no clear evidence that any variants have been lost. All the mainland populations and all the island populations of Berry's data appear to be polymorphic for all characters, though some of the frequencies approach zero. This is an interesting example of the wealth of variation found in natural populations. The importance for the argument here, though, is that a mouse with a particular set of characteristics, say state 1 for character *A*, state 2 for character *B*, state 1 for character *C*, and so on, could, on the basis of its spectrum over the 35 epigenetic characters studied, come from almost any population. This being so, there is in that sense no difference amongst the genotypes available on the mainland and on the islands, and therefore no reason to suppose that a new genetic balance has been struck.

Berry (1964) gives the frequency of skull variants in fifteen populations: five from Pembrokeshire (Wales), one from southern England, six from the east of Scotland (Fife and East Lothian) and three island populations, Skokholm, the Isle of May, and St. Kilda (Fig. 6.3). For all except St. Kilda he gives figures for post-cranial variants too. All these populations are compared in Fig. 6.1 which is explained below. The weights of mice in these populations (Fig. 6.2) will be discussed later. Unlike the other island mice, those on St. Kilda were commensal.

There are two problems when using multiple comparisons of genetic distances, as in Fig. 6.1. The first is the scaling of the distances, the second the consequences of summing many characters into one measure. Smith's distance (Table 6.1) is the average of the squares of the differences between the frequencies of characters in the two populations, that is, it is a square measure, like a variance. (The frequencies

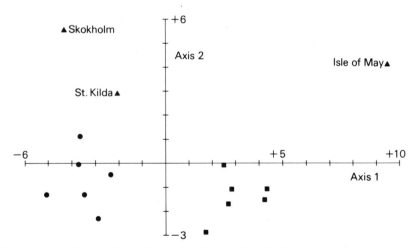

FIG. 6.1. Principal coordinate analysis of skull characters of mouse populations. This is a two-dimensional representation of all the genetic distances using the square root of Smith's measure (see Table 6.1). The scale is in hundredths of a radian per character; the distances are derived from 24 characters. ● Southern English and Welsh populations (five Pembrokeshire, one Hampshire), ■ south-east Scottish populations (five Fife, one East Lothian), ▲ island populations.

are transformed to angular measures, for well-known statistical reasons.) Distances are more naturally thought of as linear measures. If only the rank order of the different distances is wanted, then it matters not whether the measure is square or linear. For multiple comparisons, the scaling can affect the conclusions.

Figure 6.1 is a principal co-ordinate analysis of the frequencies of 24 skull variants in the 15 populations, using the square root of Smith's measure. A true representation of the genetic distance apart of the 15 populations requires 14 dimensions. A principal co-ordinate analysis allows the distances to be shown in fewer dimensions, while retaining as much of the original variance as possible. Figure 6.1 is then, in a statistical sense, the best two-dimensional representation of the genetic distances between the 15 populations. The Welsh and English populations form one cluster and the Scottish populations form another. Skokholm is nearest the Welsh cluster, the Isle of May to the Scottish, exactly as stated by Berry. However, all the island populations have diverged from the mainland ones in the same direction on the second axis, the commensal St. Kilda population rather less than the two feral ones. A reasonable hypothesis is that the second axis records the response of mouse populations to the selective effects of maritime climates.

It is now necessary to disentangle the effects of the individual characters that have been summed to produce the genetic distances. The major differences of Skokholm mice from all other wild mice is in the frequency of the character No. 2, *interfrontal present*. This has a frequency of 50.3 per cent in Skokholm mice, 7.9 per cent on St. Kilda, and less than 2 per cent everywhere else, indeed frequently not being observed in samples. It occurs at about the same frequency as in Skokholm mice in some laboratory inbred strains. The frequency varies between 58 per cent and 90 per cent in different sub-strains of C57BL/Gr mice (Berry and Searle 1963). Similarly, the Isle of May mice differ notably in a few characters. Character 7, *maxillary foramen I absent*, has a rather variable frequency, between 6 and 30 per cent on the mainland, but 40 per cent on the Isle of May. More strikingly, Character 24, *mandibular foramen double*, has a frequency of 10 per cent or below on the mainland, but of 56 per cent on the Isle of May. The frequency on Skokholm is 9.7 per cent. So in these epigenetic characters, the island mice have shown marked changes in frequency, not in presence or absence, of a few characters each. The characters that have changed greatly in proportion in this way have indeed been different on the two islands, which is why Berry finds a large genetic distance between them, and why they are so far apart in Fig. 6.1.

An important change that has happened in the same direction on both islands, and which certainly makes the interpretation of the other changes difficult, is that in both cases the mice appear to have increased in size. Figure 6.2 shows, for twelve populations, the mean weight of male mice, with plus and minus one standard deviation. The standard errors of the means are, of course, much smaller than the standard deviations, and most of the differences between the means are statistically significant. Populations from the main island of Britain form a set, and have a mean weight of 15–18 g. A second set are mice on islands, whose positions are shown in Fig. 6.3, and the mean weight is now between 18 and 22 g, although the St. Kilda mice are apparently much heavier at 26.5 g. However, for reasons given below, the St. Kilda mice may have been a residual population of old males, and so are perhaps unrepresentative. The Isle of May mice are intermediate in weight between mainland mice and mice on the other islands. The final population from cold stores ($-10°$ to $-15°C$) in England has a mean about the same as the island mice, and a similar range of variation.

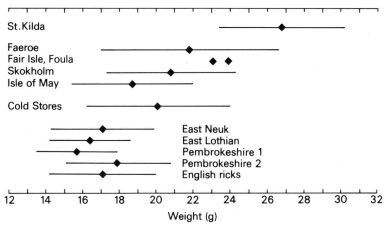

FIG. 6.2 The mean weight of male mice from various populations with one standard deviation shown on each side. Those shown above 'cold stores' are from islands, those below from the British mainland. (Data from Berry 1964; Berry and Tricker 1969.)

Possibly the major selective force changing all these island mice is adaptation to the colder and damper situation found on islands. For the skull characters, are the change in epigenetic variants genuine genetic changes in themselves, or merely pleiotropic changes resulting from a change in weight? Berry quotes data to show that dietetic changes do not greatly change the frequencies of the epigenetic variants in inbred laboratory mice. However, showing that two mice populations with the

same genotype have the same probabilities of epigenetic variants whatever their weight is not at all the same thing as saying that two
populations of different genotypes, one of a heavier weight than the
other, would also have the same frequency, even if the same genes were
present. It is certainly difficult to ascribe such changes to founder
principle or genetic balance. Simple selection changing the proportions
of genes which are polymorphic in both populations seems to be more
than enough.

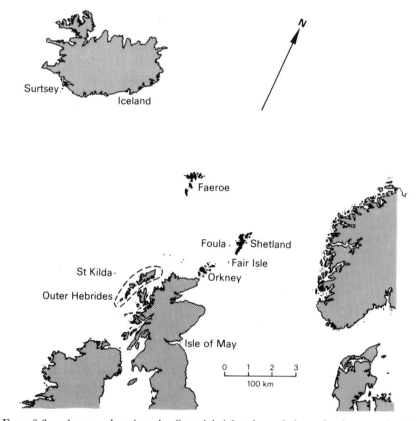

F IG. 6.3.   A map showing the Scottish islands and those further north with
populations of mice or wrens, mentioned in the text.

The house mice on St. Kilda and on the Faeroes have been described
as distinct subspecies. Figure 6.2, which gives the weights of male mice,
suggests that the St. Kilda mice were distinctive. One possible reason
for the increased size and other differences in the mice on these isolated
islands is the phenomenon, to be discussed below, of a niche shift. *Mus*

musculus is usually found in houses, warehouses, corn ricks, and other farm buildings, and so on. It is not normally found away from man's habitations, as it is on Skokholm, the Isle of May, and the Faeroes. Anticipating the discussion of Chapter 10, it would seem that competition with other rodents confines house mice to the region of houses in general. Of these particular islands, there are no other small mammals.

An interesting exception is St. Kilda, where there is a large form of long-tailed field mouse, *Apodemus sylvaticus*. Both the St. Kilda field mouse and the St. Kilda house mouse were well known to naturalists from the end of the nineteenth century, though the origin of both populations is debatable. The village of St. Kilda was evacuated in 1930. In 1931 biologists found a much diminished house mouse population, and only managing to catch (alive) 12 concluded the population was very small. The next expedition in 1939 found only field mice (Fisher 1948). This is the reason for supposing that the measurements on the size of St. Kilda house mice, given in Fig. 6.2, and based on 1931 specimens, are perhaps atypical of their population when there was a permanent village on the island.

To complete the story of genetical changes in Skokholm mice, a brief mention of electrophoretic changes is needed. Berry and Murphy (1970) classified mice at six loci and found 14 of the 15 alleles known in British-mainland populations. Berry (1977) quotes Wheeler and Selander for noting that this implies the number of founders was 'large enough to carry most of the variability present in the parental mainland population'. In this set of systems, the changes on Skokholm are, again, almost entirely changes in proportions rather than in presence or absence. Strong seasonal changes were found in the frequencies of one locus, that for haemoglobin beta, which seems to require strong selection at or associated with this locus. This cyclical variation was also detectable in some of the skeletal variant proportions. The population changes associated with these frequency changes were an approximate tenfold increase from spring to autumn, and a decrease back to the original numbers the following spring. These demographic changes certainly provide plenty of scope for a multitude of selective changes.

Another study was made by Berry's group on *Apodemus sylvaticus* populations in Scotland, Norway, Iceland, and on various Scottish islands. Again, the changes are in the frequency of certain epigenetic traits, and lead Berry to the unexpected suggestion that the Hebridean mice are descended from mice brought in by Vikings. But there are the same problems here as with the interpretation of the happenings on Skokholm. The Viking interpretation requires that mice introduced a thousand years ago have produced a set of phenotypic frequencies maintained today by selection, and that some interaction between these phenotypes prevents their converging on Scottish populations. The alternative interpretation, that these phenotypes tell us more about the similarity of the islands and Norway from the point of view of an *Apodemus*, is also worth consideration (Handford and Pernetta 1974; Berry 1975).

In none of the mice populations are the individuals sufficiently distinct to justify formal taxonomic names. Modern practice is to refer to each by its geographical locality and describe it as a local form of a particular species. The variations in size and skeleton show how the phenotype and phenotypic frequencies change in response to local conditions.

Island wrens

The wren, in fable, is the king of birds. The European species, *Troglodytes troglodytes*, is one of the smallest of European birds, a holarctic species in a family Troglodytidae which is predominantly North American. It is insectivorous, and unlike the majority of very small insectivorous birds such as the firecrest *Regulus ignicapillus*, it is resident; that is to say it does not migrate in the winter. The wren is found in a great variety of habitats, but is most commonly found in Britain and Europe in areas with low cover, like woodland, thickets, and gardens (see Figs. 5.1, 5.13). It is therefore surprising to find that it has colonized and undergone genetic change on some of the Atlantic islands. These islands are almost or completely treeless, very windy, though with a mild oceanic climate, with little frost in winter. As resident insectivorous birds, wrens suffer badly in cold weather. The effect of the winter of 1962–3 on the wren population at Bookham Common has already been noted (p. 94); hard winters also affect island wren populations (Armstrong 1955).

Islands with named forms of the wren off north-west Europe are shown in Fig. 6.3, and some details of these subspecies, most importantly their wing length, are shown in Table 6.2. Wing length is a good measure of size, in that it is little affected by the environment and generally has a small variance in birds. Armstrong (1955) gives some data for the weight of wrens, which are also shown in Table 6.2.

The habit of giving trinomials to island and other isolated populations of birds was normal in the first half of this century. Table 6.2 gives the date of publication of the names for this set of subspecies of wrens. Armstrong (1955) gives a map showing the distribution of numerous other subspecies. In that book and in Table 6.2 the British wren is regarded as being in the same subspecies as the European wren; though the British form, including birds in Ireland and the Inner Hebrides,

Table 6.2. Comparisons of island races of wrens.

Latin name	Place	Date of description	Wing length in mm	Wing length as a percentage	Notes
troglodytes	Britain and Europe		47.5	100	7.5 – 9.3 g
hebridensis	Outer Hebrides	1924	48.1	101.3	10 – 15 g
fridariensis	Fair Isle	1951	49.0	103.2	average 12.21
hirtensis	St. Kilda	1884	50.2	105.7	
zetlandicus	Shetland	1910	50.8	106.9	
borealis	Faeroe	1861	53.0	111.6	13.5 – 20 g
islandicus	Iceland	1907	56.3	118.5	

has been given the name of *T.t. indigenus* by Clancey. The present fashion is to pay less attention to such names, recognizing that much of the variation is continuous, and that any species is bound to show differences between its local races. The table does show, however, the progressively finer distinctions that were recognized.

As far as the British Isles are concerned, the proportional differences in the races are much the same as those found in races of island mice, that is only up to about 5 per cent in linear measurements, which corresponds to around 15 per cent in weight or volume. The two evolutionary questions that arise in relation to the wrens are these. Are the island forms adapted to their local environment; if so, in what way? How large has been the genetic change, and how long has it taken? Regrettably, precise answers are not possible, but it is nevertheless worth seeing what sort of answers can be given. These will throw a dim light on both the variation and ecology of island forms, and on the time span needed to produce them, and hence indirectly on rates of immigration.

The increase in size in island mice, and indeed in rodents generally, has already been noted. In discussing Foster's data (p. 49) I suggested that lowered predation and its consequent effects on competition for food might be a factor in leading rodents to become larger. Island mice resemble mice in cold stores in weight, which suggests that the climate on islands in itself leads to selection for a large form. The same suggestion is the most obvious one to make for wrens. Although there are no mammalian predators on the islands, there are bird predators, and the wren's well-known manoeuvrability near the ground, which of course enables it to catch insects efficiently, is also a protection against bird predators. A larger size, though, would enable the bird to lose heat less rapidly, and make it less liable to be blown away to sea by high winds, and generally to survive the blusterous climate on a North Atlantic island. This is particularly notable in the Iceland race, which is almost twice as heavy as the continental wren. The Iceland wren in fact migrates from the inland part of that large island down to the coast during the winter.

Little is known of the population sizes of wrens. On the island of Hirta, the main island of four in the St. Kilda group, the population in 1957 was at least 117 pairs, and for the archipelago as a whole possibly 230 pairs (Williamson and Boyd 1960). On Fair Isle the population is 40–50 pairs (49 in 1957). Fair Isle is not unlike Skokholm in that it is made of Devonian sandstone, but it is larger, about 525 ha compared with 100 ha, more northerly, more exposed, and with more varied topography; but, there are no breeding wrens at all on Skokholm. Lockley (1947) puts this absence down to a lack of cliff vegetation; the herbage on Skokholm cliffs is grazed very short by rabbits. However, in autumn and winter the wren is resident and common on Skokholm. Possibly the wrens in south-west Wales, presumably genetically almost identical with those of the rest of Europe, require thick vegetation for breeding. Possibly a genetic change is involved in the adaptation to breeding on bare, rocky sea cliffs as at Fair Isle and St. Kilda.

Although nothing is known of the genetics of these island races, something can be said of the rate of evolution. All these island populations can be presumed to be less than 10 000 years old on simple climatic grounds. While mainland wrens are frequently bigamous, the island wrens are monogamous, single brooded, and the normal clutch size is about six. That means that during a single season the wren population can increase four times, from $2n$ to $8n$, being made up of six young and the original two parents. (This is appreciably less than the tenfold seasonal increase of mice on Skokholm.) If the annual mortality of the adults is about 50 per cent, the mortality of the young would have to be between 80 and 90 per cent to give a stationary population, i.e., one neither increasing nor decreasing. This would allow the same selection intensity that can be applied per generation to laboratory-bred mice.

In laboratory mice, the heritability of size (body weight at six weeks old) is about 0.35. Falconer (1960) describes one selection experiment in which there was a 69 per cent increase in six-week weight over 25 generations. This change is of the same order as the change to produce the Iceland race of wren, and much larger than that needed for the other races. On the other hand, in the laboratory population selection was entirely for weight; in natural populations there would be much mortality other than that of selective mortality. This suggests that at the fastest, evolution in the island races would have required 100 years, while they could have been formed without any difficulty within 1000 years. These figures show that there is no problem in accounting in the time span available for the physical changes seen, provided that there was little or no immigration after the first colonization. The morphological evidence, then, suggests that immigration on to these islands from mainland wren populations is negligible in ecological time, in periods of tens to hundreds of generations.

For those unfamiliar either with Atlantic islands, or with wrens, the differences described above may seem fairly trivial. A quotation from Venables and Venables (1955) may be of interest.

The Shetland wren is only slightly larger than the typical form but the darker ground colour and more extensive markings and barrings seem to give the Shetland bird a bulkier appearance in the field. Returning to

Shetland after six years in England we were struck by the slower tempo and the loudness of the Shetland wrens' song compared with that of wrens in Oxfordshire.

They go on to note that wrens are found on almost all islands in Shetland, giving as a limiting case the low island of Greena in Weisdale Voe, with an area of about 5 ha and a maximum height of less than 15 m, and one breeding pair in the years 1945–7 when it was studied.

Polynesian dialects

The next example is from man, and shows the importance of migration patterns. One of the major difficulties in studying phenotypic differences between island forms is to know how much of it is genetic. One form of variation in which the genetic component is likely to be minimal is in the divergence of human languages. Claims have been made that there are inherited pre-dispositions to produce certain sounds, but these have been greeted with scepticism. It is certainly possible that human genetic variation, leading to slight variations in the shape of the voice-making system, may lead to some people being better able to make some sounds than others, and so leading, even with a change of proportion of types, to a drift of sounds. Such a hypothesis seems flimsy, and rendered less plausible by the ability of young children of all races to speak new languages with quite different systems of sounds, accurately. In any case, with speech so very much a derived character, affected by a very large number of genes, involved both in the physics of voice production and in more complex traits of social behaviour, it is likely that heritability of speech would be low.

Overall comparisons of the differences between languages are difficult to make, although the differences themselves have received detailed study. No doubt such comparisons could be made; they have not been. So all that can be shown about the evolution of languages is the pattern of present dialects and something of their history, without quantifying the extent of these dialectical differences.

The Polynesian peoples and language are, more than any other, associated with islands. Other peoples have managed to colonize some oceanic islands: for instance, the Vikings reached Iceland; the Canaries were populated when the Spanish first arrived there; and in the Pacific large numbers of islands have been colonized by Micronesians and Melanesians. The really isolated islands in the Atlantic and Indian Oceans were found to be uninhabited, with no trace of former inhabitants when they were first discovered by Europeans, starting with the Portuguese voyages of the fifteenth century. In contrast, all the inhabitable Pacific islands from Asia out to Hawaii and Easter Island either were inhabited, or, like Pitcairn, had traces of former inhabitants. Inhabitants of these very isolated islands all spoke dialects of one language, Polynesian, and had other common features of phenotype and culture.

There has been much dispute about where the Polynesians come from, but there seems little doubt now, on linguistic and cultural grounds, that they derive from around Fiji in the Western Pacific. This is not to say that they necessarily have only one origin. The occurrence of the sweet potato, *Ipomoea batatas*, and one, but only one, structure of apparently South American type, points to some slight contact with South America (Bellwood 1978). The structure is an ahu (stone temple platform) at Vinapu on Easter Island, dated at *c.* 1500 A D. There is no record of any South American element in the language, and the latest thoughts on its phylogeny are shown in Table 6.3, while Fig. 6.4 is a map showing the inhabited islands, their types, the distribution of the major dialect groups, and a possible set of colonization routes.

Apart from the intrinsic interest of this diagram, some points are relevant to the biology of islands. The first is the occurrence of what are generally called the Polynesian outliers in the far west of the Pacific. These are all small islands, generally atolls and occur near larger higher islands inhabited by Melanesians and Micronesians. There is considerable evidence that these are not areas that were inhabited in the eastward movement of the Polynesian people, but they have been re-occupied by Polynesians from the general area of Samoa. One of the most striking examples is the atoll of West Uvea in the Loyalty Islands, which is known to have been founded by Polynesians from East Uvea, which is just to the west of Samoa. One of these Polynesian outlier islands is the atoll of Kapingamarangi mentioned in Chapters 3 and 5. These outliers show that colonization is not always from the nearest source.

The other interesting point biologically is the origin of the Hawaiians and the Maoris of New Zealand from the central Pacific. The Maoris may have come from the Society Islands via the Cook Islands. The Hawaiians may have come either from the Society Islands or from the Marquesas or both; the evidence is still not entirely clear. It is in fact possible that the original migration into the centre of the Pacific went from Samoa, past the Society and Tuamotus to the Marquesas, and from thence back again as shown in Figure 6.4 (Bellwood 1978). The biological point is that Hawaii was colonized from Polynesia. In Chapter 9, it will be seen that this is an unusual but by no means unknown route for biotic colonizations of Hawaii.

The pattern of Polynesian dialects shows, on a small scale, the type of

Table 6.3. A possible phylogenetic classification of Polynesian dialects

Proto-Polynesian		
	Proto-Tongic	
		Tongan
		Niuean
	Proto-Nuclear Polynesian	
	Proto-Samoic-Outlier	
		East Uvean
		East Futunan
		Samoan
		Pukapukan
		Tokelauan
		Ellicean
		⎰ Nukuoroan
		⎱ Kapingamarangian
		⎧ Takuan
		⎨ Luangiuan
		⎩ Sikaianan
		Rennellese
		Tikopian
		Maean
		⎰ Filan
		⎱ West Futunan
		West Uvean
Proto-Eastern Polynesian		
?..		Easter Islandic
Proto-Central Polynesian		
Proto-Marquesic		
		Hawaiian
		SE Marquesan
		NW Marquesan
		Mangarevan
		Rapan
Proto-Tahitic		
		Australan
		Tahitian
		Rarotongan
		Tuamotuan
		Maori

Dialects bracketed together are particularly similar.
From Bellwood 1978, Green 1966, and Kuschel 1975.

pattern that can be expected in biotic change. The main radiation has taken place in a period of about a thousand years. Each island group has developed its own dialect, but its descent from another group, the small number of generations, and the occasional voyaging between groups of islands, have kept all these dialects as dialects. That is to say, they remain mutually intelligible, even the most isolated one on Easter Island. The process of forming a distinct language, which could be compared to speciation, has not occurred.

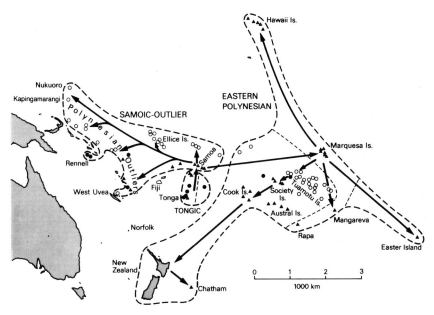

FIG. 6.4.   Possible migration routes of the Polynesian peoples, and the major groups of dialects. The islands shown are inhabited. ▲ High islands, ○ atolls, ● raised atolls. Data from Bellwood 1978 and Douglas 1969. (See also Table 6.3.)

There are, however, other languages and peoples with whom the Polynesians have interacted. This is most noticeable in the Polynesian outliers. These populations are found only on small islands and not on the neighbouring larger ones. The Polynesians are notably skilled at surviving on low islands, atolls, so perhaps it is not surprising that many of the outliers are atolls. Nevertheless there are peoples in the Pacific who are also skilled at living on atolls, particularly the Micronesians. Within the last century, many of the inhabitants of Kapingamarangi were killed by a canoeful of warriors from the Marshall Islands in Micronesia. The Polynesians have a history of fighting, like most human races. Many of the voyages that discovered uninhabited archipelagos appear to have been made by losers in a war setting out in their canoes in the hope of finding a new home.

The pattern of Polynesian dialects shows the importance of the first colonization, possibly from an unexpected source, in determining the type of population found on an island. Similar patterns will be seen in the anoline lizards of the West Indies, in Chapter 9, and the occasional successful colonization, against the odds, has played a major part in the evolution of the Hawaiian Drosophilidae, described in Chapter 8.

Niche shift

A common observation, and particularly amongst ornithologists, is that an island form of a species may have a distinctly different ecology from some other races. That is, the habitat may differ, and with it there may be changes in feeding behaviour, nesting sites, and in relations to other species, such as predators or competitors. All this can be referred to as a shift in the ecological niche. An example has already been seen in the island wrens, which appear to have adapted to life on rocky cliffs, in contrast to life amongst undergrowth that characterizes continental forms. Lack (1942) gives this and a number of other examples from British island birds, which are listed in Table 6.4. These shifts occur on fairly large, inhabited islands like the Outer Hebrides and the Orkneys, but the island races of wren occur both on such islands and on smaller ones.

Table 6.4. *Lack's examples of niche shifts in Orkney birds*

Species		Normal mode	Orkney mode and occurrences
Fulmarus glacialis	Fulmar	Nests on cliffs	North Ronaldsay, Sanday Nests on flat ground* and sand-dunes
Columba palumbus	Woodpigeon	Nests in trees	Orkney Mainland, Rousay Nests in heather (*Calluna*)
Turdus philomelos	Song thrush	Nests in bushes and trees	Westray, Papa Westray Nests in walls and ditches*
Turdus merula	Blackbird	Habitat: woods + bushy places	Most islands Rocky and wet moorland
Anthus spinoletta	Rock pipit	Sea cliffs	Papa Westray Out of sight of sea*
Acanthis cannabina	Linnet	Bushes and scrub	Sanday, Stronsay, Westray Cultivated land without bushes, reedy marshes

The normal mode is also found in Orkney in all cases.
* Also on other northern islands of the British Isles.

From Lack 1942, 1942–3 and Sharrock 1976.

Niche shifts of this sort are also seen on larger islands. Some well-known cases come from the British Isles, and illustrate some of the difficulties in interpreting this phenomenon. For instance, the red squirrel, *Sciurus vulgaris*, a palaearctic species, is found characteristically over most of its range in coniferous forest. Before the Forestry Commission started work at the end of the First World War, such forest was scarce over most of Britain, and the only natural one was a remnant of the Caledonian pine forest in Scotland. Consequently, the red squirrel was usually seen in deciduous woods. It had in fact died out in Ireland, perhaps in the sixteenth century, and was reintroduced in the nineteenth century, again into deciduous woods. Whether the grey squirrel, *Sciurus carolensis*, is in competition with the red squirrel is disputed, an argument which partly depends on what one imagines the phenomenon of competition to be. Perhaps it is safer to use the term introduced by Holt (1977) of 'apparent competition'. At least there is no doubt that in most places where a grey squirrel population has been established for 15 years or so, red squirrels are usually not found, though there are some interesting exceptions (Williamson 1972; see also the maps in Arnold 1978 and Crichton 1974). The British red squirrel is a fairly well marked subspecies, *S.v. leucourus*, but it would be a bold biologist who proposed that the genes responsible for the morphological differences also fitted it for life in deciduous woods rather than in coniferous woods. Indeed, the persistence of the red squirrel in the coniferous forests of East Anglia and Scotland suggests that it is still most suited to that habitat.

Another example of niche shift is found in the pine marten, *Martes martes*. On the continent of Europe there is another related species, the beech marten, *Martes foina*. The pine marten is characteristic of coniferous woods, but also of mixed woods, while the beech marten is found particularly at wood margins and even away from woods. In the Lake District in the British Isles, where there was very drastic deforestation, pine martens have been recorded in rocky areas. For martens, unlike the red squirrel, it is possible to postulate that competition between the two species (or perhaps, better, apparent competition between them), determines to some extent the niche of each. In Britain, where only one species occurs, the niche can be broader, or at least different.

A rather similar example in birds comes from the treecreeper, *Certhia familiaris*. This is the only species of treecreeper in the British Isles, but on the continent of Europe (including the Channel Islands) there is another species, the short-toed treecreeper, *C. brachydactyla*. The two species can be distinguished only with difficulty in the field but tend to occur in different habitats where they are sympatric. *C. familiaris* is particularly a mountain species where the two occur together. World distribution maps for these two species are given by Voous (1960), but the point here is that in the British Isles *C. familiaris* appears to take up the habitat which would typically be that of *C. bracydactyla* in Central Europe.

Possibly the best indication of niche shift related to competition comes from the Irish hare, *Lepus timidus hibernicus*. Competition between hares will be discussed more fully in Chapter 10; here it suffices to say that on the island of Britain, lowlands are occupied by the brown hare, *Lepus capensis*, and its distribution scarcely overlaps with that of the blue hare, *L. timidus scoticus*, in the Highlands of Scotland. In Ireland *L. timidus* occupies all hare habitats. *L. capensis* has been introduced in a few places in Ireland, and seems to have managed to maintain itself without spreading (Corbet and Southern 1977). The palaearctic distributions of *Sciurus*, *Martes*, and *Lepus* are given by Corbet (1978).

These examples raise the question of the definition of competition. The importance of this on islands will be discussed in Chapter 10. Many biologists think of competition as a demand for the same resources, or possibly as well, as a direct interaction between species. Others prefer to use the term competition for any interaction between populations that leads to a reduction of both populations. To overcome this semantic difficulty, Holt (1977) introduces the term 'apparent competition' to cover this second phenomenon, which also encompasses the first. This is a helpful innovation, and makes it easier to discuss the effects of predation and competition simultaneously, because apparent competition includes cases where two species tend to exclude each other by having a common predator.

This brings us to the topic of niche shifts which are induced by changes of predators. Such changes may well be important on islands because populations of predators are, as we saw in Chapter 3, often lower or even absent on islands. A now classic example of such a niche shift is shown by the plant *Hypericum perforatum*, called in Britain Common St. John's wort, and in California Klamath weed. In the British Isles it is found in woodland and grassland, and, although common, is never a pest. It was introduced into North America, where it became a serious weed of grassland. It was brought under control by the introduction of the herbivorous beetle, *Chrysolina quadrigemina*, with the interesting result that the plant in California is now almost entirely confined to the shade of trees (Huffaker and Messenger 1964). The beetle reduces the plant to very low densities in open grassland, but does not enter the shade. The result is a niche shift in the plant population, perhaps better described as a niche narrowing. There is no reason to suppose that this niche narrowing has been accompanied by genetic change, though the possibility appears not to have been examined. The importance of this example is the change of ecology brought about by a predatory species. Other, less striking examples can be found in the literature on biological control.

Given the plasticity and adaptability of natural populations, and the great amount of genetic variation in them, it is to be expected that cases of niche shift, whether based on genetic change or just phenotypic adaptability, will be found quite commonly. The examples given above are a very small selection of those in the literature. For instance, examples relating to island birds in the south-west Pacific are given by Diamond (1970).

The phenomena of niche shifts, and our knowledge of them, may be summarized with reference to Lack's examples shown in Table 6.4. The genetic basis, if any, of the shift is generally unknown. The causes of the shift could be a change in the spectrum of available habitats, or a change in biological interactions, or both. Again, the causes are often unknown. In Table 6.4, the change of habitats in *Anthus spinoletta*, the rock pipit, and *Turdus merula*, the blackbird, could come from the absence of, and so the absence of competition from, the closely related species which frequently occupy such habitats: *Anthus pratensis*, the meadow pipit, and *Turdus torquatus*, the ring ouzel, respectively. The two species of *Anthus* sometimes occupy exclusive contiguous areas, as on Ailsa Craig in the Firth of Clyde (Vevers 1948) again suggesting an interaction between these species. But the two niche shifts in the Orkneys may result from having isolated, and in the case of the black-bird, marginal populations, and not be related to competition at all. Explanations in terms of competition with a closely related species are not available for the other four cases of Table 6.4, nor for island wrens. So both the mechanism and causes of niche shift are usually unknown, and may well be quite different in different cases. The phenomenon is of considerable interest in showing the early stages of evolutionary change, and its genetics deserve more study.

Niche width

Population phenomena need at least two parameters for their full description, namely a mean and a variance. Niche shift is concerned with changes of the mean. It is seldom possible to ask if the variance changes at the same time, partly because if the mean changes sufficiently, whether or not the variance changes depends on the scaling used. It is, however, possible to ask a different question, and that is whether there are cases in which the variance changes while the mean stays still. Cases in which the variance increases are described as niche widening. The case of *Hypericum perforatum* is an example of niche narrowing, in which the variance of the environmental conditions under which the plant is found decreased as a result of the predation by *Chrysolina quadrigemina*. There has been considerable argument about whether niche widening occurs on islands. The important point is not whether it has ever occurred, but whether it occurs with sufficient frequency to be a phenomenon worth taking note of, and so influencing our views on the structure of ecological communities on islands.

Darwin, in *The origin of species* (1859) was the first, and for quite a long time the only, person to point out that commoner species were more variable. Fisher and Ford, working on British moths, and Fisher on the eggs of British birds, showed that Darwin was right. The evidence, which is not of direct relevance to island populations, is reviewed by Soulé (1971). He also presented some results of his own which relate to islands, which are shown here in Fig. 6.6. He studied meristic characters in populations of the lizard, *Uta stansburiana*, on islands in the Gulf of California, Mexico (Fig. 6.5). He used eight characters, six of which were counts of scales on various parts of the body, the other two counts of pores and of plaques. He combined his observations to obtain a generalized variance, G, and Fig. 6.6 shows that G is significantly smaller on small islands, and on his two largest islands matches the same measurement in two mainland areas, one in Baja California, opposite the islands, the other from much farther north in Nevada, USA. Although the relationship is statistically significant, the variance in it is quite high, and two quite small islands, San Ildefonso and San Francisco, have values for G as high as that of the Nevada population. (Both Spaniards and Scots have an unfortunate habit of using the same name repeatedly for different places.)

While the data for lizards suggest that on small islands variation is less, Van Valen (1965) had put forward data, in a paper that led to much of the recent controversy on niche variation, that some island populations of birds varied more in their physical measurements than their mainland counterparts. He studied birds on islands in the Atlantic, and used six species, testing males and females separately. The

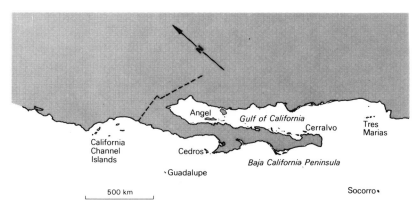

F I G. 6.5.   Islands off California and Mexico, the Baja California peninsula and the Gulf of California. Soulé studied islands from Angel to Cerralvo. The 'California Islands' of the text are those from the California Channel Islands to Guadalupe and the Cedros group.

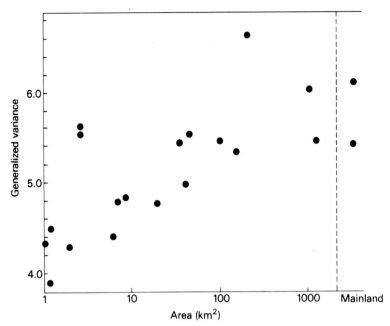

F I G. 6.6. The relationship between the generalized variance of lizards on islands in the Gulf of California and the area of the islands. (Modified from Soulé 1971.)

species were *Mimus gilvus*, the southern mocking bird, from Curaçao, *Parus caeruleus*, the blue tit, and *Phylloscopus collybita*, the chiffchaff, from the Canaries, *Regulus regulus*, the goldcrest, *Motacilla cinerea*, the grey wagtail from the Azores, and *Fringilla coelebs*, the chaffinch, from both the Azores and from the islands of Tenerife and Gran Canaria in the Canaries. From others' observations in the field, he expected all these to be cases of niche widening, compared with mainland populations, except for the chaffinch in the Canaries. A closely related species, *Fringilla teydea*, the blue chaffinch, occurs on Tenerife and Gran Canaria, so Van Valen's expectation was that *F. coelebs* would show niche narrowing there, and that both the niche widening and niche narrowing would be reflected in the variance of measurements of the birds' bills.

While all the changes in variance were in the direction predicted, of the fourteen tests only two were significant at the 1 per cent level (*M. gilvus* males and *P. caeruleus* males) and three at the 5 per cent level (*R. regulus* males, *M. cinerea* females and *F. coelebs* males on the Azores). Further, it is not clear that his populations were homogeneous. In the Azores there are three subspecies of *R. regulus*, and in the Canaries two of *P. collybita* and four of *P. caeruleus*, quite apart from any local variation there might be on any one island (Soulé 1970).

Both Soulé's and Van Valen's tests were statistically significant, and so no doubt demonstrate real phenomena. They could indeed both represent the same phenomenon, namely, niche availability. It might be that the niches available to lizards on small islands are narrow compared with niches on larger islands. Similarly, it might be the niches available to birds on oceanic islands were, because of the smaller number of species, wider than those on the mainland. Soulé, however, contrasts two distinct views. On the first, the niche-width variation hypothesis, the individuals within a population exploit different parts of the habitat resources, and this exploitation is determined by genetic differences that produce the measured phenotypic differences. The second, the gene-flow variation hypothesis, is that populations in different places are exposed to quantitatively different selection intensities. That is to say, the larger islands in the Gulf of California will have greater environmental heterogeneity, and so a greater width of environmental selective pressures.

These two hypotheses are by no means the only ones possible, and both are difficult to test. The niche variation hypothesis requires a demonstration of an appropriate scale in environmental heterogeneity and a demonstration of corresponding selective pressures combined with dispersal of the individuals in sub-populations. Rothstein (1973) attempted to test the niche variation model by arguing, *inter alia*, that niche widths should be roughly proportional to abundance for species within the same community. He was able to show, again using birds, that the more abundant species were more variable, using the coefficient of variation as his measure. But there seems no particular reason why niche width should be proportional to the abundance. Population density is most naturally thought of as a measure of the amount of niche available, rather than of its variability.

There is another school of thought, of which Carson is a distinguished member, which suggests that species with either increasing populations or with high population densities, are less subject to selection than populations decreasing in number or of low population densities. There are numerous variants within this general view. There has also been a lot of discussion about the characteristics of populations at their physiological limit, that is to say marginal populations. This brings us back to the discussion above about the founder effect. Marginal populations are thought by some to be maladapted, because of the perpetual influx of genes from the central population which prevents selection producing a suitable adaptation in the marginal areas. In that case, islands, provided they are sufficiently isolated and immigration is low, might be expected to show better adaptation than populations in otherwise similar habitats on the mainland.

This proposition is again difficult to test because there will always be some differences between the mainland and the island. Indeed, if the islands have a low level of immigrants, they are likely to have a different biotic balance altogether, leading to a different set of biotic pressures.

It seems, then, that not much progress has been made since Darwin wrote in *The origin of species*

> I thought that some interesting results might be obtained in regard to the nature and relations of the species which vary most, . . . At first this seemed a simple task; but Mr. H. C. Watson . . . soon convinced me there were many difficulties, as did subsequently Dr. Hooker, even in stronger terms. I shall reserve for a future work the discussion of these difficulties.

That work was never published.

One problem in this field is that there is no necessarily simple connection between the widths of the niche, however one might like to define that, and the morphological or other variance of the species. Wide niches can be utilized either by morphological variation, possibly involving polymorphism, or alternatively by the production of individuals which are capable of using the niche widely. Roughgarden (1972) distinguished these as two components of a population's niche widths, calling them the 'between phenotype component' and the 'within phenotype component'; this is a useful distinction. Many species undoubtedly exploit a between-phenotype component, an exteme case being the (unfortunately extinct) huia bird, *Heteralocha acutirostris*, from New Zealand. Females had long curved beaks, males shorter, less curved ones, and the two sexes collaborated in extracting insects from vegetation. The male would probe and the female would catch. This example is striking, yet it is not clear that the two sexes can in any sense be said to have different niches. Other similar, but less striking, cases are reviewed by Selander (1966). Roughgarden attempted to apply his theory to *Anolis* lizards, which will be discussed more in Chapter 9. His concept was that different sized lizards would take different sizes of food, but his conclusions about niche widths have been queried by Lister and McMurtrie (1976).

If there is a variation of niche widths, as opposed to the well observed phenomenon on niche shift, on islands it seems neither to be a major phenomenon nor one that is easy to show. For the moment it looks as though this must be a problem that will have to be set aside, until much more is known about the demography of different genotypes in polymorphic populations. If different genotypes could be shown to be subject to different density-dependent selective factors, then an important advance in the understanding of populations would have been made. But that aspect of the problem is as likely to be forwarded by studying mainland populations as by studying those on islands.

7 Speciation on islands and the taxon cycle

In the last chapter the variation of one species in different places was considered. The splitting of one species into two is an important early stage of the processes of speciation. For those groups in which the biological species concept holds, that is, in almost all sexually reproducing organisms, the essential step in speciation is reproductive isolation. When there are two sets of individuals which do not exchange genes between their populations, the sets are two distinct species. There are plenty of problems for this definition of species. For instance, there are groups like the classical ring species of the gulls, *Larus argentatus* and *Larus fuscus*, in which the ends of the chain behave as two sympatric species, although connected by a continuous chain of interbreeding populations. While populations of herring gulls and lesser black-backed gulls do not exchange genes in Europe (though there are very rare hybrids), the populations are, in theory at any rate, in genetic continuity through connecting populations stretching across Siberia and America. Such a taxonomic problem is much more likely to arise in species which have more or less continuous populations of wide geographic range than in species broken up into reasonably distinct populations. Species on islands normally come in the latter class so that a fairly simple concept of species is usually sufficient. A particular difficulty that arises on islands, though, is when a form has diverged to such an extent that it is as different from its nearest congener on the mainland, as are other mainland forms which are clearly separate species. If the island and mainland forms remain allopatric, it is rather seldom that experimental or genetical tests are available, and so it becomes a matter of judgment of whether or not an island form should be referred to as a separate species, or a separate subspecies. This, however, is only an extreme case of the sort of phenomena that were discussed in the last chapter. We shall now be concerned with the phenomena that arise when two sympatric forms are found, that is to say when there are two reproductively isolated populations on one island that are clearly different species.

Speciation can be looked at in two ways. The first is descriptive, and double invasions, archipelago evolution, and the taxon cycle will be described, noting some of the ecological changes that accompany the evolutionary changes. The other is analytical, to consider rates of evolution, the importance of the founder principle, and to make statistical studies of evolution. This approach will be examined after discussing archipelago speciation, but before the complex and not easily quantified taxon cycle. Finally the biological differences between oceanic and continental islands will be considered.

Double invasions

A very common way for two forms to occur on an island is by the process of double invasion. The island is first invaded by a population of the mainland species. Conditions are then such that the genetic structure of the island and the mainland forms diverge. At some later date there is another invasion from the mainland, and now the differences are such that the new invaders behave as separate species; the original island population has become an endemic species. A lack of contact between populations is normal in the evolution of an endemic form.

Amongst examples of such double invasions by birds are the two chaffinches on the Canaries (see p. 151), *Fringilla teydea* and *F. coelebs*, two thornbills in Tasmania, *Acanthiza ewengi* and *A. pusilla* (Keast 1972*a*) and the rock-buntings, *Fringillaria socotrana* and *F. tahapisi* on Socotra (Fig. 1.5). In each case the endemic species has been named first. The phenomenon is less well known in other groups, but an interesting example in butterflies is the two swallowtails, *Papilio hospiton* and *P. machaon*, in Corsica and Sicily. *P. hospiton* is genetically close to, and may have been derived from, the North African *P.m. saharae*, while the island *machaons* are closer to European forms (Clarke and Sheppard 1955). Holloway (1970) gives no fewer than nine further examples in the montane lepidoptera of Borneo. The occurrence of double invasions is reviewed by Mayr (1942).

The ecological relations of the old and new invaders vary. *F. teydea*, the blue chaffinch, is found in forests of the endemic pine, *Pinus canariensis*, on the islands of Tenerife and Gran Canaria; the two populations have been given different subspecific names. *F. coelebs*, the chaffinch, occurs in both deciduous and coniferous woods in Europe. It is not found in pine woods on those two Canary islands, a simple case of ecological separation by habitat. The Canary Island populations of *F. coelebs* have been placed in three subspecies, one on Hierro, one on La Palma, and one on Gomera, Tenerife, and Gran Canaria. There are forests of the pine on Hierro and La Palma, where *F. teydea* is absent and *F. coelebs* behaves as in Europe. The nearest, and only close relative of the pine is *Pinus roxburghii* in the Himalayas, 8000 km away (Critchfield and Little 1966) which is beyond the range of the chaffinch (Voous 1960).

Less distinct habitat-separation is found in the rock-buntings of Socotra. *F. socotrana* is found in thickets and on narrow ledges on rock-faces; *F. tahapisi* is found in the edges of dry gullies, especially where there are rock outcrops near thickets, but not found in thickets. Although the ranges of the two species on Socotra overlap, the two species are scarcely ever seen together (Ripley and Bond 1966). *F. tahapisi* on Socotra is an endemic subspecies of a widespread African species (Hall and Moreau 1970). Both *Fringilla* and *Fringillaria* fit Hooker's observation (p. 31) that the older endemic is rarer.

In other cases of double invasions, the two forms are sympatric, and *Acanthiza* is an example. Grant (1968, 1971) discusses the morphological divergence between 14 pairs of species which appear to have arisen through double invasions, and which occur sympatrically on their islands. Ecological separation through size differences is usually plausible. Mayr (1969) in reviewing the evolution of birds on tropical islands, notes that it is usual for the invasion to go from mainland to island, and rare for it to go the other way round.

Archipelago speciation

Double invasions, involving the repeated colonization of an island from the mainland, are clearly an important part of speciation processes in birds. Another possible mechanism is where birds form new species by invasion from island to island in an archipelago, without invasions from the mainland. Diamond (1977) indicates that this has happened only rarely on archipelagos of the Pacific. Apart from the famous cases on Hawaiian islands and the Galapagos, some features of which will be reviewed in Chapter 9, he finds archipelago speciation only in Fiji, Society Islands, Marquesas, and New Zealand. Requirements for archipelago speciation in birds seem to be considerable isolation, and quite large islands in the archipelago. These two factors can counterbalance each other. There is, for instance, archipelago speciation on Tristan da Cunha (*Neospiza*, Table 2.2) where the islands are very small but isolated, and none at all on the Azores, where the islands are much larger, but where taxonomic divergence has been so low, not going beyond a few endemic subspecies, so that immigration must be thought to be quite common.

With forms that are less vagile than birds, however, archipelago speciation can be expected to be very common. A simple example of the beetles of the Tristan archipelago is shown in Table 7.1.

Table 7.1. Distribution of the sixteen species of Curcuclionid beetles (weevils) known from the Tristan archipelago

Species group	Nightingale	Inaccessible	Tristan	Gough
Pentathrum carmichaeli	*P.c.*	*P.c.*	*P.c.*	*P.c.*
Palaechtus glabratus	*P.g.*	—	—	—
Palaechtodes cossonoides	*P.c.*	*P.c.*	—	—
Inaccodes oblongus	—	*I.o.*	—	—
Gunodes major	*G.m.*	—	—	—
Tristanodes integer	*T. sivertseni*	*T.i.*	—	—
T. attai	*T. minor*	*T. medius*	*T.a.*	—
T. scirpophilus	—	{ *T. reppetonis* { *T. conicus*	*T.s.*	*T.s.*
T. craterophilus	*T. insolidus*	*T. echinatus*	*T.c.*	—
Total species	7	8	4	2

All species are flightless except *Pentathrum carmichaeli*. All are endemic.
From Holdgate 1960*a* and Kuschel 1962.

Rates of speciation

There are two evolutionary phenomena involved in speciation by double invasions and archipelago speciation, generally known as cladogenesis and anagenesis. Anagenesis is the production of a new species through time by progressive genetic change in a population. Cladogenesis is the splitting of one line into two distinct species, and involves anagenesis in at least one of the lines (Fig. 7.1). Advocates of the founder principle would argue that a critical event in cladogenesis is frequently a rather rapid change in genetic constitution, associated with the small size of the founder population, leading to a new genetic balance. If this balance involves a constitution sufficiently different from the original population, then, when they meet again, they will have been found to be sufficiently isolated reproductively to be good species. On this view, the rate of evolutionary change would be bi-modal, either fast while the population is going through its founding revolution, or slow at other times. There will, of course, be many other factors affecting the rate of evolutionary change, and so bimodality might be difficult to show. The set of speciation events large enough to show the bimodality might also be large enough to have too many other effects for the bimodality to be apparent. Opponents of the genetic revolution view would expect there to be a much more continuous spectrum of evolutionary rates.

A related discussion about whether speciation is gradual or sal-tational is going on amongst palaeontologists. In one sense, the discussion goes back to Simpson (1944), who distinguished between horotelic and tachytelic rates of evolution, suggesting that major adaptive changes involve unusually rapid (tachytelic) evolution. The view that many changes are saltational is argued in a balanced way in Raup and Stanley (1976). Contrary views are certainly held, as may be seen, for instance, in Bookstein, Gingerich, and Kluge (1978).

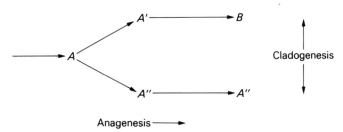

FIG. 7.1. A diagram of two modes of evolution, showing that speciation by splitting (cladogenesis) always involves change in time (anagenesis) in at least one line. *A* ancestral form, *A′* and *A″* genetically different forms, still in species *A*, *B* a new species.

The difficulty with the palaeontological data is partly a matter of the material, partly of definition. As far as the material is concerned, if a gradually changing line can be found through geological time, it would be natural to accept that as a change within one population. On the other hand, if a sudden change is found in the geological record, it can be argued either that that represents a sudden change in one line or the immigration of another line from elsewhere where it has itself been changing gradually. There will inevitably be a rather few geological lineages so complete that the second alternative can be definitely discounted. The second difficulty, the problem of definition, comes in the form: how saltational is saltation? There is no suggestion that there is a lack of genetic continuity. Consequently, the phenotypic changes per generation can not be so great as to break the genetic continuity. No saltational change is likely to be an absolute jump; it will merely be a very fast gradual change. This seems to come back to the view of the proponents of the founder principle, that there will be a bimodality of rates. Critical tests of the hypothesis in that form are again difficult, and have not yet been made.

A difficulty that should perhaps be mentioned, partly because it was buried in Simpson's ideas, is that there is a natural tendency to measure evolutionary rates in taxonomic terms. Mammalian orders, for instance, are defined by the characters of species existing today, at least in the first instance. These orders separated from each other at the beginning of the Tertiary. It should be possible to find some speciation events in the early Tertiary in which the two branches led to different mammalian orders. Such a speciation event might well not be a saltational one. The initial divergence, even though it might involve a group of characters which later came to characterize the orders, could be quite slight. The importance of these characters would develop later on, as each lineage underwent its own evolutionary development. I shall mention the origin of characters distinguishing taxa again in Chapter 8, when discussing the Hawaiian Drosophilidae.

The question of whether or not there is a bimodality in rates would seem to be answered more readily by a detailed genetical analysis of modern species. Usually there is no geological record of the history of the lineages, but the wealth of genetic information over a large set of species whose ecology and distribution can be studied more than compensates for this. By far the best information on this is in the genus *Drosophila*. The particular variation shown in Hawaiian Drosophilidae will be studied in the next chapter. At this point it is only necessary to refer to Throckmorton (1977) who surveys what is known about evolutionary speed and variation in a number of groups within the genus. His conclusion is perfectly clear: in all the groups studied, the information on allozymes points to a gradual process of evolution with a spectrum of rates. Throckmorton was one of the pioneers in the use of gel electrophoresis, and one of his reasons for using this technique was to test the soundness of the ideas associated with the founder principle.

Throckmorton's survey attacks a number of popular views. The first is that there is an extensive reorganization of gene pool during speciation. As he says 'investigators have been nearly unanimous in agreeing that there is no evidence for extensive reorganization'. In general, the amount of genetic difference between the two forms increases with their taxonomic distinctness. Sibling species are more alike genetically than randomly chosen pairs of species in the same genus, subspecies more alike than sibling species, and so on. However, within this general rule there is an inconstancy of evolutionary rates, which tells strongly against a second view, popular in some quarters, that genetic variation can be used as a molecular clock.

The third popular view attacked by Throckmorton is that phylogenies can be derived reliably by the methods of numerical taxonomy, and in particular by phenetic clustering methods, or by methods based on an assumption of maximum parsimony. In *Drosophila*, phylogenetic sequences can be established with certainty from inversions, and we shall see this very clearly in the Hawaiian *Drosophila*. These sequences normally differ appreciably from those derived from phenetic clustering. Clustering methods often use implicitly a principle of parsimony, assuming that the simplest pattern is the true one. It seems that evolution, to an appreciable extent, goes at variable speeds and in random directions; both effects that would lead to complex patterns. Studying land snails in the genus *Partula* from Moorea and Tahiti in the Society Islands and from Saipan, 8000 km away in the Marianas, Johnson, Clarke, and Murray (1977) come to the following conclusion: 'The study provides strong evidence that the conditions for morphological divergence and reproductive isolation are not necessarily the same as those for divergence at the enzyme level'. Reproductive isolation is the critical step in cladogenesis. If it is not related to enzyme variation, then enzymes will give at best weak evidence about phylogenies.

When considering the possible importance of founder effect on island populations of mice, little evidence was found for the predicted loss of genetic variability and for the reforming of a balanced genome. On the other hand, the hypothesis that mainland populations in contact with each other are prevented from diverging by gene flow was left as a possibility. Throckmorton's review of mass of *Drosophila* work leads to much the same point. Speciation appears to be on the whole gradual, but moving at different speeds in different lines. It is still quite possible that the process of isolation, whether on an island or some other place, is an important part in speeding up the process. Acceleration would come both from the selective pressures of a novel environment, and from the lack of migration pressure from other demes of the species.

Statistical studies on speciation

There have been a few studies which have attempted to quantify the process of speciation, by relating it to measurable environmental variables. These studies on the whole show little more than that isolation is important for speciation. For instance, Hamilton and Rubinoff (1967) found the following multiple regression for the number of endemic subspecies of Darwin's finches on the Galapagos—

$$N = -0.04 + 0.003 \, x_a + 0.148 \, x_n,$$

where x_a is the average isolation, that is to say the average distance in kilometres to 15 other islands in the archipelago, while x_n is the distance to the nearest island. x_a are, in general, inevitably larger than x_n, but in fact the second regression coefficient was significant at the 1 per cent level, the first only at the 5 per cent level. Both show the effects of isolation.

A less direct, but possibly more informative, way of looking at speciation statistically was used by Scott (1972). He studied the distribution of butterflies in the Greater and Lesser Antilles [all the

Caribbean Islands from the Florida keys to Trinidad (Fig. 9.2)]. He calculated species–area curves for four sets. The first was the total set of his species, the second for species which were endemic in the Antilles, that is, are not found on the continent. Some are, of course, endemic on one island; many of them are more widespread. The remaining species he referred to as continental species and split into two more sets. The third are restricted continental species, the fourth widespread ones, the restricted ones being those that are found only on a few islands in the Antilles. Of the entire 285 Antillean species (set 1), endemic species (set 2) were 45 per cent, restricted continental (set 3) 40 per cent, and the widespread continental (set 4) 15 per cent. The species–area curves had a slope of 0.255 for the total, but widely different slopes for the other three. The widespread species were almost horizontal, with a slope of only 0.08, the restricted species had what was often thought of as a fairly standard slope for an island group of 0.355, while the endemic species had the very steep slope of 0.520.

A procedural note is necessary. The distribution of butterflies on many of the islands is imperfectly known, so Scott grouped the islands into 13 sets. He found that the best regression of species on area came if the area used in each set was that of the largest island, rather than the total area of the island group, or one of a number of other alternative possible measures. This makes good sense where there is one major island and some satellite islands round it; it is less obviously right when the set includes islands of similar sizes as in St. Vincent, Granada, and Barbados. Nevertheless, with the limited information at his disposal, it is clearly a sensible course, and he has taken steps to make the best possible use of the data.

The very steep slope of the species–area curve for endemic butterflies is a most striking point in the analysis. Scott notes, but does not give the figures for, another interesting relationship. The number of endemic species is strongly affected by the altitude on the island. For instance, Hispaniola has 72 endemic species, against Cuba's 51; Cuba is the larger island, Hispaniola the higher. It would seem that a reasonably large area and considerable environmental heterogeneity on an island are conducive to the process of speciation. The consequences for the evolution of anoline lizards on Puerto Rico will be seen in Chapter 9.

The very flat curve for the widespread continental species is consistent with the very flat curves for members of bird species on oceanic archipelagos. An example is shown in Fig. 2.4, for birds on the Azores.

The Lesser Antilles form an island arc stretching from Puerto Rico down to the South American coast. The fauna of Lesser Antilles is derived partly from South America, partly from Hispaniola, to the west of Puerto Rico. Scott uses a simple and informative index of faunal resemblance. He considered two areas with *n* and *m* species in each, and *j* as the number of species that are found in both. Then Scott's index is *j* as a percentage of whichever is the smaller of *n* and *m*. Applying this to the butterflies of the Lesser Antilles gives the figure shown in Fig. 7.2 where the effect of the double filter on these islands is seen. An even more striking effect of this arc will be seen with the anoline lizards on these islands, in Chapter 9.

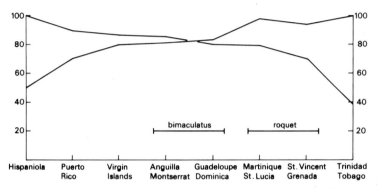

FIG. 7.2. Indices of faunal resemblance for butterflies in the West Indies. From top left, resemblance to the Hispaniola fauna. From top right, resemblance to the South American fauna. The islands of the Lesser Antilles occupied by *Anolis* lizards of the *bimaculatus* and *roquet* groups (Chapter 9) are also shown. (Modified from Scott 1972.)

These statistical studies, then, add up to the conclusion that well-isolated, reasonably large and environmentally heterogeneous islands are those best suited to speciation. In a phrase, geography is all important.

The taxon cycle

When the set of species involved in speciation on islands is enlarged beyond the fairly small sets so far considered in this chapter, another phenomenon sometimes arises. This was named the taxon cycle by Wilson (1961) who previously had introduced all the component concepts (Wilson 1959). In the earlier paper he considered the ecological changes and type of dispersal seen in ants moving from the Oriental region, and particularly its rain forests, to the south-west Pacific islands. The major route of this migration is across the continental islands of Indonesia through to New Guinea, then out across the Bismarck Archipelago, the Solomon Islands and on to the Vanuatu, Fiji, and Samoa. A spur from this route leads from New

Guinea down into north-eastern Australia, which is still a rain forest zone, and from Australia to New Caledonia. The effect of this migration is to make New Guinea and Queensland in Australia bear a strong faunistic resemblance to the Oriental region, a resemblance I earlier noted holds for insects in general (Fig. 1.14). Tropical rain forest ants are, in general, rather poor dispersers. The only dispersal period in their life history is the mating flight.

Wilson describes three characteristic stages (Fig. 7.3) in the dispersal process out on to the oceanic islands. In Stage I, species showed a continuous distribution, and no tendency to break up into local geographical races, that is to say no taxonomic divergence. An example showing different eastern limits of distribution is four species of ponerine ant, all widespread in Indonesia, the Philippines, and New Guinea. *Diacamma rugosum* does not extend beyond New Guinea (limit 1 in Fig. 2.5), *Mypopone castanea* extends to the Solomons (limit 3), *Trachymesopus darwini* is found further out in the Santa Cruz islands and Vanuatu (limit 4, but excluding New Caledonia), while *T. stigma*, again not found in New Caledonia, reaches Fiji and Samoa (limit 6 in Fig. 2.5).

In Stage II, the species have differentiated to species level in Melanesia, forming either superspecies, in which the individual members are allopatric, or species groups where the distributions overlap. Examples are found in *Leptogenys*, another genus of ponerine ant. (*Leptogenys* has many species in the Oriental region and Indonesia that do

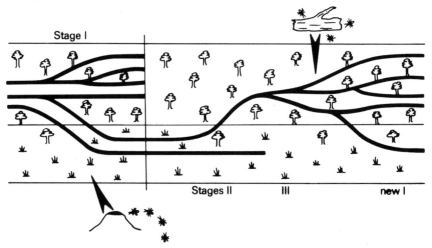

Fig. 7.3. The taxon cycle in Melanesian ants. The upper part of the diagram refers to rain forest, the lower half to marginal habitats. The left-hand part of the diagram refers to the continent of Asia, the right-hand part to the islands of Melanesia. (Modified from Wilson 1969.)

not reach New Guinea.) Amongst Stage II species, *L. breviceps* is confined to New Guinea, *L. fallax* is confined to the Cape York peninsula of Australia, and *L. oresbia* is known only from the island of Malaita in the Solomons. Finally, in Wilson's Stage III, evolution has proceeded so far that the set of species is centred on Melanesia, and no longer has close relatives in Asia.

This progressive geographical pattern of evolution is, in itself, not surprising, but the ecological phenomena associated with it are most interesting. Stage I species are found partly in what Wilson describes as marginal habitats. Marginal in this case is defined as being open lowland forest, grassland, and littoral habitats. All these are marginal compared with the dominant vegetation type, of tropical rain forest. However, the Stage I species are not restricted to these marginal habitats; they are merely proportionally better represented in them, and as a set show a greater ecological amplitude than the Stage II and Stage III species. They also tend to be characteristically trail-making ants, rather than being confined to logs or such-like habitats. This is indicated diagrammatically in Fig. 7.3.

Stage II species have, by and large, returned to the dominant vegetation type, and are found in the interior of the lowland rain forest and in the montane rain forest. The species that occupy this habitat in Asia are not the species that form Stage I. Stage III species show this return too, the individual species being even more restricted in their range of habitats. Occasionally, Stage III species show a new lease of evolutionary life and become secondary Stage I species. This, too, is shown in Fig. 7.3.

The taxon cycle has been demonstrated with other groups by a number of authors. One of the most striking is the work by Greenslade (1968) on the birds of the Solomon group. His general conclusion is shown in Fig. 7.4. He also used three stages, which bear a resemblance to Wilson's but are not identical with them. Stage I are expanding species distributed fully over the archipelago, and showing no geographical divergence. Such species are characteristic of coastal and cultivated habitats. In Stage II there is a fragmentary distribution, leading to subspeciation, rather than to full speciation as in Wilson's Stage II. These species are characteristic of the lowland rain forests. Their fragmentary distribution indicates some extinction. The final stage, III, is a much fragmented contracting stage, in which the species occur in the mountain forest. Rather similar stages were shown in the birds of the West Indies by Ricklefs and Cox (1972, 1978). They use essentially the same three stages as Greenslade, but add a fourth at the end for endemic species.

All these examples seem to indicate that evolution on an island tends

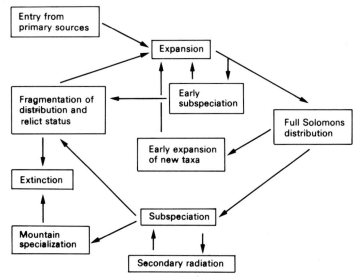

FIG. 7.4.   The taxon cycle in the birds of the Solomon Islands. (After Greenslade 1968.)

to lead to eventual extinction. Sometimes the extinction can be ascribed to invasion by later forms, which have presumably meanwhile evolved rather faster, in an anagenic manner on the mainland. Other cases may be related to over-specialization in small habitats, making the population vulnerable to environmental changes.

Only a few cases of the taxon cycle have been described, but no studies have been published showing it to be inapplicable. How general a phenomenon the cycle is remains to be determined.

What is an oceanic island?

Wallace's concept of an oceanic island, described in Chapter 2, was an island well out into the ocean, lacking certain groups of species. Essentially it is one to which dispersion is difficult, as measured over the whole set of species on the continent. However, some groups, such as birds and ferns, are good dispersers; others such as conifers and mammals are bad ones.

In the discussion of biogeographic regions, it was noted that the tendency of some biologists to talk merely in terms of regions was a rather limited way of examining distributions. It is useful also to talk about the biota of a region, and to discuss the spectrum of relationships with other regions. In the same way it is too simple just to talk of oceanic and continental islands. It is useful also to talk of the biota on an island, and distinguish between those groups for which the island is continental, readily reached by dispersal, and those for which the island is oceanic leading to little dispersal. The distinction between high dispersal rates and low dispersal rates may be measured in terms of evolutionary rates.

This leads to a possibly novel way of looking at island biota. On oceanic islands, evolution is faster than immigration. On continental islands immigration is faster than evolution. For instance the Azores, which were considered on p. 52, are clearly oceanic for forms like beetles which have undergone much speciation there. They are much more nearly continental for the birds, as there are no endemic species of birds, and few endemic subspecies. They are also continental for the ferns, for again all the species occur on the continent of Europe. Nevertheless, the bird list is remarkably short (Fig. 2.4). So both on the grounds of lack of species, and on the grounds of some slight evolutionary change, even for birds the Azores are reasonably regarded as oceanic islands, which is as it should be. For islands closer to the continent, the dissection of the biota into those for which the island is oceanic and those for which it is continental may be helpful, but this approach has not yet been applied systematically.

8 Hawaiian Drosophilidae

The present fauna

Of all the groups of organisms, plants or animals, that can be studied on islands, the Hawaiian Drosophilidae are supreme. This is why. There are a great many species; their ecology is very varied; and, most important, a genetic analysis is possible. In other groups of organisms, it is possible to study allozyme frequencies, metaphase chromosomes and so on. So far though, only in the Drosophilidae can we study the evolution on an archipelago of a group with polytene chromosomes. These giant chromosomes, found in the salivary glands and other parts of the fly larvae, show complex sequences of bands down their length whose patterns differ in different species. This variation in banding produces detailed and sound evidence of phylogenetic history. In the Hawaiian Drosophilidae, this allows us to postulate at which points in evolutionary history the stock has immigrated to a different island and at what point it has evolved on one island. The extent to which our knowledge of the Hawaiian Drosophilidae allows us to be definite about these points will be discussed towards the end of this chapter. Other points about the evolution of this group will be dealt with first.

The Hawaiian islands can claim to be the most isolated archipelago in the world (Figs. 1.7, 1.9). The Marquesas are further from any continent, but less isolated because they come at the end of a set of Pacific archipelagos (Fig. 6.4). Other isolated islands are much smaller than the Hawaiian chain. The chain can be divided into the Leeward islands, which are all small islands, spanning from Kure to Nihoa (Fig. 1.7), described by Carlquist (1970), and the main islands or Windward chain from Kauai to Hawaii (Fig. 8.3). In this and the next chapter we shall be concerned almost entirely with species found on the main islands. Some further aspects of the geography and ecosystems on the main islands will be considered as we go along, and particularly the background necessary to an understanding of the phylogeny of the Drosophilidae (p. 182).

That there are very unusual flies in the family Drosophilidae on the Hawaiian islands has been known since the 1890s. Perkins (quoted by Hardy 1974) reported in 1913 that there must be at least 250 species in the family on the islands, and possibly twice that number. After the

Second World War, Zimmerman (1948), in launching the massive *Insects of Hawaii*, drew attention to the importance of drosophilids, and later (Zimmerman 1958) threw out a challenge to geneticists and evolutionists with the suggestion that there were 300 species of *Drosophila* on Hawaii. Intensive work on the morphology and taxonomy of the groups started with the arrival of D. Elmo Hardy in 1948. Eventually, he interested W. S. Stone of the University of Texas, and a co-operative research project resulted between the University of Hawaii and the University of Texas. Their project began in 1963; Hardy's work on the taxonomy of Hawaiian Drosophilidae, Volume 12 of the *Insects of Hawaii*, was published in 1965. This history, and other background points, are to be found in Hardy (1974).

So the variation of morphology was fully described for the first time about 15 years ago, while detailed work on the genetics, behaviour, and ecology is more recent. While the main outlines of evolution in the group are now clearly established, many fascinating details are undoubtedly still to come, and this chapter can be no more than a report on our present state of knowledge. Detailed reviews of various aspects will be found in Carson, Hardy, Spieth, and Stone (1970), Carson and Kaneshiro (1976), and the other papers accompanying Hardy (1974). White (1978) discussed the evolution of the group in relation to speciation patterns in general.

The Hawaiian islands have a tragic history of loss of endemic species, particularly amongst their birds, which will be considered in the next chapter. These extinctions have resulted from the great spread of agriculture and the growth of the human population on the islands. As on other oceanic islands, the Hawaiian fauna and flora have suffered from the introduction of foreign species. The insect fauna in particular has been harmed by the introduction of an ant, *Pheidole megacephala*, which occurs in the lowlands. There are no native ants. Native *Drosophila* are scarcely ever found below an elevation of 200 m, but the role of this exotic ant in limiting the distributions or the very existence of certain species of native Drosophilidae is uncertain because no collections of these flies were made before the ant arrived in the islands about a century ago. Further, the destruction of most of the endemic lowland vegetation can only have meant the destruction of many drosophilid species.

The number of species

Drosophila is a familiar organism to all biologists. Much less well-known is the genus *Scaptomyza*, a taxon very close to *Drosophila*, and which has indeed sometimes been included as a subgenus in *Drosophila*. In both genera there are many species still to be discovered, both in Hawaii and in the rest of the world. *Scaptomyza* has been distinctly less studied than *Drosophila*. It looks as though there may well be 1500 *Drosophila* species worldwide, of which probably no fewer than 500 are Hawaiian endemics. That is to say, one *Drosophila* species in three may well be Hawaiian. For *Scaptomyza*, the figures are much less certain, but nevertheless even more startling. There may possibly be 400 species worldwide, 300 of them in Hawaii. If these figures turn out to be correct, then over 40 per cent of the species in these two genera combined are endemic on this one group of oceanic islands. Allowing for the island species that must have been lost, the importance of Hawaii for the study of *Drosophila* is clear.

The importance of *Drosophila* for the study of insect faunas on Hawaii itself is less easy to give in quantitative terms. The number of species alone indicates their importance, and there are numerous remarks in the literature on the commonness of drosophilids in the native ecosystems. The vegetation is species poor, but with many interesting endemic forms (Carlquist 1970). Many Hawaiian Drosophilidae are so unlike *Drosophila* from other parts of the world that they were for many years placed in distinct genera in that family. It is now clear that all the Hawaiian flies are in two closely related groups called drosophiloids and scaptomyzoids (Carson and Kaneshiro 1976). The term scaptomyzoid, meaning *Scaptomyza*-like, includes two genera on Hawaii, *Scaptomyza*, with several subgenera, and the endemic *Titanochaeta*, discussed below (p. 180). All Hawaiian drosophiloids (i.e. *Drosophila*-like) are now regarded as *Drosophila* (see below, p. 181). Scaptomyzoids and drosophiloids are the only Hawaiian native Drosophilidae; collectively they will be referred to as drosophilids.

In the British fauna, for comparison, there are nine other genera in the family Drosophilidae. An attempt to indicate the relative importance of *Drosophila* in different faunas is shown in Table 8.1. The British lists can be regarded as reasonably complete. Figures for North America and for Hawaii must be much more doubtful, because of the relatively small amount of taxonomic work in relation to the richness of the faunas. In Britain and North America, *Drosophila* comprise less than one per cent of the diptera; in Hawaii, *Drosophila* (with *Scaptomyza*) are perhaps 12 per cent of all insect species.

To date, 359 species of endemic Hawaiian *Drosophila* have been described, with an estimate that there are well over 100 more to come; indeed the estimate of 500 in total may be conservative even for the extant species. In *Scaptomyza*, where much less work has been done, 132 species have been named, but this is probably of the order of half the total species, and there may well be 300 in all. These two figures lead to a suggestion that there are 800 Hawaiian drosophilids. The more

Table 8.1. The numerical position of *Drosophila* in three faunas.

	British Isles (Species recorded)	North America (Species recorded)	Hawaiian archipelago (Estimates of native species)
Drosophila	32	108	500
Scaptomyza	5	19	300
Total *Drosophila* s. lat.	37	127	800
Other Drosophilidae	14	52	0
Total Drosophilidae	51	179	800
Other cyclorrhapha	2836	6523	
Total cyclorrhapha	2887	6702	
Other diptera	3063	9428	
Total diptera	5950	16 130	
Other insects	15 883		5700
Total insects	21 833		6500

Data from Kloet and Hincks 1964–78, Stone, Sabrosky, Wirth, Foote, and Coulson 1965, and Zimmerman 1972.

cautious might prefer to say 750–800, but estimates of these numbers have consistently been revised upwards, and so it seems sensible to take the higher figure for the moment.

Appearance

Drosophila in other parts of the world are well known as small or very small flies, with bright red eyes, and rather little sex dimorphism. *Drosophila melanogaster* is about 2–3 mm long, with each wing also about that length. This is a fairly typical size, though some of the species are larger, 3–4 mm long. Male *D. melanogaster* and *D. pseudoobscura* have sex combs on their legs, but many other species lack even this slight amount of dimorphism.

The Hawaiian Drosophilidae are quite different as a set, although plenty are similar in appearance to those in other parts of the world. Many of the species are strongly dimorphic, with females not much modified, but with males with extraordinary structures on the head or legs. In the picture-wing group of over 100 species there are maculations on the wings, making the flies look like the rather distantly related family Tephritidae (also known as Trypetidae). Tephritids are known colloquially as large fruit flies or gall flies, in contrast to the Drosophilidae which are known as small fruit flies. Illustrations of a picture wing, and of some of the heads and legs, are shown in Fig. 8.1. Picture-wing *Drosophila* are typically rather large, with a body length of about 5 mm. Some of them are enormous for *Drosophila*, 7 or 8 mm long, so that the largest species, *D. cyrtoloma* in the *planitibia* group and found on the island of Maui, has a wing span of almost 20 mm. At the other end of

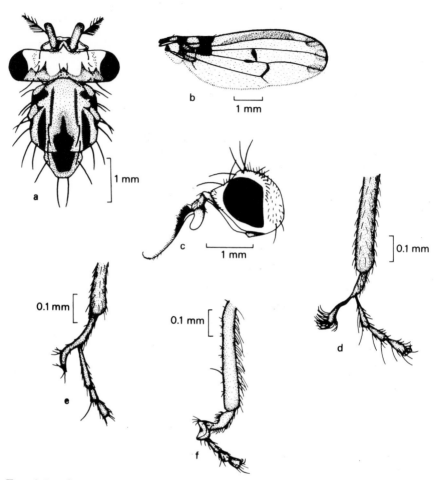

FIG. 8.1.   Some morphological variants found in the Hawaiian *Drosophila*. a, b. *D. heteroneura* (Hawaii) head and thorax, wing. The wing is a 'picture-wing', the upper of the two vertical cross-veins is the vein that characterizes 'Idiomyia'. c. *D. longiseta* (Molokai) showing the 'antopocerus' antenna. d, e. *D. capitata* (Kauai) and *D. ancyla* (Maui) front tarsi, showing the 'forked tarsus' condition. f. *D. contorta* (Maui) front tarsus, a 'spoon tarsus'. After Hardy 1965.

the scale, Hawaiian scaptomyzoids are mostly between 1.5 and 2 mm in body length.

   Several groups in the endemic flies are named by their characteristic modifications. As well as picture-wings there are groups called modified mouth parts, ciliated tarsi, bristle tarsi, fork tarsi, spoon tarsi, and white-tipped scutellum. Other groups, which were once given generic names, may still be referred to by those names even though the genus has been synonymized with *Drosophila* (Carson and Kaneshiro 1976). An example is antopocerus, in which the male antenna has a remarkable structure (Fig. 8.1). The first segment is very large, almost equal in length to the third segment, which is much the largest in most *Drosophila*. The arista (the bristle that sticks forward from the third segment) is in antopocerus densely covered with short hairs on the dorsal surface and almost bare on the ventral. It seems that all these modifications of the males are related to courtship behaviour, which will be considered more fully below, as will the taxonomic divisions in *Drosophila* and *Scaptomyza*.

Food

In most parts of the world, *Drosophila* larvae feed primarily on yeast. This indeed is why they are known as fruit flies, as the eggs are laid in decaying fruit, in which yeasts are present. Some species have consequently become commensal with man, attending the manufacture of beer, cider, vinegar, or pickles. Wild species are found round rotting fruit, and also at sap flows from tree wounds (which produce slime fluxes). Most species can be attracted by fermenting bananas.

Scaptomyza is different. In this genus the larvae are normally leaf miners, and all, it seems, develop in vegetable matter.

Hawaiian *Drosophila* cannot be maintained in the ordinary *Drosophila* medium. Though some will feed on yeast as part of their diet, the normal requirement, in the sense of that found in most species, is for bacteria. The discovery of how to raise Hawaiian Drosophilidae, particularly the picture-wing group, was a major success of the 1960s; the story of this is told by Hardy (1974). So far, about 140 species have been raised in the laboratory, but there are still many which have been brought in, but for which the right conditions have not been found.

An important discovery was that larvae of many species are to be found in the rotting leaves and rotting bark of endemic plants. Two important genera are *Clermontia* in the Lobeliaceae (occasionally regarded as part of the Campanulaceae) and *Cheirodendron* in the Araliaceae. Though these are the two most important genera, larvae have also been found in rotting leaves, bark and stems of many other plants of over 40 genera including some ferns. Heed (1971) estimated that 70 per cent of the Hawaiian drosophilids are specialized in their larval food habits, occurring only in one part of species in one genus. For instance, all nine species of antopocerus come from rotting leaves of *Cheirodendron*. The larvae of several species, not necessarily closely related, may be found close together. Heed found 9 species in 17 specimens from a small sample of *Ilex* (Aquifoliaceae) from Hawaii.

Varying degrees of generalization are also found. *D. adiastola* has larvae in the leaves, bark, roots and fruits of *Clermontia*; *D. imparisetae* in the fruits of *Sapindus*, *Myrsine*, and *Pittosporum* (all nominate genera of their families); while *D. crucigera* has been taken from 21 different plant families (Montgomery 1975). Most of the generalists are in the groups with many species, the picture-wings, the modified-mouthparts group and in the largest subgenus of *Scaptomyza*, *Trogloscaptomyza* (Heed 1971).

Other specializations are also found. Some species, including apparently all 50 odd in the white-tipped scutellum group, grow in fleshy fungi. A few grow in slime fluxes, a well-known habitat for continental *Drosophila*. *Scaptomyza* (*Exalloscaptomyza*) develop in the flowers of Morning Glory (*Ipomoea*, Convolvulaceae). *Titanochaeta*, the other genus of scaptomyzoids, has larvae which are parasitic on crab spiders (Araneae, Thomisidae).

On the basis of the distribution of food preferences, Montgomery (1975) suggested that the first Hawaiian drosophilids lived in rotting plants of the family Araliaceae. For instance, on the island of Kauai, the oldest of the large Hawaiian islands, there are four species, all of which seem to be primitive amongst the Hawaiian endemics, namely *D. primaeva*, *D. attigua*, *D. anomalipes*, and *D. quasianomalipes*. On the few occasions on which larvae of these have been found, they have been in rotting bark of araliaceans. However, a standard bait that attracts many species of picture-wings is made from bananas and inoculated with yeast derived from the lobeliad *Clermontia*. This bait also attracts *anomalipes* and *quasianomalipes*. So it looks as though the Hawaiian Drosophilidae may have evolved through forms that grew on the rotting parts of plants where both bacteria and yeast were found. These plants might have been either lobeliads or perhaps somewhat more probably araliaceans.

(The family Araliaceae is a largely tropical one, quite closely related to the Umbelliferae. In Europe the only species is ivy, *Hedera helix*. In North America there are a few species, including wild sarsaparilla in *Aralia* and the Devil's Club, *Echinopanax horridum*.)

Behaviour

Drosophila melanogaster may be taken as an example showing a fairly typical simple courtship pattern in this genus. The sexes meet at food sites, where the females devote most of their time to feeding and ovipositing. The males spend a short time feeding and then persistently approach to court the females. The courtship pattern has various elements, leg vibration, wing vibration, circling the female, and licking the ovipositor. Whether successful or not, the courtship is over quite soon. Receptive females mate readily; unreceptive ones brush off the male which will then normally pursue another female. Feeding, courtship, and oviposition all take place at the same site, and that is normal in *Drosophila* irrespective of how simple or complex the courtship is. The same pattern is found in *Scaptomyza*, including the Hawaiian species. It is also found in the white-tipped scutellum group of Hawaiian *Drosophila* and in the endemic subgenus *D. (Engiscaptomyza)* (Spieth 1966).

In contrast, many Hawaiian *Drosophila* do not court at the food sites. Instead both sexes are quiet and tolerant of each other, and arrive and leave the food site discreetly, by short, quick flights or slow walking. In the vegetation near the food site, sexually-mature males each select and defend an individual small territory. It may be the surface of a leaf, or an area a few inches in diameter on the trunk of a tree. Normally the males select positions from which they may intercept females as they leave the food site. Interception is by advertisement; there are three forms this may take. The male may wave both wings and walk about, giving a visual signal. He may sit immobile with the tip of the abdomen elevated and pulsating an anal droplet, or he may walk about and drag the tip of his abdomen over the substrate depositing a thin film of liquid. These last two produce olfactory stimuli. If the female is attracted by the advertisement, then the detailed courtship is more complex than that of mainland *Drosophila*. The specially-developed parts of the body of the male are displayed in front of the female. Spieth (1968) gives pictures of three species, showing each male displaying on his own patch.

Spieth calls such behaviour lek behaviour, but this seems not quite accurate. The term lek originally referred to the behaviour of a game bird, the black grouse, *Lyrurus tetrix*. In this bird, both sexes assemble at special display grounds and the females choose from amongst all the males present. The term lek was apparently derived from a Scandinavian word for a game or activity where a group play together. This communal, lek behaviour is found in several species of birds (Lack 1968a, Wilson 1975). The contrasting behaviour in birds is the much more usual type in which the species is monogomous, the male establishes its territory and attracts the female to it; nesting and the feeding and raising of the young occur in the territory, or mostly so. The behaviour of some Hawaiian drosophiloids is clearly intermediate between these two types, and seems to lack an appropriate name. As most papers on the behaviour of Hawaiian drosophiloids refer to leks, it is perhaps simplest just to call the displays lek-like. It is not clear if any Hawaiian drosophiloids have a true lek, with a communal display ground, though such a lek has been reported for the Australian *D. polypori* (Parsons 1977).

There are other features of reproduction in Hawaiian drosophiloids in which they stand in contrast to mainland *Drosophila*, in addition to having lek-like behaviour. In most flies, individuals are fully alert during copulation. In Hawaiian drosophiloids, however, the pair becomes immobile, and another individual can walk on them without eliciting a response. At the end of the copulation the pair just falls apart; indeed in some species the male may stay in a cataleptic posture for a minute or two.

Another feature of reproduction in the Hawaiian drosophiloids associated with lek-like behaviour, is a fairly high level of agonistic behaviour. In mainland *Drosophila*, males and females may fend each other away, especially with their middle legs, and may show other ritualized movements. In the Hawaiian species there may be a fierce ritualized behaviour which Spieth (1974) has called slashing. The wings are scissored outward horizontally with increasing amplitude. When this action reaches 90° or rather more from the median line the fly thrusts and slashes with its fore legs held stiffly. This is usually done at such a distance that there is no contact. In the large planitibias of the picture-wing group the male flies may physically wrestle with each other, thrusting at each other with their legs and heads, with their bodies upright.

All these modifications of courtship behaviour fit in with the other behaviour of the Hawaiian species. Commensal *Drosophila* are readily recognizable, having a slow, ponderous, hovering sort of flight, the abdomen hanging downward, and so despite their small size, readily coming to one's attention. In contrast the general behaviour of the Hawaiian drosophiloid species can be described as secretive, wary, and cryptic. They never hover over food sites. They choose substrates to rest upon with which their colour pattern blends. If approached slowly they remain immobile. When disturbed, they make a rapid darting flight downward towards the substrate (Spieth 1974). The Hawaiian scaptomyzoids (and a few drosophiloids) behave more like typical mainland flies. For instance the litter-dwelling *D. mimica* flies upwards when disturbed, other drosophiloids fly downwards. *D. anomalipes* stays around the food site (Carson *et al.* 1970); other drosophiloids in general pay only fleeting visits to the food sites.

Enemies

Many species on oceanic islands either have fewer predators than their congeners on the mainland, or none at all. For instance, the birds on Tristan da Cunha have neither bird, mammal, nor reptile native predators, and the flora of Tristan da Cunha has no native vertebrate grazers or browsers. This lack of predators has to be considered when

discussing island communities: some of its consequences will be considered more fully in Chapter 10. However, this immunity does not apply
to insects, which frequently have at least as many predators, even
though of a different sort, on islands as on continents. This is certainly
true of the Hawaiian Drosophilidae.

The birds of the Hawaiian islands will be considered in detail in the
next chapter. Here it is sufficient to point out that the endemic family of
honeycreepers, the Drepanididae, are nectar and insect feeders. Like
the *Drosophila*, they are ecologically intertwined with the lobeliads,
including *Clermontia*. The birds feed upon the nectar, and are the prime
pollinators; the insect-feeding species will no doubt find many larval
and adult *Drosophila*. There is also an endemic flycatcher, *Chasiempis
sandwichensis*, which catches insects both on the wing and by picking
them from the bark and leaves.

There are also important insect predators of the *Drosophila* (Montgomery 1975). An important set are the hundred or so endemic species
of *Lispocephala*, which is a muscid dipteran. The genus is not endemic.
The larvae of *Lispocephala* attack drosophilid larvae; the adults prey on
the *Drosophila* adults. However, neither these flies nor, it seems, the
Hawaiian birds, attack at all readily the larger picture-wing species.
However, it would be rash to be dogmatic with the present rarity of
many of the honey-creepers, and without detailed studies of the mus-
cids. Some of the *Lispocephala* are very large, 10 mm or more in length.
Montgomery (1975) records one feeding on the picture-wing *D. seto-
simentum*, and of another attaching a tipulid, presumably even larger,
but perhaps less able to put off its attacker by buzzing as a picture-wing
can.

Another prominent family of dipteran predators are the Dolichopo-
didae. Two hundred and eight species have been described from the
archipelago, and again they are notably predacious both as larvae and
adults. They are, though, much smaller than *Lispocephala*, ranging only
up to a maximum of 4 mm in the adult. So only the smaller species,
particularly *Scaptomyza*, might be attacked and it seems likely that even
they are not often taken.

Other insect predators of drosophilids are known. There are, for
instance, predatory hymenoptera, such as eucoiline wasps, and various
hymenopterous parasites. Montgomery records a bizarre mantis-like
geometrid moth caterpillar, *Eupithecia*, which has been raised on
picture-wing *Drosophila* in the laboratory.

So Hawaiian drosophilids of all sizes are not short of predators.
Spieth [(1974) and in Carson *et al.* (1970)], has argued that these
predators, and in particular *Lispocephala*, are responsible for the evolution of the behaviour of the picture-wing group. The argument seems

insufficient by itself. Predators of this sort occur on the continents, but there the *Drosophila* have not evolved in this manner. On the other hand, the existence of a vacant set of niches, combined with the presence of the predator, could plausibly be regarded as important circumstances determining the course of evolution.

Continental *Drosophila* lay many eggs a day. For these species, the evolutionary strategy seems to be to get as many larvae as possible into the food supply, which perhaps has the effect of keeping that supply from other competing species. Certainly the slow, hovering flight of the adults could lead one to suppose that predation pressure is not important, with the possible corollary that larval competition is. Amongst the Hawaiian Drosophilidae there is wide variation in the rate of egg production. Some, like *D. sejuncta*, lay large numbers of eggs in clusters; others like *D. mimica* produce many eggs but lay them singly; still others rather few eggs, one per female per day. An example is *Engiscaptomyza*, whose taxonomic position is considered below. A critical part of its life history may be finding a suitable site to lay the egg, leading to low fecundity and high survival. Such a life history is clearly more vulnerable to predator pressure. So a third element in the evolution of elaborate courtship may be a shift of larval food from yeasts growing in a favourable medium to bacteria growing in a rather poor one. However, there is no simple relationship between courtship behaviour and the fecundity pattern. Some picture-wings, such as *D. conspicua*, are in the high fecundity group, while *Engiscaptomyza* show typical scaptomyzoid behaviour (Carson *et al.* 1970).

In addition to ascribing the evolution of the lek-like behaviour and other less elaborate courtship systems to the presence of predators, Spieth (1974) suggests that microallopatric evolution on any one island becomes much more probable after the evolution of lek-like behaviour. This comes about both by a species occupying small geographical areas on the island, and because the complex courtship behaviour allows rapid development of sexual isolating mechanisms. Classical allopatric evolution, with the divergence of species in different places, could then take place on a micro scale, in different areas of one island.

Taxonomic points

In most of the world, *Drosophila* and *Scaptomyza*, although clearly closely related and rather similar, can be easily separated. *Scaptomyza* usually have one or no ventral hairs on the arista behind the apical fork, and two or four rows of acrostichal bristles. The acrostichals in the Drosophilidae are small bristles lying between the much larger dorsocentrals. One ventral aristal hair and four rows of acrostichal bristles can be seen in *S. frustulifera* (Fig. 2.8). *Drosophila* has two to many ventral hairs on the arista and six or eight rows of acrostichals.

On Hawaii, *Drosophila* may have only one ventral hair on the arista, and some *Scaptomyza* (*Trogloscaptomyza*) have six rows of acrostichals. To distinguish the two genera, it is necessary to take several characters into account. *Scaptomyza* generally have more complex male genitalia than *Drosophila*. However, a major feature of the Hawaiian drosophilids is that there is no sharp distinction between drosophiloids and scaptomyzoids. An indication of the interdigitation can only be given by a discussion of several species and groups. Some detail is necessary to show the complexity of the evolutionary patterns amongst Hawaiian drosophilids and their relationship to *Drosophila* and *Scaptomyza* elsewhere in the world. The association of *Scaptomyza* with islands, and the likely origin of this genus on Hawaii, are points of particular interest for the study of island biogeography. This account is based on a variety of sources, particularly Carson *et al.* (1970), Carson and Kaneshiro (1976), Hardy (1965), and Throckmorton (1966, 1975).

The relationship of the Hawaiian Drosophilidae to those elsewhere became clearer when it was found that part of the polytene sequence of chromosome 5, known as inversion *h*, could be matched in several species (Stalker 1972). Amongst continental species, the sequence is found in the *robusta* group which has many species in east Asia, though the closest match to the chromosome so far is in *D. colorata* of North America. The Hawaiian species with the sequence are two sibling primitive relatives of the picture-wings, *primaeva* and *attigua* from Kauai, and one of the modified-mouthparts group, *mimica*. This sequence is not found in any other picture-wings, but polytene chromosomes have yet to be examined in many other drosophiloid groups.

From *primaeva* and *attigua* it may be a fairly small step to another pair on Kauai, *anomalipes* and *quasianomalipes*. Of these Spieth said they 'show a queer mixture of drosophiloid and scaptomyzoid characters plus certain non-Hawaiian features' in their courtship behaviour. The wings of *primaeva*, *attigua* and *quasianomalipes* are evenly tinged yellow–brown, with slight darkenings over some of the veins, but *anomalipes* has a hyaline wing with a dark brown spot at the base and another at the tip of the wing. All the groups with specialized tarsi, bristle-, fork-, comb-, spoon- and ciliated-tarsi are perhaps derived from a form somewhere near *anomalipes*, and through the ciliated-tarsus *imparisetae* there seems to be a link to the white-tipped scutellum group.

The scutellum is the dorsal rear part of the thorax, and so the name of the group refers to a conspicuous feature. In some species the tip is yellow, so Throckmorton refers to the light-tip scutellum group. They have, to the trained eye, a characteristic low, lean look. On external characters they are drosophiloid, but in behaviour and on some internal characters scaptomyzoid.

Engiscaptomyza, with at least six species whose phylogeny will be considered below, is even harder to place. Most of the external characters are drosophiloid, and it is still in the size range of all the species mentioned so far, with a body length of 3–5 mm. But the behaviour, internal characters, the metaphase chromosomes, and the male genitalia all point to *Scaptomyza*. Carson and Kaneshiro (1976) have classed it as a subgenus of *Drosophila* and Throckmorton (1975) as a genus of its own, near *Scaptomyza*.

Next there are a few smaller species, originally placed in *Drosophila*, now generally regarded as *Scaptomyza*. The male genitalia of *reducta* and *taractica* are definitely *Scaptomyza*-like, and the flies are about 2.5 mm long. There is probably a group of species near *parva* which, as its name implies, is small, 1.5–2 mm. On internal and genital characters the group could be the link between three groups, white-tipped scutellum, *Engiscaptomyza*, and *Scaptomyza*.

In *Scaptomyza* a number of subgenera are still recognized, and *Titanochaeta* is also scaptomyzoid. Nearly all are about 2 mm long. The central subgenus may be *Bunostoma*, which are predominantly polished black flies, with two or three ventral hairs on the arista. From *Bunostoma* there may be two lines, one leading to *Alloscaptomyza* and *Exalloscaptomyza*, the other to *Trogloscaptomyza*, *Tantalia*, *Rosenwaldia* and *Titanochaeta*. All these groups have less than a dozen known species except *Trogloscaptomyza* which has 87.

The known distribution of *Scaptomyza* in the world (Hackman 1959; Wheeler and Takada 1966) is remarkable. There are a few cosmopolitan or widespread species, such as the leaf miners *pallida* and *graminum*, many species in North and South America, Europe, east Asia, and Japan, very few species in Africa, Indonesia, and Australia. To some extent this reflects the distribution of dipterists. There are two known endemic *Scaptomyza* in New Zealand. But then, besides Hawaii, there are species of *Scaptomyza* in the Marquesas, Society Islands, Samoa, Tristan da Cunha, St. Helena (Tsacas and Cogan 1976), Cape Verde Islands, Canaries, Azores, and Bermuda. The group is remarkably prevalent on oceanic islands. *Trogloscaptomyza* emphasizes this; 86 of the 87 species are Hawaiian endemics, the other (the type of the subgenus) is *S. (T.) brevilamellata* of the Tristan archipelago. Specimens were caught on fly paper at a temporary camp on Nightingale Island (Fig. 2.3) by the Norwegian Scientific Expedition of 1937–8. The camp was near multitudes of sea birds. The simplest explanation for the distribution of *Scaptomyza* would be that many species are associated with sea-bird colonies, and that they are dispersed from island to island, albeit very rarely, by sea birds.

The remarkable interdigitation of *Drosophila* and *Scaptomyza* on Hawaii requires an explanation; three can be put forward. The first is that there were two immigrant populations to Hawaii, one droso-philoid and one scaptomyzoid, and that they have converged. This seems rather unlikely in view of the complex reticulation of characters, which appears much more consistent with an evolutionary divergence. The second explanation is that the original immigrant was a primitive form intermediate between *Drosophila* and *Scaptomyza*, and that the stages of separation of these two genera have persisted in Hawaii, while similar evolution has led to the loss of intermediates elsewhere in the world. While this is consistent with the range of forms found on Hawaii, it begs the question of why there are two distinct sets elsewhere, and indeed rather presumes what it attempts to explain, by assuming that the intermediates which are not found have become extinct. It is also inconsistent with the relationships of the Hawaiian *Drosophila* to con-tinental *Drosophila* shown by polytene sequence 5*h* (Stalker 1972). This leaves a third explanation, that starting with an ordinary *Drosophila*, there has been evolution to *Scaptomyza* on Hawaii. This then requires that all other *Scaptomyza* round the world have been derived from the Hawaiian form. In one respect this is plausible: there are twice as many species of *Scaptomyza* on Hawaii as in the rest of the world. But it is at first sight a remarkable explanation. No other case is known to me of a group having evolved on an oceanic island, and from there spread to one continent, let alone all of them, and to many other oceanic islands as well. The possible association of *Scaptomyza* with sea birds and their colonies should be investigated. The probable role of sea birds in the dispersal of insects has already been noted (p. 37). On the present evidence, it seems that all the Hawaiian drosophiloids and scaptomy-zoids have been derived from a single immigrant population.

In *Scaptomyza* sub-generic names are still used, but they have been abandoned for the Hawaiian drosophiloids. The reason is that the original names given to genera have turned out either to refer to polyphyletic groups, or to refer to sets of species which have close relatives amongst typical *Drosophila*. A striking example is found in the picture-wings. One of the earliest names given in the Hawaiian dro-sophilids was *Idiomyia*. These are large flies with a characteristic vena-tion of the wing not found in typical *Drosophila*. There is an extra crossvein in cell R_5 In Fig. 8.1 this extra crossvein can be seen: it is the upper of the two vertical veins in the central part of the wing. Now that the phylogeny of the picture-wings has been worked out (and this will be discussed below), it is clear that the *Idiomyia* wing type has evolved at

least twice. The change of venation is apparently a consequence of the
change in size and life pattern, and no doubt will one day be shown to
have a straightforward mechanical function. *Idiomyia* was the first of the
generic names given to endemic Hawaiian drosophiloids to be abandoned. The last to go was *Antopocerus*, a name given to nine species in
which the males have the distinctive antennae already described (Fig.
8.1) (Hardy 1974; Carson and Kaneshiro 1976). The females, however,
are very like other *Drosophila*, and the group is no longer thought to be
sufficiently distinct to be considered a different genus. Meanwhile, with
the discovery of the great variety of drosophiloids it has become clear
that some other subdivision, assuming any subdivision is needed,
would be more satisfactory.

All of this is relevant to one perennial question in evolutionary
biology. Do the characteristic features of the higher taxonomic categories, that is to say genera, families, and orders, appear by saltation,
or by the same sort of evolution that gives rise to new species? The
evidence from the Hawaiian Drosophilidae is that speciation is a
gradual process, and that some elements of this gradual process quite
readily give rise to the characters which are recognized in other groups
as distinguishing genera. On this evidence, there is no difference between the evolution of species and of higher groups, and the changes
involved in speciation are quite small, though they may possibly be
sudden.

Evolution of the fauna

Phylogeny

At this point it is perhaps necessary to explain briefly the principles of
constructing phylogenies from polytene chromosomes. More fully-
illustrated descriptions are available in any number of text books.

The sequence of banding patterns down a chromosome is recognizable even when a segment of the chromosome has been split at two
points and inverted, or where two chromosomes have joined, or
another chromosomal rearrangement, because each of the thousands of
bands has a number of distinguishable characteristics. In the whole of
the picture-wing group, over 100 species, all of the bands are recognizable in every one of the species, if one allows in that statement a
small deletion in one species. An inversion of a segment of a chromosome requires two breaks and two junctions, and so the probability of
any one inversion being formed more than once is very small indeed.
Whenever an inversion overlaps another inverted pattern, so that there
are three inversion types, the original, that with the first inversion, and

that with the second inversion, then the middle type can be identified unambiguously as the middle one. On the other hand, the first might be the last or the last first; that is to say the direction of evolution is not demonstrated by this evidence alone; see Fig. 8.2. Nevertheless, from a study of overlapping inversions, what is known mathematically as a tree, and regarded by biologists as an evolutionary tree, can be produced. If the oldest species can be identified, then the tree becomes what is called by mathematicians a rooted tree, or in other words the course of evolution is made clear.

a	b	c	d	e	f	g	h	i	j	k		1
a	b	g	f	e	d	c	h	i	j	k		2
a	b	g	f	e	i	h	c	d	j	k		3

FIG. 8.2. The reconstruction of phylogenies from chromosome inversions. The letters stand for individual bands in polytene chromosomes. Condition 2 is derived from 1 by inverting the sequence c to g, condition 3 from 2 by inverting d to i. As these two inversions overlap, 3 cannot be derived by a single inversion from 1. For this set of three sequences, 2 must be intermediate, but the phylogeny could be $1 \rightarrow 2 \rightarrow 3$ or $3 \rightarrow 2 \rightarrow 1$ or $1 \leftarrow 2 \rightarrow 3$.

The course of evolution on Hawaii has been affected greatly by its physical setting. The origin of the islands by the movement of a hot spot was discussed in Chapter 1, and Fig. 1.7 shows the island chain, and its predecessor, the Emperor Seamounts. It is now necessary to look at this chain in somewhat greater detail. The Hawaiian Islands can be divided into two groups, the small fragments of the Leeward chain from Nihoa out to Kure, and the large inhabitable islands of the Windward chain. This last set is shown in Fig. 8.3. For Molokai, Maui, Lanai, and Kahoolawe the greatest depth of sea between neighbouring islands is less than 100 m and is indeed less than 50 m between Lanai and Maui. All the other channels between the islands of the Windward chain are much deeper than this—over 500 m. The four islands of Maui and its neighbours have, from time to time in the Pleistocene, been one island. It is therefore possible as a first approximation to treat the Windward chain as four distinct blocks, Kauai, Oahu, the Maui complex, and the big island of Hawaii. An interesting part of the evolutionary pattern is the changes that happened with immigration from one of these groups to another. As will be seen, however, evolution appears to have been more rapid, leading to great numbers of species, on the Maui complex, no doubt reflecting its history of fusion and separation.

Because of the motion of the hot spot, the islands are progressively younger from west to east. Kauai is the oldest island, Hawaii the youngest. The sizes, and estimates of the ages (from potassium argon datings), are shown in Table 8.2. Two smaller islands (see endpapers) in the Windward chain will not be mentioned again, Niihau, south-east of Kauai, and Kahoolawe. Native species of drosophilids are not known from them; access is forbidden by the owners. Niihau is mostly plantations; Kahoolawe is a bombing range. Endemic drosophilids have not been recorded from any of the Leeward chain either, though it has been suggested that some *Scaptomyza* might be found there.

Table 8.2. Minimum number of inter-island founders in the picture-winged *Drosophila* of Hawaii

	No. of founders				
To:	Kauai	Oahu	Maui, Molokai and Lanai	Hawaii	Total emigrant founders
From:					
Kauai	–	5	2	1	8
Oahu	0	–	6	1	7
Maui group	1	10	–	11	22
Hawaii	0	1	1	–	2
Total immigrant founders	1	16	9	13	
Total number of picture-wing species known	11	29	39	25	
Age of islands 10^6 years	5.6	2.55–3.6	1.3–1.84	0.68	
Area, km²	1437	1564	2924	10 440	

Ages from Clague and Jarrard 1973.

Two other features of the Hawaiian islands deserve mention. The first is that, as high islands in the North-East Trades, parts of the islands have very heavy rainfall, and these parts have a rain forest. Other parts, though, are in the rain shadow and relatively dry. The variation in climate over quite a short distance is therefore surprisingly large. The second feature is that the lava flows on the islands are still new, and indeed on Hawaii are still active in places. These flows quite frequently surround areas on which forest still grows. These isolated patches are called kipukas. The fauna on different kipukas can differ considerably, and it is a reasonable hypothesis that in many cases isolation on a kipuka has been involved in evolutionary divergence.

One of the most striking features of the distribution of Hawaiian

Drosophilidae is that, treating the Maui complex as one, almost every species is found only on a single island.

In the 101 species of picture-wings shown in Fig. 8.3, which is explained in detail below, only two occur on more than one island. *D. crucigera* (97) is on Kauai and Oahu, *grimshawi* (81) on these two and all three islands of the Maui complex as well. Even in the Maui complex most species are only known from one island. *Adiastola* (8) and *ortho-fascia* (95) are on Lanai and Maui, *neopicta* (26) and *spectabilis* (10) on Molokai and Maui, *balioptera* (91) is on all three. Lanai is mostly plantations and only four picture-wings are known from it; all are also found on at least one other island. For Hawaiian drosophilids as a whole, it is possible that as many as 98 per cent are single-island endemics (Hardy 1974).

As an example of single-island endemism and of the methods used in deriving phylogenies, consider *Engiscaptomyza*. There are two groups of species in this genus, *crassifemur* and *nasalis*. The latter has two known species, *nasalis* from Maui and Molokai, *undulata* from Hawaii. The four sibling species of the *crassifemur* group are discussed by Yoon, Resch, Wheeler, and Richardson (1975). On chromosome 4, the standard sequence only is found in *amplilobus* from Kauai and *inflatus* from Oahu, the standard and two inversions, P and Q, occur in *crassifemur* from Maui and Molokai, and all these sequences and two more, S and T, are found in *reducta* on Hawaii. In addition, *amplilobus* differs from all the other species in two inversions on chromosome 2 and one on chromosome 5. The simplest interpretation is that the phylogeny follows the sequence of the islands, starting on Kauai and ending on Hawaii. However, it could start with *inflatus* on Oahu, leading on the one hand to *amplilobus* and on the other to *crassifemur* and on to *reducta*. Either way, three inter-island immigrations are needed.

The major work on the phylogeny of the *Drosophila* of Hawaii has been done with the picture-wing group. There are over a hundred species now known in this group, and Fig. 8.3 shows the probable phylogeny, using data up to that published by Carson and Kaneshiro (1976). This figure shows the tree of species, and also shows on which of the four islands, treating the Maui complex as one, the species occur. White circles indicate hypothetical species. There is a certain amount of ambiguity in constructing this tree, in that certain species have identical chromosome patterns, that is to say are homosequential. In the whole of this diagram, as was noted above, there are only two species that occur on more than one island, *grimshawi* (81) and *crucigera* (97).

In Fig. 8.3 the frequent occurrence of inter-island jumps is obvious, and there also appears to be quite a lot of speciation within islands.

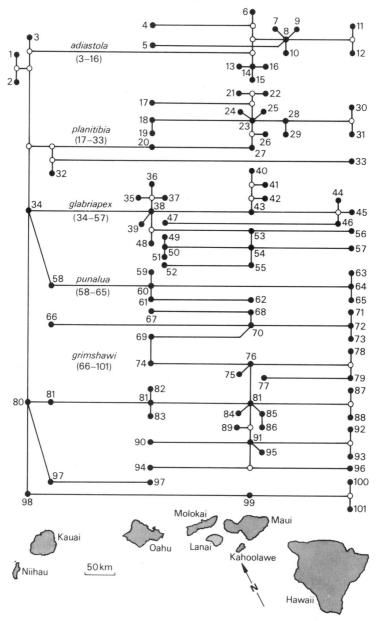

FIG. 8.3.　A phylogeny of the picture-wing *Drosophila* of Hawaii, based on chromosome inversions. ● Known species, key to names below, ○ hypothetical intermediates. The species are placed vertically above the island on which they are found (treating Maui, Molokai and Lanai as one island). The phylogeny starts with species 1 and 2, *primaeva* and *attigua* on the oldest island,

That on the Maui complex may, of course, be simply allopatric, because there are now, and have been at various stages in the past, three main islands in the group. In other cases, apparent species formation within an island may just reflect our lack of knowledge. For instance, in the 1970 diagrams *hirtipalpus* (77) of Maui was derived directly from *villitibia* (76) of Molokai, as part of the speciation of the *grimshawi* subgroup of Maui. Since then, *psilotarsalis* (79) has been found on the island of Hawaii, and is intermediate with two of the three inversions that distinguish *hirtipalpus* from *villitibia*, thus adding two more inter-island jumps to the phylogeny.

The diagram in Fig. 8.3 is what has already been described above as a tree. This particular tree can be rooted because the two species on the

---

Kauai. When the chromosome sequences allow more than one phylogeny, an arrangement that uses the minimum number of inter-island transitions is chosen. Species shown as 'parents' may well be 'uncles': to show no species as directly derived from an existing one requires 33 more hypothetical species.

1 *primaeva*	2 *attigua*	3 *ornata*	4 *neogrimshawi*
5 *touchardiae*	6 *clavisetae*	7 *cilifera*	8 *adiastola*
9 *peniculipedis*	10 *spectabilis*	11 *setosimentum*	12 *ochrobasis*
13 *hamifera*	14 *paenehamifera*	15 *truncipenna*	16 *varipennis*
17 *nigribasis*	18 *oahuensis*	19 *hemipeza*	20 *substenoptera*
21 *melanocephala*	22 *ingens*	23 *neoperkinsi*	24 *cyrtoloma*
25 *hanaulae*	26 *neopicta*	27 *obscuripes*	28 *planitibia*
29 *differens*	30 *silvestris*	31 *heteroneura*	32 *picticornis*
33 *setosifrons*	34 *glabriapex*	35 *inedita*	36 *distinguenda*
37 *divaricata*	38 *pilimana*	39 *aglaia*	40 *discreta*
41 *lineosetae*	42 *fasciculisetae*	43 *vesciseta*	44 *alsophila*
45 *conspicua*	46 *assita*	47 *montgomeryi*	48 *hexachaetae*
49 *spaniothrix*	50 *tarphytrichia*	51 *psilophallus*	52 *gymnophallus*
53 *virgulata*	54 *odontophallus*	55 *liophallus*	56 *digressa*
57 *macrothrix*	58 *ocellata*	59 *uniseriata*	60 *punalua*
61 *paucicilia*	62 *prostopalpis*	63 *basisetae*	64 *paucipuncta*
65 *prolaticilia*	66 *musaphilia*	67 *turbata*	68 *recticilia*
69 *gradata*	70 *gymnobasis*	71 *heedi*	72 *hawaiiensis*
73 *silvarentis*	74 *flexipes*	75 *lasiopoda*	76 *villitibia*
77 *hirtipalpus*	78 *formella*	79 *psilotarsalis*	80 *villosipedis*
81 *grimshawi*	82 *atrimentum*	83 *obatai*	84 *sodomae*
85 *disjuncta*	86 *bostrycha*	87 *sproati*	88 *pullipes*
89 *orphnopeza*	90 *sobrina*	91 *balioptera*	92 *murphyi*
93 *engyochracea*	94 *reynoldsiae*	95 *orthofascia*	96 *ciliaticrus*
97 *crucigera*	98 *sejuncta*	99 *limitata*	100 *ochracea*
101 *claytonae*			

(Data from Carson and Kaneshiro 1976.) See note on p. 196.

left-hand side, *primaeva* (1) and *attigua* (2), a pair of sibling species found together in the same habitat on Mount Kahili, Kauai are primitive, having chromosome inversion 5*h* (Stalker 1972; see above, p. 179). *Primaeva* is also known from Kokee, on the same island. For the moment it is sufficient to note that all the five main subgroups, *adiastola*, *planitibia*, *glabriapex*, *punalua* and *grimshawi*, originated on Kauai. It might perhaps be safer to say they originated on Kauai or on some island farther west. The islands to the west of Kauai have all become very small and it is conceivable that some of the early evolution of the picture-wing group, and for that matter other sections of *Drosophila*, took place on those islands when they were larger.

The pattern of inter-island founders is mostly of immigration from west to east, which is in fact against the prevailing wind, and from older islands to newer islands. This is brought out more clearly in Table 8.2, which shows the number of founder events now known to have occurred in the picture-wing group from one island to another. There has been only one immigration recorded on to Kauai, and only two emigrations from Hawaii.

The phylogeny based on inversions is mostly unambiguous, except where species are homosequential. Figure 8.3 does not show the number of inversions involved, but these are given by Carson and Kaneshiro (1976). One difficulty in showing the pattern of inversions is that a certain amount of the evolution has been through inversion polymorphism. A striking case is in *neopicta* (26) in the *planitibia* group. This species has two chromosome inversions on each of the second, fourth and X chromosomes, symbolically 2 $m/+$, X $t/+$, 4 $f3/+$, where the + sequences are those found in the Kauai species and also in *substenoptera* (20) and *obscuripes* (27). The t inversion is fixed, homozygous, in all species past *neopicta* in the phylogenetic tree (17–19, 21–25, 28–31). The m inversion is fixed in *nigribasis*, *ingens* and *melanocephala* (17, 21, 22) while 2 + is fixed in the rest of the tree beyond *neopicta* and *neoperkinsi* (23) (Carson 1973).

This group of species (20 onwards) is one of the two sets once placed in *Idiomyia*. The other set is *neogrimshawi* (4) and *clavisetae* (6), while *picticornis* (32) and *setosifrons* (33) have the standard *Drosophila* wing venation.

The phylogeny of *planitibia* (28), *differens* (29), *silvestris* (30) and *heteroneura* (31) shows some of the ambiguities met in constructing the tree. *Planitibia* (Maui) and *differens* (Molokai) are homosequential and have no polymorphisms; the two Hawaiian species *heteroneura* and *silvestris* are in addition polymorphic for an inversion m on chromosome 3 (not related in any way to m of chromosome 2, a separate alphabetical sequence is used for each chromosome). In Fig. 8.3, *planitibia* is shown as ancestral, *differens* equally well could have been. On the basis of mating preferences, Kaneshiro (1976) suggests that *differens* gave rise directly to *heteroneura*, and also to *planitibia* and thence to *silvestris*. His scheme has two jumps from the Maui complex to Hawaii; the scheme in Fig. 8.3 is preferred here as it has only one jump, and Fig. 8.3 is based on using the minimum number of island jumps where there is ambiguity. Figure 8.3 also makes the simplest assumption about the origin of inversion 3 *m*, namely that it originated on Hawaii.

Another genetic system, which is well known for its polymorphism, comprises the genes responsible for production of a variety of soluble enzymes. The variants are called isozymes. When isozymes are shown to be formed by different alleles at the same locus, they may be referred to as allozymes. This usage is not adhered to as closely as might be desired. An isozyme occurring in two different species cannot usually be shown to be allozymic, simply because hybridization is impossible. Nevertheless, many authors refer to isozymes with identical bands as being the same allozyme. The assumption is reasonable, but cannot be proved. Working with the frequencies of different isozymes, including in the term 'frequency' the presence or absence of certain types, it is possible, using the methods of numerical taxonomy, to construct dendrograms. For many groups of organisms, this is the closest one can get to an objective phylogeny. The Hawaiian Drosophilidae show that it is not guaranteed to produce a right answer.

Figure 8.4 shows a dendrogram for isozymes in the *planitibia* group of picture-wings, taken from Johnson, Carson, Kaneshiro, Steiner, and Cooper (1975) and with the species numbered as in Fig. 8.3. In this dendrogram two major groups can be picked out, a group of seven species running from *heteroneura* to *neopicta*, and a group of six species from *hanaulae* to *oahuensis*. *Nigribasis* and *picticornis* form a pair, not particularly closely related, while *obscuripes* is even less closely related to any of the others though fitting closest to the second major group. The parts of the dendrogram that do not match Fig. 8.3 are shown by dashed lines, long dashes for very bad fits, short dashes for poor ones. The isozyme classification cuts across the chromosome phylogeny in a surprisingly large number of places. The first major group contains the four species close to *differens* discussed above and a natural group, but the other three in this isozyme group are separated in the chromosome tree by species which are isozymically different. The second isozymic group is a compact part of the phylogenetic tree, based on *hanaulae* but the details of the dendrogram and the phylogenetic tree are not identical. *Obscuripes*, the most isolated species on its isozymes, is in a central position in the chromosome phylogeny. Perhaps the most striking example of cross-classification in this group occurs on the island of Oahu. There there are four species (17–20), classified by the chromosomes into a pair (18, 19) with the other two more distantly related. On the isozymes, this pair is separated into different clusters, while *nigribasis* (17) is paired, albeit weakly, with *picticornis* (32), the most isolated species on the chromosome phylogeny.

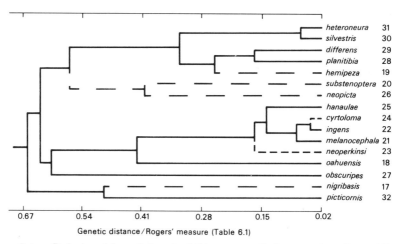

heteroneura	31
silvestris	30
differens	29
planitibia	28
hemipeza	19
substenoptera	20
neopicta	26
hanaulae	25
cyrtoloma	24
ingens	22
melanocephala	21
neoperkinsi	23
oahuensis	18
obscuripes	27
nigribasis	17
picticornis	32

0.67   0.54   0.41   0.28   0.15   0.02

Genetic distance/Rogers' measure (Table 6.1)

F ɪ ɢ. 8.4.   Relationships of the *planitibia* group of picture-wing *Drosophila* as shown by isozyme frequencies. Species badly misplaced from their position in the chromosome phylogeny (Fig. 8.3) are connected by long dashes; those somewhat misplaced by short dashes. The numbers after the names are the numbers of Fig. 8.3. (Modified from Johnson *et al.* 1975.)

On this evidence, isozyme phylogenies should not be taken too seriously, though it is evident that they can be useful for approximations to a true phylogeny. The reason why the isozyme phylogeny does not work better is not clear, but two partial explanations can be suggested. The first is that the isozyme clustering is done mostly on variations in gene frequency, though some isozymes are either absent or homozygous in species of the set. Chromosome phylogeny is done entirely on the presence and absence of inversions, with polymorphic forms taken as intermediates. If isozyme phylogenies were worked on the same principle, they might be more reliable, but also would frequently give scarcely any information at all. The second possible reason is associated with the numerical techniques involved. Dendrograms are attractive and readily intelligible. It is not so immediately apparent that some rather arbitrary rules are necessary in order to construct them. Figure 8.3 is not shown as a dendrogram as to do so would be incompatible with showing the inter-island jumps. However, quite apart from that, it is not possible to put information on inversion changes into a dendrogram form. Let me explain.

Suppose there is an ancestral species which continues unchanged to the present day. This may give rise by a single inversion type to a divergent line. In that line suppose there are species which go in for rapid evolutionary changes involving many inversions, while there are other more conservative ones. Then on the similarity of their inversion types the more conservative ones will be like the ancestral ones, rather than like the more recently evolved ones. To put it another way, the true chromosome phylogeny cannot be deduced by adding up the number of inversion differences because the sequence in which the inversions have evolved is critical. To construct a dendrogram, at each fusion a group characteristic is normally required, and for chromosome inversions this group characteristic makes no biological sense. So, although it would be possible to distort the information in Fig. 8.3. into a tree diagram, with all the existent species on the same level, the successive levels of fusions could not be related in a hierarchial way to the number of inversions. It could indeed be argued that one reason why dendrograms are so easy to understand is that they hide confusing information.

Phenotype, ecology, and evolution

The detailed phylogeny of the picture-wing group allows us to examine a number of issues that have been frequently discussed in relation to the evolution of other groups. The first is the relative speed of evolution in different systems. In the picture-wing group it is possible to find species which are homosequential in their chromosomes, with similar isozyme frequencies, and similar morphologies. An example are the pair *heedi* (71) and *silvarentis* (73) which are sympatric on the island of Hawaii and whose ecology is discussed below. There are also many cases in which there has been considerable evolution in one system, with conservatism in another. Species that have almost indistinguishable external morphology are called sibling species, and are well known in other *Drosophila* groups across the world. In most of the picture-wings the species are readily distinguishable in the males. If they were only known from the females, they might in many cases be described as sibling. However, *heedi* and *silvarentis* are close enough even in the males to be reasonably described as sibling species.

Another sibling pair is *primaeva* (1) and *attigua* (2); the latter species was discovered when some laboratory crosses gave unexpected results. However, they differ by no fewer than 12 chromosome inversions. The opposite situation is found in the apparently recently evolved pair of species on Hawaii, *heteroneura* (31) and *silvestris* (30). These are not only homosequential, and with one chromosome polymorphism in common. Nevertheless, they are strikingly different in the morphology of the head; *silvestris* is normal, *heteroneura* is shown in Fig. 8.1. For the genetics of this difference, see Val (1977). In the same way, *oahuensis* (18) and *hanaulae* (25), occurring on the islands of Oahu and Maui respectively, are homosequential but markedly different in their isozymes. The converse situation is found in *cyrtoloma* (24) and *ingens* (22) both from Maui, which have almost identical isozymes, but differ by six inversions.

Another contrast in different systems is that *picticornis* (32) and *silvestris* (30) are both highly polymorphic in their isozymes, but *picticornis* is monomorphic in its chromosomes, *silvestris* has eleven inversion polymorphisms. It is clear that different system evolve at different rates in different lines. The differences in pace can be expressed by saying that no system behaves as an evolutionary clock (Throckmorton 1977).

Turning from morphological to ecological characters, it is well known that the ecological differences that keep *Drosophila* species apart worldwide have been difficult to study. The same is true for many of the Hawaiian species, where closely related species appear to be completely sympatric, and whose larvae are found in the same leaf samples (see p. 173). There have, however, been some cases where niche separation is striking. One example is in *heedi* and *silvarentis*, as has been mentioned. These two occur together on an area in Hawaii which is, for those islands, remarkably dry and cold (Kaneshiro, Carson, Clayton, and Heed 1973). They occur at an altitude of about 2000 m in the saddle between the two major volcanoes Mauna Loa and Mauna Kea. The dry, powdery soils of recent cinder cones support a park-like and sparse vegetation consisting largely of two species of tree. One is *Myoporum sandwicense*, for which the Polynesian name is Naio, a member of the Myoporaceae, a small family centred on Australia. Naio has slime fluxes from time to time on its trunk and branches. Some of these fluxes run down the trunk to the soil; some drip from the branches to the soil below.

Larvae of the two species of *Drosophila* live in these slime fluxes, but those of *silvarentis* are found in those on the tree; those of *heedi* are confined to those on the ground. Occasional *silvarentis* larvae work their way down the tree and might be found in a slime flux at the foot. Both species pupate underground. The niche separation here is very obvious, possibly because the ecosystem is so simple.

In Fig. 8.3 classical allopatric speciation is evident in all the interisland jumps. The abundance of species on the Maui complex is also an indication of allopatric speciation. However, many species are found on the same island as their nearest known relative, which leads to the

question: has there been sympatric speciation in the Hawaiian Drosophilidae? (Sympatric speciation is defined here to be when the reproductive individuals of the population dividing into two, and their
descendants as two new species, intermingle and could mate.) With
such small animals as *Drosophila*, with the marked variation in the
physical environment in different parts of the same island, and with the
island-like kipukas, allopatric speciation on one island is clearly a
possibility. Heed (1971) examined the distribution of larval food requirements, and concluded that related species usually used the same
food, and that most foods used were continuously available throughout
the year, and that therefore sympatric speciation had probably not
been important. Spieth (1974) has emphasized the role that lek-like
behaviour might play in microallopatric speciation, and says firmly
that no case in the Hawaiian Drosophilidae requires sympatric speciation. While lek-like behaviour may be an important component of the
evolution of hundreds of species of drosophiloids, this behaviour is
absent in the scaptomyzoids that have also produced hundreds of
species.

Sympatric speciation has been suggested for *heedi* and *silvarentis*
(White 1978) on the grounds of niche separation, discussed above,
and that they are homosequential. However, three other species,
hawaiiensis (72) from Hawaii, *gymnobasis* (70) from Maui, and *musaphilia*
(66) from Kauai have the same sequences. Separate immigrations from
Maui, microallopatric evolution on Hawaii and sympatric speciation
are all possibilities; there is no evidence as yet to distinguish between
them. Richardson (1974) argued for sympatric speciation as the origin
of two closely related species of the modified-mouthparts drosophiloids, *mimica* and *kambysellisi*. They occur in Kipuka Puaulu and Kipuka Ki on Hawaii. These are the only known localities for *kambysellisi*,
though *mimica* is known from elsewhere. The two predominant trees in
the kipukas are *Sapindus saponaria* (Sapindaceae) and *Pisonia brunonianum*
(Nyctaginaceae). *Kambysellisi* has been reared only from the rotting
leaves of *Pisonia* and *mimica* mostly from the fruits of *Sapindus* (along
with *imparisetae*, p. 174). The evidence for sympatric speciation is again
niche separation and close relationship. However, it now seems that
both are members of species groups found elsewhere on the islands.
The closest-known relative of *mimica* is *reschae* from Oahu (Carson and
Kaneshiro 1976).

While sympatric speciation is at most rare, founder principle might
be important in the evolution of Hawaiian Drosophilidae. Carson has
been at once one of the most senior and distinguished geneticists
studying the Hawaiian Drosophilidae, and one of the best known and
most persuasive proponents of the theory of founder principle. The

most clear description of his views is perhaps in Carson (1976), where he postulates a marked reduction in genetic variability from the reduction of a population to low size, followed by a decrease in selection pressure as the population increases, with a final phase where selection is re-established and the population stabilizes. It is therefore to be expected that he would argue strongly that the inter-island founders, at least, have led to speciation by this process.

To what extent is the pattern of speciation consistent with this view? Most of the Hawaiian *Drosophila* occur only on one island, but that fact seems neutral in relation to the founder principle, as the isolation on islands is certainly marked, and that in itself would tend to lead to different selective pressures. Information on chromosome polymorphism is also not very helpful. Most species are, again, monomorphic; 60 per cent of inversions are fixed (Carson and Kaneshiro 1976). Those that are polymorphic in general only have two types on any one chromosome. *D. neopicta* is polymorphic for three inversions, but these are on three different chromosomes. It is therefore quite feasible for this sort of polymorphism to be carried by a single heterozygous fertilized founding female. However, with so few polymorphic populations, there is simply not enough information to test whether inter-island founders tend to be significantly less polymorphic than intra-island founders, even assuming that these could be identified with certainty.

The evidence from isozyme polymorphism is perhaps better suited to studying this problem. There the evidence is, as White (1978) noted, rather against Carson. Derived species, whether derived between islands or within islands, seem not only to maintain a high polymorphism of isozymes, but frequently the same polymorphisms.

One difficulty in resolving this problem is that successful founder events are very rare. Taking the data in Table 8.2, there are 39 successful founder events, including in that the spread of *grimshawi* and *crucigera*. Those going to Hawaii have all taken place in less than the last 700 000 years, but others, particularly those going from Kauai to Oahu, may well be much older. There are also no doubt quite a few founder events of which we have no knowledge, because the species are still extant but have not been found, or because the phylogenies have been incompletely worked out, or because the species have become extinct. The last is perhaps the most important. To get some feeling for the frequency of founding events, however, it might be sensible to regard the 39 events as having happened within a million years, which leads to an average of one event every 25 000 years or so. *Drosophila* must be blown from island to island more frequently than that, so it is possible to argue that it takes a freak occurrence, with a group of flies immigrating together, for a population to be established. Still, even that does not necessarily speak against the founder principle, because even such a group would presumably be measured in tens or hundreds and so still be a very small population.

To put this extraordinarily low rate of founding populations into context, once every 25 000 years, perhaps it is worth pointing out that the great bulk of the British flora and fauna has become established in the last 10 000 years, or that the rate is only four founding events in Hawaii in each glacial cycle of 100 000 years through the Pleistocene.

One thing is certain, and that is that the evolution of the Hawaiian Drosophilidae, provided their habitat is maintained, is far from finished. With such a slow time-constant, the time between successful inter-island founding events, this is perhaps hardly surprising. Another indication of this may be the species–area curve for the picture-wings, which is shown in Fig. 8.5. In this figure, the number of picture-wings on the three islands of Lanai, Molokai, and Maui have been separated. Taken as a whole, the set has a slope of 0.514, though this is not in fact significantly different from a slope of zero. Hawaii and Lanai have relatively few species for their area. The former may reflect its youth as an island, and so the lack of evolution, the latter may be an artefact of habitat destruction.

Figure 8.5 also shows the species–area curve for the indigenous birds. The slope is 0.335, and is significantly different from zero at the 1 per cent level. This group will be studied in the next chapter, together

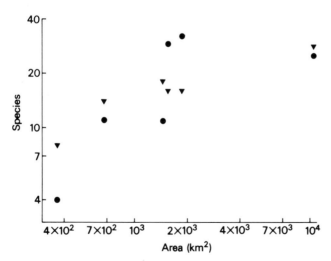

FIG. 8.5. Species–area plot for native land and freshwater birds ▼, and for picture-wing *Drosophila* ●. (Data from Hawaii Audobon Society 1975, Carson and Kaneshiro 1976.)

with some other points about Hawaii. Taking both sets of species–area data, it seems that evolutionary processes can be important in producing such a relationship.

Conclusion

Any other study of evolution must surely seem inadequate after the study of the Hawaiian Drosophilidae. In no other group is so much known, are there so many species, and can the ecological relationships be clarified so well. They also show the advantages of studying evolutionary phenomena on islands where one group dominates the evolutionary scene in a limited theatre. There is still an immense amount of work to be done on the group, but the work carried out so far clearly establishes their supremacy.

Note added 1982: Two additional species to, and some minor differences in interpretation of, the phylogeny of Fig. 8.3 (p. 186), as well as a mass of interesting data, can be found in Carson, H. L. and Yoon, J. S. (1982). Genetics and evolution of Hawaiian *Drosophila*. In *The genetics and biology of* Drosophila (ed. M. Ashburner, H. L. Carson, and J. N. Thompson) Vol. 3b, pp. 297–344. Academic Press, London.

9 Evolution on archipelagos

While the Hawaiian Drosophilidae are supreme in showing the general pattern that evolution may take on archipelagos, there are some phenomena of interest which cannot be shown with them. In this chapter I shall discuss the birds on Hawaii, the birds on Tristan, the birds and other vertebrates on the Galapagos, and the evolution of *Anolis* lizards in the West Indies. Each of these topics brings out some new points; the data for Hawaii and the Galapagos in particular give some indication of how the disharmonic set of species on oceanic islands is brought together. The *Anolis* lizards show some variations in evolutionary patterns and sequences, which are rather distinct from any shown on Hawaii, and which contrast with the patterns that might be expected under the MacArthur–Wilson theory.

What this chapter will not deal with is adaptive radiation in the Darwin's finches or in the Hawaiian drepanidids. These topics have been dealt with at more than sufficient length in more than enough books. The evolution of these groups has also been subjected to excessive compression in too many elementary text books, compression, as so often, leading in many cases to rather severe distortion. A proper study of the Darwin's finches requires a reading of Lack (1947, 1971) and several of the works to which he refers. Carlquist (1965) describes the Galapagos and some of its fauna, and gives a good, short account of adaptive radiation in the finches. For the Hawaiian honeycreepers, Wilson *et al.* (1973) give a useful introduction, while good pictures and accounts of their distribution and some notes on their ecology are to be found in Hawaii Audubon Society (1975). Some superficial familiarity with these two groups is assumed in this chapter.

Hawaii's flora and fauna

Hawaii is an almost tropical archipelago, set in the centre of the largest ocean. The large islands of Hawaii are remarkably large for oceanic islands. The areas of a number of islands are shown in the endpapers. Here we may note that over 60 per cent of the total land area of the archipelago is in the one island of Hawaii. The next-largest island of Maui is rather smaller than the Outer Hebridean island of Lewis and Harris and half the size of Long Island, while the smallest of the large islands that we will be considering, Lanai, is about the same size as the Isle of Wight and bigger than Mount Desert Island, Maine. The big island of Hawaii is, then, larger than any of the satellite islands in the British Isles, though much smaller than Ireland. Perhaps its size is best indicated by saying it is intermediate between Jamaica and Puerto Rico, two islands that will be considered later on in this chapter.

In the last chapter the number of species of *Drosophila* on Hawaii was compared with the number in the British Isles, and this comparison can perhaps be extended, not merely because of familiarity, but also because the tropicality and isolation of Hawaii might be thought perhaps to balance the temperate, continental position of the British Isles. Similarly, the smaller area of Hawaii might be compensated by its much greater height. For the British Isles, it is easy to remember in round figures that there are 200 species of breeding birds, 2000 species of vascular plants, and 20 000 species of insects. The first of these includes sea birds, but a comparison with Hawaii should preferably exclude sea birds. This is because the north-west chain of the Leeward Islands contains such vast populations of sea birds that including them makes comparisons with plants and insects unbalanced. So confining ourselves to land and freshwater birds, there appear to be 43 species of Hawaiian birds, living or recently extinct. The corresponding figure for Britain would be about 180, depending on which species were thought not to be sea birds. The Hawaiian birds are listed in Table 9.1 and this information is considered further below.

There are perhaps 2000 species of higher plants on the archipelago, derived from only about 275 ancestral stocks (Zimmerman 1972). Allowing for the difficulties of defining species limits in certain apomictic and other critical groups of plants, this is by any standard remarkably close to the total number in the British list, though there, of course, the number of original immigrants will also be near 2000 species. Many groups of plants have undergone spectacular evolution on Hawaii, as these figures indicate. One of the most famous groups is the lobeliads, including *Clermontia*, which has already been mentioned as an important habitat for the native *Drosophila*. The flora is also notably disharmonic. There are no gymnosperms, and no oaks, elms, willows, maples, no mangroves, or figs, only one genus of palms, and few orchids.

The insect fauna is also markedly disharmonic. To take one example, there are no endemic ants. The present number of 6500 endemic species, already given in Table 8.1, is thought to have arisen from about 250 original immigrants.

Comparisons amongst these three groups are also interesting. As a proportion of the British species, the ancestral plants represent about

Table 9.1. The status and relationship of native Hawaiian land and freshwater birds

Status	Latin name	English name (Polynesian)	No. species	No. subspecies	Nearest relative
Endemic family	Drepanididae	Hawaiian Honeycreepers	23	40	a holarctic passerine
Endemic genera	*Phaeornis*	Thrush	2	6	*Myadestes*, Turdidae N. American
	Chasiempis	(Elepaio)	1	3	*Monarcha* etc., Muscicapidae Polynesian
	Moho	('O'o)	4	4	*Amoromyza* etc. Meliphagidae Australasian
	Chaetoptila	(Kioea)	1	1	
Endemic species	*Branta sandvicensis*	Goose (Nene)	1	1	*B. canadensis* N. American
	Buteo solitarius	Hawk	1	1	*B. swainsonii* N. American
	Porzana palmeri	Laysan rail	1	1	*P. pusilla* Palaearctic
	Porzana sandwichensis	Hawaiian rail	1	1	Inderterminate: *Porzana* holarctic + Polynesian
	Himantopus knudseni	Stilt	1	1	Indeterminate: 7 other species worldwide
	Corvus tropicus	Crow	1	1	*C. cryptoleucus* N. American
	Acrocephalus familiaris	Laysan + Nihoa millerbird	1	2	Polynesian or palaearctic
Endemic subspecies	*Anas platyrhynchos wyvilliana*	Hawaiian duck	1	2	Holarctic Mallard
	A. p. laysanensis	Laysan duck	1	1	
	Gallinula chloropus sandvichensis	Gallinule	1	1	Holarctic Moorhen
	Fulica americana alai	Coot	1	1	North American
	Asio flameus sandwichensis	Short-eared owl	1	1	Holarctic
Indigenous	*Nycticorax n. hoactli*	Black-crowned night heron	1	1	North American

Compiled from Mayr and Short 1970, Mayr 1976, and Hawaii Audobon Society 1975.

15 per cent, the birds 10 per cent, but the insects only 1 per cent, while in the evolved biota, plants are about 100 per cent, birds 25 per cent and insects 30 per cent. There seems little doubt that plants are the best dispersers, insects the worst of these, though of course by far from the worst of all groups. There are no land mammals, reptiles or amphibians, for instance, except one species of bat, *Lasiurus cinereus*, the hoary bat of North America. In terms of evolutionary potential, the order is different. The insects have increased twenty-six-fold, the plants seven-fold, but the birds only two-and-a-half-fold. None of this is surprising, but the figures illustrate the size of the differences between different groups.

The Hawaiian avifauna

In Table 9.1 are listed the endemic and indigenous land and freshwater birds on the Hawaiian islands. This list includes not only those on the four main island groups, described in the last chapter, but also those on two islands of the Leeward group, Laysan and Nihoa (Fig. 1.7). The table lists the species by their current taxonomic status, indicates their nearest relative where known, and their geographical origin as far as it can be ascertained.

The first thing that can be deduced from this table is that there have been at least 15 separate immigrations, and quite possibly 18, leading to the species known to exist now or recently. On that figure, and from the known ages of the islands given in Table 8.2, it would appear that the average time between successful immigrations was hundreds of thousands of years. Possibly if there had been many other successful immigrations that have become extinct, the interval might be shorter, but it seems unlikely that there would have been enough to upset the order of magnitude of the process. For the size of the islands, for the number of possible immigrants in Asia, North America, and Polynesia, and for the great length of time in which a favourable habitat may be presumed to have existed, the number of immigrants is clearly very low. In this respect the Hawaiian Island fit, *par excellence*, the definition of an oceanic island offered at the end of Chapter 7, one where evolution is faster than immigration.

The next aspect that can be examined is the taxonomic divergence which has taken place. Here the situation is very much less clear, simply because of the changes of taxonomic criteria over the years. There are, in fact, only two immigrants whose status is totally agreed, and these occur at the two ends of the scale. The Drepanididae are regarded as an endemic family by all authorities, and their relationship to any other family of Passerines is uncertain. At the other end of the list, the reef heron, *Nycticorax*, is agreed to be not distinguishable from the North American populations of the same species. Working up the list, three of the forms, the owl, *Asio*, the gallinule or moorhen, *Gallinula*, and the coot, *Fulica*, are generally regarded as representing distinguishable subspecies. The two island ducks were for a long time regarded as distinct species, but the current opinion is that they are just well-marked subspecies of the mallard. This question of taxonomic status is very common with island populations. It is generally agreed that all populations are distinguishable on their average characters from all other populations. The convention in naming subspecies has been that all specimens should be identifiable unambiguously, or in the weaker form that three-quarters of them should be. Once all individuals are distinguishable, the taxonomist can call them a subspecies, or if he thinks the divergence has gone sufficiently far, an allopatric species. In the extreme he can give the distinct species its own generic name. The tendency in this century has been that forms that were originally described as distinct genera have become just distinct species, while forms that were originally given a specific name have frequently been demoted to subspecies.

Some examples of this process can be seen in the list of six endemic species. The Hawaiian state bird, the Ne-ne, was once put in its own genus *Neochen*. It is now generally regarded as a very distinct offshoot of the Canada goose, *Branta canadensis*, but still regarded as a distinct species. *B. canadensis* is a North American species, and is a member of a species group which has three other species in the holarctic, the brent goose, *B. bernicla*, the red-breasted goose, *B. ruficollis*, and the barnacle goose, *B. leucopsis*.

A similar case is the extinct Laysan rail, *Porzana palmeri*. Like the rails in the Tristan da Cunha group considered in Chapter 1, this was a flightless rail. Olson (1973*a*) in reviewing the rails on the Atlantic islands, pointed out that the Laysan rail was probably derived from *P. pusilla*, Bouillon's crake, which is a widespread Palaearctic and African species, and which also seems to have given rise to another endemic, flighless form, now extinct, on the mid-Atlantic island of St. Helena.

Himantopus knudseni, the Hawaiian stilt, is another species with a chequered taxonomic history. Most works of reference declare either that it is a subspecies, or not even that, of *H. himantopus*, otherwise known as *H. mexicanus*. However, Mayr and Short (1970) regard *Himantopus* worldwide as consisting of eight allopatric species, that is to say a superspecies, and that it is not possible to be sure to which one the Hawaiian form is most closely related. Other authorities regard all these allopatric species as merely subspecies of one widespread one, but that still leaves the relationship of the Hawaiian one to the other geographical forms uncertain.

Of the other four endemic species, *Corvus tropicus*, the crow, is related to a North American form, the white-necked raven. *Buteo solitarius*, the hawk, is also related to an American form. *Acrocephalus familiaris*, the millerbird with two subspecies, one on Laysan and one on Nihoa, the former unfortunately extinct, is a member of a generally Palaearctic family, but the Hawaiian forms are probably derived from a widespread Polynesian species. The millerbird is particularly interesting as an endemic species not found on any of the main islands. The Hawaiian rail (now extinct) has generally been placed in a genus by itself, *Pennula*. Olson (1973*b*) considers it to belong in the genus *Porzana*, which has species in North America as well as Palaearctic ones. It was quite a lot larger than the Laysan rail, and so presumably represents a separate immigration, where from is not clear.

The next group in Table 9.1 is the forms placed in endemic genera, and here the taxonomic problems become more acute. The flycatcher, *Chasiempis*, which has distinct subspecies on Kauai, Oahu, and Hawaii, is related to Polynesian flycatchers, but again the closest relative is uncertain. The same applies to the two genera of honeyeaters, *Moho* and *Chaetoptila*, both as to their origin and uncertain relationship. All are extinct except the Kauai species of honeyeater. The four species that were in *Moho* were in fact on different islands, and conceivably if they were still living, might have been reduced to a subspecies by some taxonomist. With such uncertainty of relationship, it is conceivable that they represented only one immigration, but they are conventionally regarded as two. In the analysis below, the assumption is made that there were two immigrations of rails, two of honeyeaters and two of ducks, making 18 in all, but each one of these might have been only one immigration, which would reduce the number to 15.

The remaining endemic genus, the thrush, *Phaeornis*, is quite closely related to the American Townsend's solitaire, *Myadestes*, a genus with several species in Central America and the West Indies as well. The Hawaiian thrush is interesting in that, with two species on Kauai, it is the only case apart from the Drepanididae in which there has clearly been speciation on the islands.

Finally in this section on the taxonomy of the Hawaiian avifauna, we come to the remarkable family, the Drepanididae. At the moment there are 40 races placed in 23 species; eight species and ten other subspecies are extinct. The most convenient list, with notes on the island occurrences and pictures, is to be found in Hawaii Audubon Society (1975). The standard account of drepanidid morphology and ecology is Amadon (1950). He discusses their relationships and comes to no definite conclusion. The group itself is undoubtedly derived from a nectar-eating bird. All species have a frilled, forked, tubular tongue, and the course of evolution is most rationally presumed to have been from a nectar-eating form to the variety of insect eaters. Unfortunately, there is rather a large number of different nectar-eating Passerines, in a series of closely related families. One likely ancestor was the family Coerebidae, but that only illustrates the difficulty in finding the closest relative: this family is now regarded as an artificial one, and its members have been distributed amongst other families. Other families which are considered by Amadon to be possible ancestors are the Thraupidae, Parulidae, Icteridae, and Vireonidae. The Coerebidae have been distributed amongst the Thraupidae and the Parulidae in recent revisions.

The drepanidids were a highly successful and very abundant family until the end of the last century. There were even two forms out on Laysan. However, with the spread of agriculture, the introduction of foreign birds, and possibly from diseases from these birds, many of them have become extremely scarce, and quite a few extinct. Probably some became extinct before specimens were collected. On the other hand, the discovery of a new species in the mountains of Maui in 1973 (as already noted on p. 17) also shows that the family has been incompletely known. Its adaptive radiation is remarkable, but adaptive radiation is not a phenomenon peculiar to islands. Unlike Darwin's finches on the Galapagos, to be considered below, the species are all readily distinguishable, and in no case can the geographical course of evolution now be disentangled.

As there were so many drepanidid species, they dominate the species lists on each of the islands. Consequently, the graph of endemic and indigenous species against area, in Fig. 8.5, largely represents the known occurrence of drepanidids. With so much uncertainty about the real number of species in this group, the slope of that relationship, about 0.3, may be representative of the activities of taxonomists, rather than of the distribution of birds in the Hawaiian archipelago.

The geographical origin of the Hawaiian avifuana is reasonably clear in Table 9.1. Hawaii is closer to North America than to any other continent; furthermore, the prevailing winds blow from America. It is therefore not surprising that more species have American rather than other relatives.

There are seven forms that may reasonably be regarded as American, *Phaeornis*, *Branta*, *Corvus*, *Buteo*, *Gallinula*, *Fulica* and *Nycticorax*. Of these the two rails, *Gallinula* and *Fulica*, are very widespread, and indeed *Gallinula* is found on both the Galapagos and Tristan. In *Fulica* the Nearctic and Palaearctic forms are close but at the moment generally put in separate species.

There is only one form clearly derived from a Palaearctic species, the Laysan rail. The Polynesian and South-West Pacific forms are the two honeyeaters, *Moho* and *Chaetoptila*, the flycatcher, *Chasiempis*, and the millerbird, *Acrocephalus*. That leaves six immigrants, of which four are clearly Holarctic, either American or Asian. Two which might be American, Australian, or even Polynesian, are the Hawaiian rail, *Porzana sandwichensis*, and the stilt, *Himantopus*. However, in most cases those taxonomists who have expressed an opinion have regarded them as American. Similarly, the four Holarctic immigrants, the original drepanidid, the two mallards, and the owl, *Asio*, also might well all have been of American origin.

So the major features of the Hawaiian avifauna are its small number of species, its predominantly North American origin, and the occurrence of archipelago speciation only in the Drepanididae and *Phaeornis*.

A comparison with Tristan

The birds of Tristan have already been discussed and tabulated in Chapter 2, Table 2.2. Regarding Tristan and Gough as two separate groups, then there are four immigrants to Tristan, two rails, *Atlantisia* and *Gallinula*, both flightless, but occurring on different islands, and the two Passerines, *Nesocichla*, a thrush, and *Neospiza*, a bunting. The origin of all four is uncertain, though a South American origin has been suggested for the Passerines and an African one for the rails. The Tristan rail, like the Gough rail, is clearly closely related to the common widespread moorhen, *Gallinula chloropus*, which occurs also in Hawaii and in the Galapagos. Both the Tristan and the Gough forms are flightless, unlike the Hawaiian and Galapagos forms. Olson (1973*a*) suggests they derive from separate immigrations. It is presumably somewhat more likely that there were two immigrations, rather than that one immigrated to, say, Tristan and then managed, before losing its flight, to be taken to Gough. Tristan is ten times nearer to Gough than to any of the continents, but it is also smaller by a much larger factor.

The rail on Inaccessible Island, *Atlantisia rogersi*, is presumably a very ancient species, as there are no other close relatives anywhere in the world. Most remarkably, Olson (1975, 1977) has described fossil remains of two other species in this genus, one on Ascension Island and another on St. Helena (Fig. 2.2). It is again surely more probable that *Atlantisia* was widespread on the continent of either Africa or South America and made three separate immigrations to these islands, rather than that these three extremely widespread isolated groups colonized one to another. This view is strengthened by the three island forms being quite markedly different in size, with the Inaccessible one being the middle-sized one.

Turning now to Gough, the bunting, *Rowettia goughensis*, is fairly clearly related to the South American and Falkland Island buntings, *Melanodera*, while its flightless moorhen has already been mentioned. Holdgate in Baird *et al.* (1965) discusses the antiquity of all these species, but can come to no clear conclusion. The oldest known rocks from Gough island are six million years old, but it is quite possible it became uninhabitable by land birds at some stage in the Pleistocene. On the islands south of the antarctic convergence (the well-marked boundary between antarctic and sub-antarctic waters) there is no native rail and only one endemic passerine, namely the pipit on South Georgia. This species *Anthus antarcticus* is derived from a widespread pipit of South America *A. correndera* (Hall and Moreau 1970) which has, *inter alia*, a subspecies on the Falkland Islands. On Macquarie Island (Fig. 1.4), which lies on the antarctic convergence South of New Zealand and Tasmania, a New Zealand rail has been introduced and established itself. This is the Weka, *Gallirallus australis*. On the same island, there are records of redpolls, *Acanthis flammea*, breeding. This is another bunting, a Holarctic form introduced into New Zealand. From New Zealand it has flown to a number of outlying islands, including Chatham, Snares, Aukland, and Campbell as well as to Macquarie (Watson 1975).

So on that evidence it might be suggested that both the Gough island forms are post-Pleistocene, that is to say less than 10 000 years old. However, their taxonomic distinctness argues rather strongly for a greater age. For the Tristan forms, a rate of immigration comparable to that on Hawaii, of one species every few hundred thousand years or even less frequently, seems perfectly reasonable.

Cocos and the Galapagos

It is almost impossible to read a book or see a film about animal life, especially about evolution, without hearing about the Galapagos. Many of us have been over-exposed to accounts of Darwin's finches. The adaptive radiation of this group is discussed more than adequately elsewhere, as was noted above. On the other hand, the taxonomic diversity, origin, and variety of the avifauna on the Galapagos is usually treated rather briefly, if at all. It is worth giving enough information here so that a comparison may be made with Hawaii.

In such a comparison, it is sensible to include the avifauna of Cocos, as it is quite likely that some of the species, and particularly Darwin's finches, have originated from there. It is, just, the nearest land to the Galapagos, as can be seen in Fig. 9.1, and is quite small, 47 km².

Cocos, like the Galapagos, is a volcanic island. It is very steep, with tall cliffs rising to some 600 m. It is densely wooded, the trees rising to more than 20 m, and has a high rainfall. A description of the island and its birds is given by Slud (1967). Fosberg and Klawe (1966) give a preliminary list of the plants; but more work on this is needed. Their list names 108 species of angiosperm, about 10 of them introduced and about 8 endemic, and 39 species of pteridophytes, none endemic.

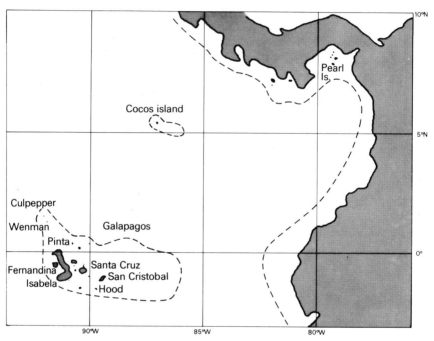

FIG. 9.1. Map showing the relation of Cocos Island and the Galapagos islands to Central and South America. The dashed line approximates the 1000 fathom (1800 m) depth contour. Five degrees on the equator are approximately 560 km.

There are only four species of land birds. Comparing this tropical island with those in the South Atlantic, there are only two species on Gough on an area slightly larger than Cocos, but Inaccessible, with an area a quarter the size, also has four species, including the two species of bunting which must have speciated on the Tristan archipelago. Cocos is a single island, and so there has been no possibility of archipelago speciation.

The four Cocos birds are a cuckoo, *Coccyzus minor* (Cuculidae), a flycatcher, *Nesotriccus ridgwayi* (Tyrannidae), a bright yellow warbler, frequently called a canary, *Dendroica petechia* (Parulidae), and the outlying member of the Darwin's finches, *Pinaroloxias inornata* (Geospizinae). *Pinaroloxias* is an endemic genus, the flycatcher is an endemic species, the warbler is, a bit doubtfully, an endemic subspecies, while the cuckoo, *C. m. ferrugineus*, is a well marked subspecies. The warbler is, indeed, put in the same subspecies as the populations on the Galapagos, but it is only a weakly differentiated form. Slud (1967) considers that the Cocos race sang much better (that is more musically, more richly, and louder) than birds in the Eastern United States, but he honourably quotes two other accounts whose authors thought the song was indistinguishable.

From this flimsy and superficial taxonomic evidence only guesses can be made about the rate of immigration. One species every ten thousand years is perhaps plausible, and with the relationship of *Pinaroloxias* to the Darwin's finches, which have undergone archipelago speciation into 14 currently recognized species, a slower average rate is possible. Slud (1976) notes there has been no turnover in the indigenous avifauna in the last 73 years. Some of those who have taken the MacArthur–Wilson theory to imply that there is a high turnover rate have been impressed by this. With the evidence from the other oceanic archipelagos of Hawaii and Tristan already considered, and the Galapagos considered below, the probability of observing a population becoming successfully established in any one period of 100 years is anything from 10 per cent down to 1 per cent down to fractions of 1 per cent. Extinction rates on oceanic islands have been high, but have largely been associated with man's activity. Cocos is uninhabited.

The land and freshwater birds of the Galapagos are listed in Table 9.2. Unlike the Hawaiian avifauna, the local populations have not had many critical ornithologists working on them, but again, as in Hawaii, quite a number of the local races are regarded as being in distinct species. The taxonomy used in Harris (1973a) is shown in the table.

On Hawaii, only two of the immigrants had undergone speciation on the islands, namely the original drepanidid and the thrush, *Phaeornis*. On Tristan, one immigrant, the bunting, *Neospiza*, has speciated producing, like the Hawaiian thrush, a mere two species. On the Galapagos, there is again only one form that has produced sympatric species, the ancestral Darwin's finch. The next largest taxonomic change comes in the mocking bird, where four endemic species of an endemic genus *Nesomimus* are recognized, but all are allopatric.

One feature which is apparent in comparing Tables 9.1 and 9.2 is that certain species are particularly good dispersers. The short-eared

Table 9.2. Breeding land and freshwater birds of the Galapagos

Endemic subfamily	Geospizinae	Darwin's finches. 13 species
Endemic genus	*Nesomimus*	Galapagos mockingbird. 4 allopatric species
Endemic species	*Butorides sundevalli*	Lava heron. *B. striatus* may occur, may hybridize
	Buteo galapagoensis	Galapagos hawk
	Laterallus spilonotus	Galapagos rail
	Zenaida galapagoensis	Galapagos dove
	Myiarchus magnirostris	Large-billed flycatcher
	Progne modesta	Galapagos martin
Indigenous species	*Ardea herodias*	Great blue heron
	Anas bahamensis	White-cheeked pintail (duck)
	Neocrex erythrops	Paint-billed crake
	Gallinula chloropus	Common gallinule or moorhen
	Haematopus ostralegus	Oystercatcher
	Himantopus himantopus	Common stilt
	Coccyzus melacoryphus	Dark-billed cuckoo
	Tyto alba	Barn owl
	Asio flammeus	Short-eared owl
	Pyrocephalus rubinus	Vermilion flycatcher
	Dendroica petechia	Yellow warbler

From Harris 1973*a*.

owl, *Asio flammeus*, the moorhen, *Gallinula chloropus*, and the stilt, *Himantopus*, occur on both Pacific archipelagos. On the other hand compared with Hawaii, the Galapagos hawk and duck (*Buteo, Anas*) are derived from different American species, while the two Galapagos herons, the endemic *Butorides striatus* and the great blue heron are in different genera from the night heron, *Nycticorax*, on Hawaii. Nevertheless, the general statement that hawks, owls, ducks, herons, waders and, particularly rails are, even as birds go, particularly good dispersers, is clearly shown in these tables.

Two species not listed in Table 9.2 because they are not land or freshwater birds, should perhaps be mentioned, as they are striking members of the Galapagos avifauna. The first is the Galapagos penguin, *Spheniscus mendiculus*, the only tropical member of an otherwise Antarctic and sub-Antarctic family, the only penguin to breed on the Equator. The other is the flightless cormorant, *Nannopterum harrisi*, already mentioned (p. 44) found only on the islands of Fernandina and Isabela, with a total population of about 800 pairs (Harris 1973*a*).

Darwin's finches

The adaptive radiation of Darwin's finches is so familiar that it will not be recounted here. It includes a clear example of allopatric speciation, in the tree finch, *Camarhynchus*, as is recounted in the classical account of Lack (1947). Lack (1969c, 1971) has also listed and recounted a variety of cases of apparent changes in size associated with competition between different species. One of the most famous is the size shift in the ground finch, *Geospiza*, on Crossman and Daphne Islands. Lack's histogram is reproduced in almost every text book on evolution, but perhaps one comment is needed here. Both these two populations were intermediate between *G. fortis* and *G. fuliginosa*. Lack records 42 specimens from Daphne, but only 16 from Crossman. However, Harris (1973a) states that the many individuals that he has seen on Daphne are 'mostly assignable to *G. fortis* and *G. fuligonosa*', so the intermediate population measured by Lack appears to have disappeared. On Crossman, Grant (1975) records the capture of four more specimens consistent with Lack's measurements, although the measurements are not in fact given.

One topic that perhaps ties the study of the Darwin's finches together, and is still unresolved, is the question of what the ancestral species looked like. Lack (1947) following some taxonomic authorities, regarded the Geospizinae as finches, i.e., members of the family Fringillidae. He thought the most ancestral form was *Geospiza difficilis*, a ground finch, which certainly has a generally finch-like appearance. Later (Lack 1968b) he opined that the group could equally well have been derived through a warbler-like form.

About the only safe statement that can be made about the Geospizinae is that they are part of the confusing assemblage known as nine-primaried oscines. The passerine birds are divided, primarily on the structure of the pharynx, into oscines and sub-oscines, the latter mostly South American and including the Tyrannidae. Amongst the oscines, the song birds, there is a group of closely-related families, mostly centred on North America, which can be distinguished by their wing feathers as nine-primaried oscines. These include not only the Vireonidae (vireos), Parulidae (wood warblers), Icteridae (American orioles, etc.) and Thraupidae (Tanagers) (any one of which could be ancestral to the Hawaiian Drepanididae), but also a series of finch-like families, with heavily built bills, the Estrildidae (waxbills), Ploceidae (weavers), Emberizidae (buntings) and the Fringillidae with two subfamilies Fringillinae (chaffinches) and Carduelinae (other finches). If the Geospizinae were derived from a finch-like ancestor, it seems likely to have been an Emberizid (Tordoff 1954; Sibley 1970). But if the ancestor were warbler-like, then any one of the first four families, the possible ancestors of the Drepanididae, is more plausible.

Harris (1973b) makes the firm suggestion that all Darwin's finches can be derived through the Cocos finch, *Pinaroloxias inornata*, and goes further and suggests that that species might well be derived from the Bananaquit, *Coereba flaveola*. This is a widespread species in South America, occurs throughout the West Indies except in Cuba, and is also found in parts of Central America. Its ecology is discussed by Lack (1976). As can be seen from its generic name, it was once in the Coerebidae. However, as was noted in discussing the origin of drepanidids, the Coerebidae is no longer recognized as a valid family, and the Bananaquit is regarded as a Parulid.

Suggesting that *Pinaroloxias* is the ancestral form, or close to the ancestral form, makes very good sense of the evolution of the Galapagos forms. Taking Lack's (1947) suggestion that a finch might form the ancestor, leads to *Certhidea* and *Pinaroloxias* being placed on an early branch, and not tied in with the other forms. This rather bald statement requires some explication.

Habitats and Darwin's finches

It is well known that the Galapagos are volcanic islands formed along the boundary separating two plates, the Cocos Plate and the Nazca Plate (see Fig. 1.1). In this respect they are like Tristan da Cunha and the other islands along the mid-Atlantic ridge, and they are certainly in the geological sense oceanic. They are also oceanic in the straight physical sense, being about 1000 km both from the coast of Ecuador, directly to the east, and 750 km from the isolated island of Cocos, to the north-east. Cocos, in its turn, is 500 km from Central America. The Galapagos Islands vary greatly in size (see endpapers). The largest is Isabela, referred to as Albemarle in the older works, 4670 km², 130 km long, with five major volcanoes strung along it. At the other extreme, the two isolated northern islands of Culpepper and Wenman are both about 2.5 km². As can be seen in Fig. 1.9, none of the peaks is as high as 2000 m, though some of these on Isabela get close to that height, but a more typical height for a Galapagos peak is 1000 m.

Apart from the mangroves, which are mostly confined to the west coast of Isabela and the island of Fernandina, the vegetation can be divided, somewhat arbitrarily, into three zones. The highest, at over 500 m above sea level, is open and grassy, with few endemic plants and no endemic birds. It is suggested that this habitat is less than 10 000 years old (Colinvaux 1972). The humid middle zone is forested, dominated by trees of the endemic genus *Scalesia* which are giant sun flowers. This zone has a foggy lichen forest at its top, and grades not particularly sharply into the low coastal strip which is essentially a desert: an arid zone dominated by prickly pear trees, of which there are several endemic species in the widespread genus *Opuntia*.

The evolution of Darwin's finches is readily comprehended if the original one were a species like *Pinaroloxias inornata*, from Cocos, which first established itself in the *Scalesia* forest. If this is correct, from this immigrant, evolution has gone in a variety of directions, and has the fairly common characteristic that evolution affecting one character markedly, has tended to leave other characters unchanged. *Pinaroloxias* is a dimorphic species, with a black male and a rather brown speckly female like the European blackbird *Turdus merula*. Slud (1967) gives a series of quotations about the behaviour of *Pinaroloxias*. Different ornithologists have described it as like a warbler; like a titmouse; with the habits of a ground-feeding finch combined with those of a tree-feeding warbler; with the habits of a honeycreeper. Slud himself says:

> the bill of the bird in life impressed me as unaesthetically long for the bodily proportions. Exploring anything and everything in its everlasting search for food, the bird kept the bill constantly employed as a tactile tool, at times even nosing it along. In the trees, the bird inserted its bill between the petals to extract the nectar from the bases of flowers. It probed the broken ends of branches, alternately picked and peered into them with one eye. It picked at bark or peeled it off, or flaked away loose bits while hugging a branch or side of a trunk. Clinging to the edge of a leaf or hanging horizontally upside down, the bird passes its half-opened beak along the rolled edges of a dried bromeliaceous whorl. . . . Afoot, at times in the exposed scree at one end of the beach, it both peered at and probed the pits and small holes in the rocks. Using its beak, the bird pried and turned over fallen leaves, fruits, and sticks, and levered up muddy small stones in mangrove-like low places. It obtained tiny seeds by passing the bill along grass stems, pecked at fallen fruits, picked apart blossoms, and it steadily gathered up specks of spilled corn meal. Only once did I see a bird with an earthworm. As a species it was hopeless at aerial sorties and usually unsuccessful though persistent in its attempt at simple fly-catching flutters. . . . In the trees, the clinging, hanging, hopping, creeping birds often flick the wings and tail as do warblers and some tanagers.

From this quotation it can be seen that *Pinaroloxias* has the habits, to some degree, of all the specializations seen on the Galapagos archipelago in its congeners.

Bearing in mind the rule of differential rates of change, it is not surprising to find that the warbler finch, *Certhidea olivacea*, is the bird closest to *Pinaroloxias* in general shape and habits, and the most different in external colour. *Certhidea* occurs in both the arid and humid zones of the Galapagos, and has formed nine subspecies, though there is only one species in the genus. The distribution of subspecies in this and the other forms are shown, for convenience of reference, in Table 9.3.

Table 9.3. *Distribution and subspecies of Geospizinae on the main Galapagos Islands*

	Large central				Small central				Medium outlying				Small outlying			
	James	Santa Cruz	Isabela	Fernandina	Jervis	Seymour	Duncan	Barrington	Pinta	Marchena	San Cristobal	Floreana	Culpepper	Wenman	Tower	Hood
Geospiza																
magnirostris	A	A	A	A	A	A	A	A	A	A	—	B	—	A	A	—
fortis	A	A	A	A	A	A	A	A	A	A	A	A	—	—	—	—
fuliginosa	A	A	A	A	A	A	A	A	A	A	A	A	—	—	—	A
difficilis	A	A	A	A	—	—	—	—	B	—	—	C	D	D	B	—
scandens	A	B	B	—	A	B	B	B	C	D	E	B	—	—	—	—
conirostris	—	—	—	—	—	—	—	—	—	—	—	—	A	B?	B	C
Platyspiza																
crassirostris	A	A	A	A	A	—	A	—	A	A	A	A	—	—	—	—
Camarhynchus																
psittacula	A	A	B	B	A	A	A–B	A	C	C	—	A	—	—	—	—
pauper	—	—	—	—	—	—	—	—	—	—	—	A	—	—	—	—
parvulus	A	A	A	A	A	A	A	A	A	—	B	A	—	—	—	—
(*Cactospiza*)																
pallidus	A	A	B	B	A	A	A	—	—	—	C	—	—	—	—	—
heliobates	—	—	A	A	—	—	—	—	—	—	—	—	—	—	—	—
Certhidea																
olivacea	A	A	A	A	A	A	A	B	C	C	D	E	F	F	G	H
No. of resident species	10	10	11	10	9	8	9	6	9	7	7	10	3	3–4	4	3

In each species, a different letter is used for each subspecies.
After Lack 1969, island names from Harris 1973*a*.

Evolving in the other direction, towards more finch-like habits, but remaining in the humid zone, are the species in *Camarhynchus* and *Platyspiza*. The vegetarian tree finch, *Platyspiza crassirostris*, has evolved the heaviest beak, and is nearest the postulated ancestor in plumage. The two species in the subgenus *Cactospiza* have evolved fastest in plumage, and remained probing insectivorous birds. These two are the classic species of tool-using birds, both using thorns and other spikes to dig out insects, thus evolving towards woodpecker-like habits.

The ground finches in *Geospiza* are the most like *Pinaroloxias* in plumage, and are least like it in bill shape, habits, and habitat. Most of them are confined to the arid zone, but the one exception is the species that Lack suggested was the nearest to the ancestor. This is *Geospiza difficilis*, which lives in the humid zone in the central islands and has distinct subspecies in the arid zone on the small outlying islands. The most interesting subspecies is the nominate one which occurs on the islands of Pinta (Abingdon) and Tower. On the former it occurs in the humid zone, in the latter in the arid zone, being a remarkable example of a single subspecies with different ecological niches in different parts of its range.

Evolutionary history taken this way makes simple good sense, and fits in with what we have already seen in the Hawaiian Drosophilidae, that different biological systems in one species evolve at different speeds. Trying to start the family tree with *Geospiza difficilis* leads to obvious difficulties in explaining why *Pinaroloxias* and *Certhidea* are rather similar in habits but quite different in appearance.

Other vertebrates on the Galapagos

Oceanic islands are characterized, in general, but having no amphibia or terrestrial mammals. Many, of course, have bats, and the Galapagos has one species, *Lasiurus brachyotis*. Seals or sea lions are frequently found, and there is an endemic subspecies of the South American fur seal, *Arctocephalus australis*. Much more surprising, there are endemic species of rice rats, which it is supposed have reached the Galapagos on rafts of vegetation from the South American coast. The habitat of rice rats in South America, along fast-flowing rivers, makes this explanation plausible. Two allopatric forms in the mainland genus and subgenus *Oryzomys* are found on Barrington and San Cristobal (Chatham). There is an endemic subgenus of *Oryzomys*, *Nesoryzomys*, with allopatric forms on Fernandina (Narborough), James, Baltra, and with two forms on the island of Santa Cruz (Indefatigable). There is also an extinct form from Santa Cruz, *Megalomys curioi*. All this suggests two, if not three, separate immigrations from the continent.

Reptiles are frequently found on oceanic islands, and the land and marine iguanas of the Galapagos, *Conolophus* with two allopatric species, *pallidus* and *subcristatus* and *Amblyrhynchus cristatus*, are famous. Less well known is a small group of snakes in the genus *Dromicus* of the family Boidae. Snakes are absent from the five small northern islands, but are found on all the other main islands. These snakes are 60–90 cm long, brown, and either spotted or striped. Two sympatric species are found on each of the islands of Fernandina, Isabela, James, and Santa Cruz (see Thornton 1971). There are also lava lizards, *Tropidurus*, and giant tortoises, *Geochelone*, in each case with only one form per island.

This small number of immigrants and the speciation on the archipelago in rice rats and snakes is all consistent with a very low rate of immigration, and so of turnover. In this, as in other ways, the Galapagos are typical oceanic islands.

Anolis in the West Indies

From the birds of the two famous archipelagos in the Pacific, we turn now to a different group, living on an archipelago of quite different form, and showing some quite new phenomena. These are lizards in the genus *Anolis* in the West Indies. The distribution of the islands, the submarine banks on which they stand, and the number of species in *Anolis* are shown in Fig. 9.2. There are two main groups of islands, the Greater Antilles, of which Puerto Rico and Jamaica are the smallest, and the Lesser Antilles forming a chain running from Puerto Rico down to the South American coast.

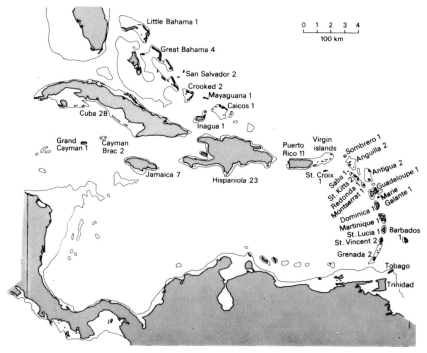

FIG. 9.2.   Islands and banks in the West Indies, contour at 200 m depth. The number next to each bank is the number of native *Anolis* species. (Data from Williams 1969.)

Anolis are small green or brown lizards, the males in some species having brightly coloured, inflatable neck sacs. They are more or less the only diurnal arboreal lizards in most of the West Indies, though other lizards are present (Williams 1972). The genus is widespread in Central and South America and one species spreads up into the United

States, though that, *carolinensis*, has clearly been derived from an Antillean origin, and forms another rare example, with *Scaptomyza*, of the
invasion of a continent from an island (Williams 1969). *Anolis* are
insectivorous, the male is larger than the female, and growth is continuous so there is much more variation in size in a population than
there is in a bird population.

   Taxonomically, the distribution of species is better taken by banks,
rather than by islands. The geological history of the Caribbean is
complex, but as a bold, possibly over-bold, statement these banks
became flooded about 7000 years ago (Lighty, Macintyre, and Stuckenrath 1979). It can be seen in Fig. 9.2 that small banks only have one
or two species on them, though the larger Antillean islands have many
more than that. Speciation and its associated evolution has taken place
on the large banks, but for the smaller islands this has taken place
between banks, a phenomenon that may tell us something about the
island size and degree of isolation needed for speciation to be possible.
On the larger banks there is the possibility that speciation could take
place to some extent by allopatric speciation on the small islands round
the banks, but it seems rather more likely to have taken place in isolated
parts on these very large islands.

   Another way of looking at this pattern of speciation is to examine
species–area curves on the Greater Antilles and neighbouring small
islands, and on the Lesser Antilles. This is done in Fig. 9.3 where it can
be seen that the relationship on the Greater Antilles is the normal one,
but that there is no relationship whatever between number of species

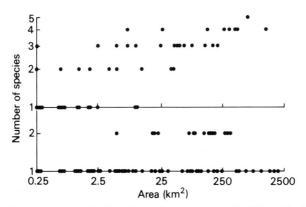

FIG. 9.3. Species–area relationships for *Anolis* in the West Indies. Upper
plot: islands round the Greater Antilles, showing a normal species–area
relationship. Lower plot: Lesser Antilles, Bahamas not on the Great Bahama
bank and other isolated islands. No island has more than two species, the
largest and the smallest only one. (Modified from Rand 1969.)

and area on the Lesser Antilles, and each bank only has one or two species.

A great deal of work has been done on the morphology, cytology, isozymic variation, ecology, and behaviour of *Anolis*, but it is only possible here to sketch a few points of interest in relation to general phenomena on islands. Herpetologists divide the hundreds of species of *Anolis* on the continent into alpha and beta types distinguished by several characters. The simplest is that the distal (autonomic) caudal vertebrae are without transverse processes in alphas but have them in betas. The difference in karyotype is perhaps more important (Williams 1969). From these hundreds there appear to have been only three stocks that have managed to invade the Antilles. A beta stock, probably starting in Yucatan, may have gone by way of Jamaica to Cuba to form the species *sagrei* and its relatives, which seem to be particularly good at colonizing. The other two invasions are apparently two separate alpha stocks. The first one, possibly from South America, appears to have invaded straight to Puerto Rico right across the Caribbean. From this stock, through *cristatellus*, there has been an invasion up to the Bahamas, side-stepping Hispaniola, and an invasion down into the Lesser Antilles, as the *bimaculatus* group discussed below. Another evolutionary branch from Puerto Rico invaded Hispaniola and so to Cuba where one of the species is *carolinensis*, already mentioned as the species that has, from Cuba, invaded the continental United States. The third invasion, another alpha from South America, has gone to the southern Lesser Antilles, to form the *roquet* group, also discussed below.

On the small islands round the Greater Antilles, that is to say the Bahamas, the Cayman Islands and some others, the species are derived from *sagrei, carolinensis, cristatellus,* and also from two other species not yet mentioned. The first is *distichus*, part of the first alpha group which evolved on Hispaniola, while there is also one invasion of the Cayman Islands from a beta *Anolis, grahami,* of Jamaica.

The phylogeny and adaptive radiation of the eleven species of the *cristatellus* group on the Puerto Rican bank has been discussed by Williams (1972). One species, *roosvelti*, occurs in shade in the tops of large trees on the island of Culebra. The other ten species occur in parts of Puerto Rico. Table 9.4 gives an indication of how these ten species separate by habitat.

Evolution of the two distinct groups on the Lesser Antilles is a fine example of the effect of isolation on species formation. Those islands that have two species have one large in size and one small. In the northern group of islands, the *bimaculatus* group has spread from *cristatellus* on Puerto Rico, through *acutus* on the island of St. Croix which is on a small isolated bank to the south-east of Puerto Rico (the Virgin

Table 9.4. Adaptive radiation of the *Anolis cristatellus* group on the island of Puerto Rico

	Large trees, canopies	Large trees, trunks	Small trees	Bushes	Cacti
Shade	*evermanni*	*gundlachi*		*krugi*	
	occultus (small)				
Sun + shade	*cuvieri* (large)				
Sun	*stratulus*	*cristatellus*	*cooki*	*pulchellus*	*poncensis*

The eleventh species on the bank, *roosvelti* is allopatric, on the island of Culebra. It is the largest species of the eleven, and occurs in the shade in the canopies of large trees. Data from Williams 1972.

Islands to the east being on the same bank as Puerto Rico). A possible phylogeny from *actutus* is shown in Fig. 9.4, which follows Lazell (1972). This phylogeny is based on a variety of morphological information: a slightly different phylogeny can be derived from isozyme frequencies. The Hawaiian Drosophilidae phylogenies in Chapter 8 showed clearly that phylogenies based essentially on principles of parsimony are likely to be wrong in some details, so the difference between these two phylogenies for the *bimaculatus* group need not concern us. The general pattern is of anagenic evolution (Fig. 7.1) on islands, coupled with dispersal to other islands, occasionally leading to the formation of two sympatric species.

Lazell's phylogeny for the *roquet* group is shown in Fig. 9.5, and again differs in details from that derived from isozymes. All authorities are agreed, however, that the first stock in this group is that on the island of St. Lucia, which is in the middle of the set of islands occupied by this group.

It is a striking phenomenon that the *roquet* and *bimaculatus* groups are not found together on the same island, and the whole of the evolution in both groups gives the strong appearance that establishment has been severely limited by interspecific competition, but the mechanism of this is unknown. Holt's (1977) term, apparent competition, seems particularly appropriate in this case.

The geographical course of evolution in the Lesser Antilles is surprising. Who would have guessed that the ancestry of *bimaculatus* was from South America to Puerto Rico to St. Croix to the St. Kitts bank, and then to Saba, the Anguilla bank, the Antigua bank and back to the St. Kitts bank (Fig. 9.4)? Or that *roquet* is descended from a South American form via St. Lucia, St. Vincent, Grenada, and Barbados before reaching Martinique (Fig. 9.5)? There seems no reason to postulate extinction of other forms at any stage. Williams (1969) points out that

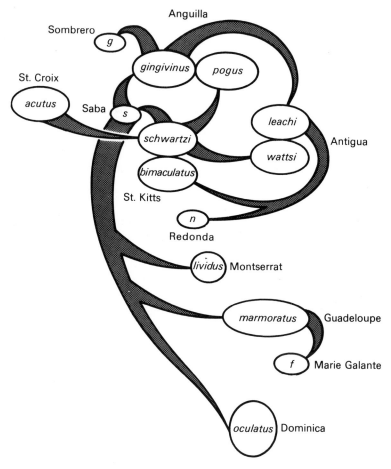

F IG. 9.4. Possible phylogeny of the *Anolis bimaculatus* group on the northern island banks of the Lesser Antilles. Names of the banks as in Fig. 9.2. *g* = *gingivinus*, *s* = *sabanus*, *n* = *nubilus*, *f* = *ferreus*. The area of the ellipses indicates the relative size of the land areas. (Modified from Lazell 1972 and Gorman and Kim 1976.)

the characters of a successful colonizing species are unusual, requiring an ecologically versatile species from an open habitat, but apparently no unusual life-history characteristics. The pattern in *Anolis* is of rare successful colonizations, producing populations which appear to compete successfully with many, but not all, succeeding invasions. Niche differentiation is important. The number of species is a consequence of these processes rather than of turnover as envisaged in the MacArthur–Wilson theory (Williams 1969).

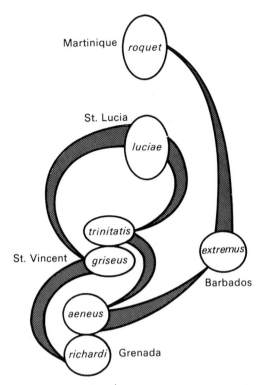

Martinique *roquet*

St. Lucia *luciae*

trinitatis

St. Vincent *griseus*

extremus

Barbados

aeneus

richardi Grenada

FIG. 9.5.   Possible phylogeny of the *Anolis roquet* group on the southern island banks of the Lesser Antilles. Names of the banks as in Fig. 9.2. (Modified from Lazell 1972 and Yang, Soulé, and Gorman 1974.)

Conclusions about archipelagos

All these studies on archipelago groups, whether of reptiles, birds or insects, strengthen the view that oceanic islands can be described as those on which evolution is faster than immigration. With the extensive disturbance on these islands by man and the introduction of many foreign species, extinctions have been common, and estimates of natural turnover from direct observation are difficult to derive. The evidence from the pattern of species formation, though, is that success-ful immigration quite commonly occurs only in periods measured in tens of thousands of years. In the Hawaiian picture-wing *Drosophila*, it seems inter-island immigrations occur on average every 25 000 years or so, but the formation of new species is faster than that. In such a situation, predictions of MacArthur and Wilson's theory about an equilibrium from immigration and extinction seem scarcely relevant. The number of species on an archipelago is determined by evolution as much as by immigration, and evolution is not at an equilibrium.

PART 4

The Structure of Island Communities

10 Ecological processes on islands: competition and feeding relationships

Up to this point, populations of species on islands have largely been considered as independent variables; their interactions through competition, predation, and other effects have been taken as secondary. In this last section some of the evidence for the effect of interactions between species on the structure of communities on islands is examined. In this chapter we look at some evidence for the importance of interactions between members of the same trophic level, and between members of different trophic levels. In the next chapter, the nature of island communities will be discussed.

A central topic in island ecology is the relationship of species to area. Three phenomena have been considered so far which could lead to the observed regularity in this relationship. The first is environmental heterogeneity and its associated habitat diversity. For this explanation there is no strong need to consider the interaction of species; the first task is to relate the set of ecological competences to the range of habitats and niches available. The second explanation is the set of phenomena, immigration, extinction, and the resulting turnover of species, considered by MacArthur and Wilson. In this theory, as was seen in Chapter 4, the original exposition was far from clear about what interactions were presumed, and in particular to what extent interaction had any influence on extinction rate. Wilson's later elaborations of the theory suggested an earlier noninteractive state, then a reduction of species as interactions became important. The third explanation is the effect of evolution, and in particular the niche shift and speciation associated with the new circumstances found on islands and, in the long run, with the adaptive radiation of groups. This effect is a major component leading to the species–area relationships in Hawaii shown in Fig. 8.5. All three explanations will generally be involved in any particular species–area relationship. In none of the three is the importance or otherwise of strong interactions between pairs of ecologically connected species clear.

Ecological interactions can perhaps be divided, at least for purposes of discussion, into two sets. One is interactions between species in the same trophic level, often subsumed under the heading of competition. The other is interactions up and down food chains, between plants and the herbivores feeding on them, between predators and prey, between parasites and hosts. There is no single accepted term for these kinds of interactions, so for convenience I shall call the latter set 'predation', though some of the examples will, in fact, be of herbivores and plants.

In the evolutionary examples considered, the major ecological effect has been in the change of the niche, again using that term somewhat loosely, of the species evolving. Examples from Hawaii and the Galapagos in particular suggest that, where sufficiently detailed studies are made, species groups have evolved by niche separation, which is perhaps no more than another way of saying that evolution involves adaptive radiation. Lack in particular was keen to emphasize the changes of phenotype associated with the presence of other species. This results in the avoidance of competition, and does not suggest that competition is a major force in the day-to-day working of island ecosystems (Williamson 1972). Only in *Anolis* on the Lesser Antilles (p. 217) do the number and distribution of species suggest that competition is important, and even here it suggests more that competition prevents the establishment of new immigrants than that competition is involved as an important interaction in ecosystems.

One difficulty in discussing the importance of ecological interactions on island communities is that ecologists hold widely different opinions on the importance of such interactions in any community. Some regard competition as almost self-evidently structuring communities; others regard strong competition as exceptional, because it is generally diminished by the pressure of natural selection. It is certainly difficult to detect competition just from the study of natural distributions (Williamson 1972). Similarly, observational evidence for the importance of food-chain effects is difficult to interpret, even with the aid of refined quantitative techniques such as k-factor analysis. The suggestion has, however, often been made that the effects of competition can be seen in the taxonomic structure of island communities, and this will be examined at end of the discussion on competition.

Experimental evidence is distinctly easier to interpret, and the best, indeed almost the only, experimental evidence for competition on islands comes from mammals. Some of the experiments considered below have been deliberate, and thus inevitably rather short term. Others come from accidental or natural introductions, or deliberate introductions for other reasons. These are longer term, but, as will be seen, lack some of the information needed for clear-cut conclusions.

Competition and the distribution of mammals on islands

Terrestrial mammals are, on the whole, rather bad dispersers. It has already been noted that many mammals that occur on islands around the British Isles have been taken there by man. Because of this, accidental and natural experimental situations have been set up, which throw some light on the importance of competition. Enough is known to be worth mentioning in three groups: voles, shrews, and hares (Rodentia, Cricetidae, Microtinae; Insectivora, Soricidae; and Lagomorpha, Leporidae respectively).

Before considering these examples it is perhaps worth noting that there are at least two distinguishable schools of thought amongst ecologists about competition. One school likes to think of competition in terms of processes, uses terms such as resources, scramble, contest and so on, and usually dislikes identifying a process as being competition unless the mechanism by which it is brought about is clearly understood. The other school thinks of competition more in terms of consequences (outcome) and defines competition as a negative interaction between two species, such that where one is more prevalent than the other is less prevalent, and *vice versa*, always bearing in mind the need to take account of the effect of varying habitats in such observed population densities. For this school, competition is any process which produces this negative–negative interaction. The differences between these two schools have led to much misunderstanding, and Holt (1977) has suggested the useful term 'apparent competition', for competition as seen by the second school.

A good example of what Holt has in mind, which indeed he uses himself, is discussed below in relation to hares. In many cases the two approaches to the concept of competition lead to the same result but there is no guarantee that this will be so, and the different interpretations that can be put on the term should always be borne in mind when considering the importance of competition either in ecology or evolution.

Voles

In the Holarctic there are two common genera of voles, *Microtus* and *Clethrionomys*. *Microtus* is typically found in grassland, has more complex teeth than *Clethrionomys* to cope with this rather abrasive type of plant, and is a large genus of 50 or more species, though only a few occur on islands. *Clethrionomys*, on the other hand, is much more typically a woodland species, the common British form being know as the bank vole. There are only three species in this genus in Europe, and perhaps another four or five elsewhere in the world.

The distribution of voles on islands has led many naturalists to suppose that some pairs of species are in competition. On the continent of Europe there are two common species, *Microtus arvalis* and *M. agrestis*, a rather smaller species and usually the rarer of the two. In Britain only *M. agrestis* is found, but *M. arvalis* is found on certain islands where *M. agrestis* is absent. These include Orkney (where it was almost certainly introduced, Berry 1977, Corbet and Southern 1977), Guernsey in the Channel Islands, and Île d'Yeu and Île de Noirmoutier off the west coast of France. Figure 10.1 is a map showing these islands off the West European coast and others that will be considered.

Although *M. arvalis* is the common vole over much of Europe, it has a distinctly more south-eastern distribution than *M. agrestis*, and, for instance, does not occur either in Brittany or Northern Denmark. Were it not for these island populations, it would be tempting to say that *M. arvalis* does not occur in Britain for the same reason that it appears not to occur in Brittany, namely that the climate is not suitable for it. The existence of a flourishing form on the Orkneys belies this. It is possible that *M. arvalis* is not able to survive in competition with *M. agrestis* under the climatic conditions found in Britain, rather than that it is the climatic conditions themselves which limit it.

The importance of chance, and man-assisted migrations, for the occurrence of voles on these islands needs to be emphasized. There are, for instance, no voles on the islands of Ouessant, Alderney, Herm, Sark, the Scilly Isles, Lundy, Shetland, many of the Hebrides or, until recently, Ireland (Arnold 1978).

The distribution of *Clethrionomys glareolus*, the only British species in its genus, is even more suggestive of competition. Both it and *Microtus* are found on the large island of Skye. *Clethrionomys* has been introduced into Ireland and is now spreading (Arnold 1978; Crichton 1974). In these cases it is apparently found in its normal habitats. *Clethrionomys* occurs without *Microtus* on, from north to south, Raasay near Skye, Skomer off the Pembrokeshire coast, Jersey in the Channel Islands, and Belle Île off the French coast (Fig. 10.1). On Jersey, Le Sueur (1976) writes 'it is in both the woodlands and hedgebanks of the interior as well as rough grasslands and gorse of the coast'. On Skomer, which is just a few kilometres from Skokholm and about three times as large, there is no woodland, but there is rather more knee-high vegetation than on Skokholm, bracken (*Pteridium aquilinum*), brambles (*Rubus fruticosus* agg.) and so on. Nevertheless, the habitat on Skomer is more like a typical *Microtus* habitat, and the success of *Clethrionomys* on Skomer appears to be a case of niche shift in the absence of competition. The house mouse, *Mus musculus*, on Skokholm possibly shows a similar niche shift, though probably because of the absence of *Apodemus sylvaticus*,

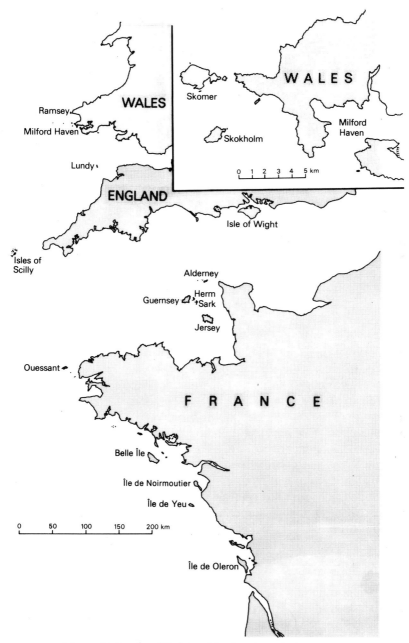

Fig. 10.1. Map of islands off Wales, England, and France. Inset : islands off the mouth of Milford Haven, Pembrokeshire, Wales.

the long-tailed field mouse, rather than *Microtus* as was noted in Chapter 6. Grant studied the possible competition between *Microtus* and *Clethrionomys*; he summarized his various experiments (Grant 1972). For instance, one 17-week experiment involved three 0.4 ha enclosures; others involved laboratory tests of behaviour. His results are as satisfactory as one could hope for in short experiments: it seems clear that *Clethrionomys* is at a disadvantage to *Microtus* in grassland, and *Microtus* is at a disadvantage to *Clethrionomys* in woodland.

Some distributional evidence for this comes from the study of small islands off North America. The islands off Europe tend to be grassy rather than wooded, and so there the presence of *Clethrionomys* suggests a release from competition, whereas off the eastern North American coast, in the maritime provinces of Canada and down into New England, islands are typically forested, and so it is the presence of *Microtus* on these islands that has suggested the escape from competition with *Clethrionomys*. The evidence for this has been summarized by Cameron (1964). Essentially the situation is that there is again one species of *Microtus* and one of *Clethrionomys*. *Microtus* is now *M. pennsylvanicus*. *Clethrionomys* is known as *C. gapperi*, but Grant (1974) has in fact managed to hybridize this experimentally with *C. glareolus*. On Newfoundland, which is, of course, far from being a small island (109 000 km²), islands in the Gulf of St. Lawrence, and small islands off the coast of Maine, both in forest and in grassland, the only vole is *Microtus*. *Clethrionomys* is found with *Microtus* on Deer Island (72 km²) and Mount Desert Island (280 km²) off Maine.

This system has been studied experimentally on small islands, of about 1 ha, off the coast of Maine by Crowell (1973) and Crowell and Pimm (1976). The islands have both wooded and grassy habitats but only *Microtus* is found. Introducing *Clethrionomys* displaces *Microtus* from the wooded habitats, but the *Clethrionomys* died out in some cases after two or three years, and some introductions failed to take at all. Both reproduction and survival of *Clethrionomys* on the small islands were poor. The experiments also involved the introduction of another cricetid, *Peromyscus maniculatus*. It seems that individual *Clethrionomys* could survive a year or two in the wooded parts of the islands, and exclude the other two species, but that permanent populations could not be maintained. In the absence of *Clethrionomys*, the other two species occurred in woodland. As far as this evidence goes, the occurrence of *Microtus* in woodland is a niche shift in the absence of a competitor, but the failure of some introduced *Clethrionomys* is unexplained, which is not surprising as they were only studied for short periods each year. Were *Clethrionomys* to be introduced to Newfoundland, it would presumably survive, as that island is well within its geographical range (Banfield 1977).

Shrews

The distributions of European shrews are good examples of the odd distributions on islands that are found in groups with poor dispersal ability. Whether the distributions have anything to do with competition is another matter.

There are five shrews listed as British, two of them only in the Channel Islands and the Isles of Scilly. The three in Britain are the water shrew, *Neomys fodiens*, and two terrestrial shrews, the common shrew, *Sorex araneus*, and the pygmy shrew, *S. minutus*. On Britain, the common shrew is much commoner than the pygmy, and both occur in a great variety of habitats (Corbet and Southern 1977). The other two species, in *Crocidura*, are considered below.

The two species of *Sorex* have both been found on a variety of small islands round Britain (Arnold 1978) such as Gigha, the southern-most of the Inner Hebrides, Great Cumbrae in the Clyde, and Skomer off Pembrokeshire (Fig. 10.1). On some small islands only the common shrew has been found. Examples include Ulva, off the west coast of Mull, and Ramsey off Pembrokeshire. The pygmy shrew has a much wider distribution, and is the only species found in Orkney (Fig. 6.3), the Isle of Man and Ireland, and on several small islands off the Irish coast. It is also the species found on, amongst other small islands, Ailsa Craig in the Clyde and Lundy in the Bristol Channel (Fig. 10.1). Until recently only the pygmy was known from any of the Outer Hebrides, but there is now a record of the common shrew near Stornoway on Lewis. Only the pygmy shrew is known from North and South Uist, Benbecula, and Barra and from the Inner Hebridean islands of Rhum, Coll, and Tiree. Neither species is known from Shetland.

The odd feature about this distribution is that the rarer species on Britain is far more widespread on small islands, and is the one found in Ireland and the Isle of Man. There are three possible explanations, not necessarily alternatives. The first is that *S. minutus* is better at dispersing naturally across water. The second is that *S. minutus* reached some of the islands, particularly Ireland, over dry land at the end of the last glaciation. The third is that *S. minutus* is more readily dispersed by man. None of these explanations is particularly satisfactory. Both shrews have a high metabolic rate and require a constant supply of food; they need to feed every hour, and die rapidly from starvation in live traps. It therefore seems unlikely that either would disperse easily over water, by swimming or rafting. The dry land explanation could also be held to apply to the two mustelid carnivores, the stoat, *Mustela erminea*, which is found in Ireland and the Isle of Man, and the weasel, *M. nivalis*, which is not. However, both *Mustela* species and both *Sorex* species range up to the far north of Scandinavia, and the hypothesis might have to include a different rate of dispersal following the retreat of the glaciers rather than an ability to stand colder climates, and there is no evidence for such a differential rate.

The presence of one or the other or both species on very small islands is consistent with the idea that they are spread by boats: many fishing boats have insect life in them. Some behavioural difference, such as a greater readiness to enter boats on a beach, may explain the wider distribution of *S. minutus*, but that is only speculation. At least there seems nothing to suggest that these distributions relate to competition, still less to suppose that the number of shrews reflects an equilibrium of immigration and extinction.

Surprising distributions are also found in the other genus of shrews, *Crocidura*. On the continent of Europe there are two species in this genus, which are white-toothed shrews unlike the red-toothed *Sorex*. Again, the larger one, *C. russula*, is also usually the commoner. It is found on the islands of Oleron, Belle Île, Noirmoutier, Guernsey, Herm, and Alderney, all round the French coast. The smaller and rather more scarce *C. suaveolens* has a distinctly more south-easterly distribution in France; from that distribution it would not be expected to be found on any islands at all. Nevertheless it is found on the Île d'Yeu, Ouessant, Jersey, Sark, and several of the Isles of Scilly. The map in Fig. 10.1 shows that Sark is much closer to Guernsey and Herm than it is to Jersey. However, Le Suer (1976) notes that Sark was colonized by Jerseymen in 1565 under Helier de Carteret, Seigneur of St. Ouen, which is the parish in the north-west corner of Jersey which gives its name to the great West Bay of the island. In this case at least transport in farm goods seems the most likely explanation for the occurrence of *C. suaveolens* on Sark, and so by extension the whole of its distribution on these islands may be ascribed to this cause.

The phenotypes of the British white-toothed shrews have been studied using multivariate statistics by Delany and Healy (1966). They find that the races of *C. suaveolens* on the Isles of Scilly, Jersey, and Sark are all distinguishable. If this variation is genetically controlled, it suggests measurable separation of populations in only a few hundred generations.

With white-toothed shrews, the occurrence of only one species on each of the five Channel Islands, and the occurrence of one on the Isles of Scilly where there is no red-toothed shrew, could be argued to indicate competition exclusion. However, there is no evidence of competition between *Crocidura* and *Sorex* elsewhere, and the occurrence of one species only of *Crocidura* on each Channel Island could well be just the result of chance dispersal. *Sorex araneus* is found on Jersey too.

The main conclusion from the study of the distribution of British shrews must be that dispersal is the most important variable.

Hares

In the Holarctic tundra there is a set of populations of hares which taxonomists now frequently regard as races of one species, *Lepus timidus*. It is found in the Highlands of Scotland, and then from Scandinavia right across Russia, in Alaska where it is sometimes given a separate specific name of *L. othus*, and then, with a gap in its distribution around the delta of the Mackenzie River, across the tundra of Canada, sometimes under the name of *L. arcticus*. In the east of Canada it is found down the Labrador coast and in Newfoundland. In parts of its range it extends beyond the tundra. It is the only native hare in Ireland (p. 148). In Siberia it occurs in the coniferous forest, though the European brown hare, *L. capensis*, has been spreading up into this zone during the last century (Timofeeff-Ressovksy, Vorontsov, and Yablokov 1977). *L. timidus* also occurred both in the coniferous forests and in the tundra above the forests on the island of Newfoundland. In the coniferous forests of continental North America, the taiga, there occurs the snow-shoe rabbit, or snow-shoe hare, *L. americanus*.

In about 1860, *L. americanus* was introduced to Newfoundland for sport. It is a smaller, more prolific species than *L. timidus* and characteristic of coniferous forests, while *L. timidus* appears to occur there only when other hares are absent.

In Newfoundland *L. americanus* is found now in the coniferous woods, while *L. timidus* is found only in some parts of the tundra. This seems a simple case of competition, but Bergerud (1967) gives a different explanation. Bergerud's process is used as a fine example of apparent competition by Holt (1977) and is certainly competition to those who regard the process as being one leading to population diminution in one competitor. It would not be regarded as a competition by those who think of it in terms of resources. It might not even be regarded as competition by those who require a population reduction in both species. Bergerud's explanation involves the lynx, *Felis lynx canadensis*, which is a native of Newfoundland, and a predator on both species of hare. When the snow-shoe hare was introduced to the Newfoundland forests, it flourished, being well adapted to the habitat. This led to an increase in the lynx population, as one of its main prey populations increased. This in turn led to increased predation pressure by lynx on the Arctic hares, leading to their elimination in the coniferous woods.

Bergerud goes further, and states that the Arctic hare is now found only in the parts of the tundra of Newfoundland where there is adequate cover for it from lynx. In more exposed areas it is absent. On this explanation, the negative effect of the snow-shoe hare on the Arctic hare is mediated through their common predator. However, there is no evidence that the presence of the Arctic hares has any deterimental effect on the population densities of snow-shoe hares.

Taxonomic indications of competition

There is one rather different field in which the suggestion has been made from time to time that competitive effects can be seen on islands. This is in the distribution of the number of species per genus. The suggestion is that in island communities the number of species per genus goes down, and that this is an indication of increased competition on islands. A proper statistical examination, however, seems to indicate that the taxonomic composition of islands is what one would expect allowing for the smaller number of species on the island (Simberloff 1970).

Simberloff took ten surveys of land birds on islands, two surveys of passerine birds on islands, one of ants and nine of vascular plants. For all these, he plotted the number of species per genus against the number of species.

Simberloff's point is that, if you take a small number of species from a larger set, then the number of species per genus will go down simply because of this sampling. In the extreme, where only one species is selected, it can only be in one genus, and so the species per genus ratio goes to one. Roughly speaking, the expected number of species per genus can be found by drawing a straight line from the point giving the number of species per genus and the total number of species in the source area to the point of one species per genus at one species. One point is fixed by observation, the other by necessity. This linear relationship slightly underestimates the expected number of species per genus at intermediate numbers of species. To get true expectations and a measure of their variance, Simberloff took random samples, on a computer, from the source sets.

The most important conclusion was that the observed species per genus was very close to that expected. The deviations were small, but tended on the whole in the direction of too many species per genus, while competition would be expected to produce too few. Some of the deviations probably come from technicalities like identifying the right source of species; others may come from the tendency of related species to have related dispersal abilities. As with the cases considered before, dispersal seems a more important biological variable than competition in determining the structure of island communities.

Predation and other food-chain effects on islands

One well-known consequence of Elton's pyramid of numbers is that predators are scarcer than herbivores. In general, this is true of the population density of predators as a whole, of the population density of individual species, and of the number of species of predator in relation to the number of species of prey. Combining these phenomena with the empirical phenomenon of the species–area curve leads to the correct expectation that predators are frequently absent from islands. This has already been discussed in relation to Tristan da Cunha birds (p. 176).

Two questions arise. First, does the absence of predators lead to changes in the balance of the community? Secondly, is the absence of predators simply a result of too few resources, or is there something about the predatory interaction that can lead to the absence of a predator even when the resources should, on average, be sufficient to support a prudent predator population?

The importance of vertical effects in food chains in having a major effect on community structure has been demonstrated in a few cases with herbivores. The island of Skokholm is heavily populated by rabbits; the island of Grassholm, 16 km farther out to sea and about a tenth the size, has none. The flora of Skokholm is very much richer, even allowing for its larger area, and this must be ascribed to some extent to the influence of rabbits allowing species to coexist, where, in the absence of severe grazing, one would overgrow the other (Gillham 1953*b*; Goodman and Gillham 1954).

A more notorious example, though without a control island, is the effect of the introduction of rabbits on Laysan (Eliot and Blair 1978; Schlanger and Gillett 1976). There the deliberate introduction of rabbits led to the extinction of two of the three native species of land birds, and great destruction of the vegetation. In this case the rabbit population overshot, so they almost all died of starvation; the island is now free of rabbits (p. 46). It is perhaps a simple example of an unstable predator to prey interaction, leading to an overshoot and crash of the population. Here there was the major tragedy of extinction for other species.

The next example is also of a herbivore, but a much larger one. Lack frequently stressed that his views about the balance of species on isolated islands depended on the assumption that all the species he was interested in were physically capable of dispersing to the islands. That is to say, he was only concerned with flying animals. So it is mildly amusing that he referred to a mythically flying animal when discussing interactions on islands: the reindeer. In northern Scandinavia the Lapps have domesticated the reindeer, but it also occurs wild in Scandinavia, Iceland, Spitzbergen, Novaya Zemlya, and right across northern Russia. The reindeer, *Rangifer tarandus*, is now regarded as conspecific with the North American caribou (Banfield 1977). In North America, caribou undergo extensive migrations, and are much hunted by local peoples. Elton (1942) gives some evidence, mostly anecdotal, of considerable fluctuations in population sizes in Ungava in eastern Canada. Reindeer have been introduced on to a number of islands on which they do not occur naturally. In the Bering Sea, the islands are two of the Pribilof islands, St. Paul and St. George, and the island of St. Matthew somewhat farther north (Fig. 10.2). The first two are about 100 km² in area; St. Matthew is rather more than three times as large as this. The population curves for these three introductions are shown in Fig. 10.3, where the data have been standardized to numbers per square kilometre, and where the maximal carrying capacity for this sort of country, based on Alaskan figures (Klein 1968), is also shown. Population data for the Pribilofs are from Scheffer (1951); those for St. Matthew from Klein (1968).

The story on St. Matthew is the more dramatic. The herd was established in 1944 by 29 yearling reindeer from Nunivak, a large island also shown in Fig. 10.2, close to the Alaskan mainland. In 1957 the herd was estimated to be 1350 and in 1963 about 6000.

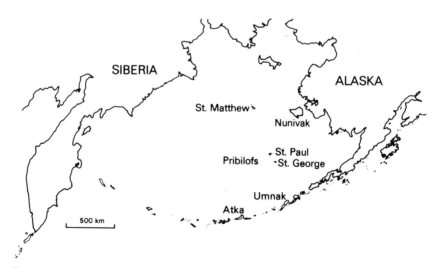

FIG. 10.2.   Map of the Bering Sea, showing the position of various islands with introduced reindeer populations.

The reindeer depends largely on lichens, particularly of the genus *Cladonia*, known colloquially as reindeer moss, for its food, especially in winter. Lichens are slow-growing, and so susceptible to over-grazing. By 1963 most of the lichen on St. Matthew had disappeared, and the island had changed to one largely covered in grasses and other higher plants. There was a hard winter in the Bering Sea area in 1963–4 and it seems that most of the herd died of starvation late that winter, possibly in March. In the summer of 1964 only 42 were left alive, and of these 41 were female. The 42nd was shot, in order to determine its sex, and turned out to be a sterile male. (Reindeer are the only deer in which both male and female have antlers, but the antlers of the female are smaller than those of the male.) Although the reindeer population was not extinguished entirely in the hard winter, it was no longer capable of reproduction, and was destined for eventual extinction.

The situation on the Pribilofs changed more slowly. On both St. Paul

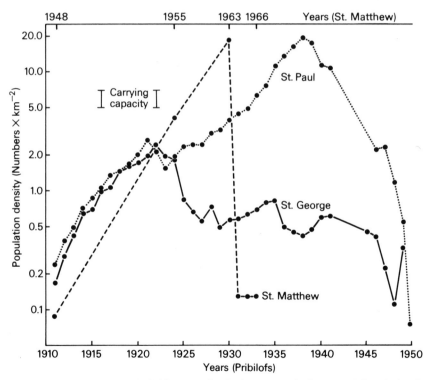

FIG. 10.3. The recorded history of reindeer populations on islands in the Bering Sea. The densities marked 'carrying capacity' show the range of estimated carrying capacity for Alaskan habitats. (Data from Klein 1968 and Scheffer 1951.)

and St. George the population rose gradually from 1911 to the mid-twenties to a density of about two per square kilometre, a figure thought to be well below carrying capacity. From there the St. George population gradually declined but did not go extinct. The St. Paul population, on the other hand, continued upwards, and reached a density which appears to have been remarkably close to that reached by the St. Matthew population before its crash, leading in this case to the St. Paul herd also becoming extinct.

St. Matthew is entirely uninhabited, but there are people on the Pribilofs, many of them concerned with the strictly regulated trade in Pribilof fur seals (*Callorhinus ursinus*). The reindeer population has survived on the larger, more populated, and slightly more southerly Aleutian islands of Atka and Umnak. No population data appear to have been published.

At the other end of the world, reindeer have been introduced in various places on South Georgia (Fig. 2.2), a very much larger, but highly mountainous island. Regular surveys have not been made, but the history of the various populations is given by Leader-Williams (1978). One, the Barff herd, was started in 1911 with 10 or 11 reindeer, and increased to a peak of about 3000 in 1958. Up to 100 animals were shot each year, though none has been since 1965. In about 1963 part of the herd spread past a glacier to form the Royal Bay herd. In 1972 the two herds numbered 1300 and 600 respectively. A quite separate herd was started in 1925 at Busen with seven animals. It increased very slowly, possibly because of much poaching. By 1972 it had apparently reached a peak of 800. Although none of the herds has maintained a steady population, none seems likely to become extinct. One possible factor is the ability of reindeer to graze the southern hemisphere *Poa flabellata*, a tussock grass. Tussock grasses are dominant in large areas of the sub-antarctic islands. On South Georgia, *Poa* sticks through the snow, and seems to be declining from grazing pressure in some areas.

The history of the herds on the Bering Sea islands is very reminiscent of the early predator–prey experiments of Gause (1934). In very simplified ecosystems the growth of the predator populations so overshoots the equilibrium that it crashes and becomes extinct. In some cases, the prey becomes extinct too, but in others it manages to survive the crisis. In real ecosystems one would expect the phenomenon shown on Laysan, namely that some of the prey species would survive but that some would become extinct with the predator. The general effect would be to reduce the number of species on islands, increase the extinction rate, and where species manage to persist, to increase their variability in population size and so their probability of eventual extinction. There are not enough data at the moment to say whether or not island populations are any more variable than populations of the same species in similar habitats on the mainland.

Predators can be stabilizing as well as unstabilizing, and so perhaps it is not worth searching for comparative data on population stability without also considering the dynamics of the interactions involved. The classic case of stabilization is that of the wolf, *Canis lupus*, on Isle Royale (Mech 1966). This is a large island, about 540 km^2, in Lake Superior. The natural vegetation is a northern coniferous forest, and its composition is apparently determined to an important extent by recurring natural forest fires. Moose (*Alces alces*), a Holarctic species known as elk in Europe, reached the island only during the first decade of this century, and are reputed to have gone through two population cycles before the arrival of the wolves in about 1949. In the early thirties there are thought to have been 3000 moose before a population crash, and there was a further build up and crash in the 1940s. Since the arrival of the wolves, the moose population appears to have been stabilized at a number which Mech puts at about 600, but Jordan, Shelton, and Allen (1967) between 800 to 1000. As Mech (1970) says, there is little reason to believe that the size of the Isle Royale moose herd has changed between the time the two censuses were taken in 1960 and 1966. Obtaining an accurate census in forested habitat on an island as large as this is difficult, and all estimates should be treated cautiously. The build up of a moose population between the wars certainly had dramatic effects on the vegetation. Mech produces very convincing evidence that at the time of his study the wolves effectively had the moose population under control, keeping it steady.

Vertebrate predators at the top of food chains frequently have territories, belonging to pairs or to packs as in the case of wolves, which must at least have a damping effect on their population fluctuations. So the introduction of such predators would also be expected to have a damping effect on population fluctuations throughout a community. This damping effect would also exert a depressing effect on prey populations, reducing them to levels below those that would be reached in the absence of the predator. As in the case of Newfoundland hares, the presence of a predator would also alter the balance between prey species, leading to changes in community structure.

The importance of predators in determining community structure has been argued by many people in recent years, perhaps most persuasively by Connell (1975). He brings together much evidence that predation, rather than competition, is the interaction that has the largest effect on community structure.

These rather fragmentary studies of food chain effects on islands indicate that these effects are important in determining the size and variability of populations on islands, and so the structure of island communities. However, the nature of the effect, whether stabilizing or destabilizing, depends on the particular biological situation, and so no general rules can be formulated for the consequences.

11 Island communities

Can studies of island populations be brought together to make quantitative studies of island communities, of island ecosystems? The answer is, not yet; but in this chapter I shall discuss some studies that have been made comparing island and mainland communities, and the prospects for a quantitative science of island communities.

Density compensation and density stasis

Islands have fewer species on them than continental areas. Does this have any consequences for the population size of individual species? Two possible effects are shown in Fig. 11.1. The top line of this figure shows the total population density of a mainland community distributed over many species. On the second line is an island community with the same total population density, but distributed over fewer species, with the result that each species has, on average, a larger population than an average mainland species. Such an effect is called density compensation. Another possible situation on islands is shown in the third line, where each island species has the same population density as a corresponding mainland species, so that the total population of the community is less than on the mainland. This I call density stasis.

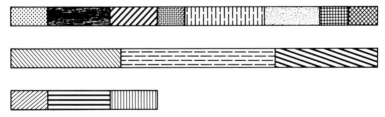

FIG. 11.1. Diagram of the concepts of density compensation and density stasis. The length of each section is proportional to the population density of one species. Top line: reference community of eight species. Middle line: community of three species with the same total density as the reference community, showing density compensation. Bottom line: community of three species with the same densities as the comparable species in the reference community, density stasis.

There are two difficulties in deciding whether island populations show either of the effects of Fig. 11.1, or for that matter intermediate or more extreme effects. The first is a general lack of data. The second comes from the consequences of the species–area relationship. We shall return to the first, with details of the technical problems and the difficulty of interpreting such data as there are, below. The second difficulty can be explained quite shortly.

The typical species–area relationship is of the form

$$\ln S = c + z \,(\ln A),$$

where S is the number of species, A the area, z a constant, often with a value near $+ 0.3$, and c is another constant. If there is no systematic variation in the total abundance of individuals of all species then, on average, the number of individuals per unit area is a constant,

$$I/A = K,$$

where I is the number of individuals and K a constant. There can be considerable variation in I/A, in the same way that there is sometimes considerable variation about the species–area relationship. All that is needed to show that studies on different size areas produce apparent density compensation, is that there should be no systematic variation in I/A. Taking logarithms, and putting $k = \ln K$,

$$\ln I = k + \ln A.$$

Now the average population size per species per unit area, P say, is given by $(I/S)/A$, or, again taking logarithms,

$$\ln P = (\ln I - \ln S) - \ln A,$$

and by substitution,

$$\ln P = [k + \ln A - (c + z \,(\ln A)\,)] - \ln A$$
$$= (k - c) - z \,(\ln A).$$

In words, the average population size per species will decline with a slope of $-z$ when measured on areas of increasing size. Surveys on large areas will generally produce smaller population sizes per species per unit area than surveys on small areas even if the assumptions above are not exactly true.

Comparing population densities in areas of different sizes will produce apparent density compensation simply because of the species–area relationship. In such cases, density compensation says nothing about population dynamics, let alone niche widening or any such phenomena. To study the effects of insularity on populations, it is essential either to use the same area of island and mainland or, equivalently, remove the effect of area by covariance techniques.

One possible consequence of the food-chain effects considered in the last chapter would be a change in population density. In general the lack of predators on islands would be expected to produce denser populations of prey. Predators may be absent because the island is too small to support them, either at all or as a stable population, or because of failure to disperse to the island. The first explanation could apply to birds and the second to mammal predators. This effect could readily be confounded with the species–area effect on density, and both effects may well be important in some studies such as Case (1975), who also discusses some other minor effects that might be involved.

What then is the evidence for thinking that compensation or stasis occurs on islands? Most of it comes from birds, some from insects, and none from plants. First some technical details of population estimation and their validity will be considered, and then the results not only for birds and insects, but also for some interesting and relevant plant data, albeit not from an island. There is a great need to study plant-population densities in comparable communities on oceanic islands and continents.

Methods

There are many ways in which bird-population densities may be estimated; obtaining reliable estimates involves a lot of work. In the British Isles the Common Bird Census has been run, using standardized census methods to count singing males, since the early 1960s (Batten and Marchant 1976). In North America, a different census, the Cooperative Breeding Bird Survey, based on road surveys made around dawn of singing males has been used (Erskine 1978). Judging by the results, and by comparing these results with the known variability of bird populations from more intensive local surveys (Williamson 1972) there is no doubt that both methods produce acceptable figures for the variation of individual species. Whether either method produces accurate figures for the relative density of different species, let alone for the absolute density of all species in a known habitat, is much less certain. The North American census does not, indeed, claim to do the latter, and it is well known that there is a considerable subjective element in estimating the number of territories in the Common Bird Census. The confidence one has in the published results is based on the assumption that the same biases have been applied throughout: but this inevitably reduces the value of the data to the relative changes of individual species. Lack (1935) describes a variety of methods for estimating the number of pairs in a open habitats, including counting nests, counting resident adults, putting up birds by drawing long ropes across the ground, and using parties of ornithologists walking in line abreast.

A method that has been used in studies of density compensation in birds is trapping by mist nets. The name comes from the fineness and invisibility of the net material. A standard size is 12 m long, set from 0.1 to 2 m above the ground, and with a mesh of sides 36 mm long (Terborgh 1977). Sometimes 20–50 such nets are used, sometimes less than 10. Diamond (1970) argues that their use is essential in tropical areas because the long breeding season of many species, and the lack of synchrony between species, precludes counts of breeding pairs. As he puts it 'many bird individuals in most localities at most times are non-breeding and non-territorial'. But there are difficulties in using mist-net data. Results are affected by the height of the vegetation, because of the height the nets can be set at; by the structure of the vegetation (Diamond 1974); by the flying habits and skulkiness of the birds; by their experience, as 'banded birds are adept at avoiding nets' (Terborgh 1977); by the size of the birds, as 'smaller species (< 8 g) occasionally slip through the mesh and larger ones (> 60 g) frequently bounce out without becoming entangled' (Terborgh 1977); not to mention the effects of weather and the skill of the ornithologist in placing the nets.

Insects may be caught in a great variety of ways (Southwood 1978), such as light traps and suction traps. The only data on density compensation known to me come from sweep netting, which is fast and reasonably standard if enough sweeps, several hundred per census, are used. Like all methods for insects, it will collect biased samples, the bias arising from the habits and activity of the insects and the structure of the vegetation being swept. Small species of 1 mm in length or less are generally badly sampled (Hespenheide 1979).

Results

Long-term censuses of bird populations show considerable variation in the total count from year to year. In the Eastern Wood counts (Table 5.1) the total pairs vary from 123 to 210 in a period of 25 years, a factor of 1.7 times. The Skokholm data vary slightly more, 1.9 times. The Common Bird Census and the Cooperative Breeding Bird Survey, averaged over many counts, show year-to-year variation in the totals of about 1.2 times, though the period is only ten years, and the totals do not represent a community but a total of indices.

For counts in different areas, Järvinen (1979) assesses data from fifteen long-term studies in Europe, five in northern communities (northern Scandinavia and Iceland) and ten in southern (southern

Scandinavia, Britain, and central Europe). The counts covered from five to ten years. The average density in northern communities varied from 68 to 298 pairs km^{-2}, and from 193 to 1058 pairs km^{-2} in the southern; ranges of 4.4 and 5.5 times. To this range must be added the year-to-year variation that has been averaged out, producing perhaps a difference in total density of five to ten times as the range for single census comparisons. Lack (1935) gives figures for British heathland bird communities that show more variation. For 27 counts, the range is from 3 to 224 birds per 100 acres (0.4 km^2), a factor of 75 times. Making allowances for some special circumstances, burning, the activities of game keepers, and so on, the data indicate a variation in the range 10 to 20 times at least. Lussenhop (1977) reports density standardized to pairs km^{-2} of from 10 to 270 in ten Chicago cemeteries in one year; excluding the smallest gives a range of 5 times. All these rather different studies suggest that a variation of up to ten times in the total population densities of birds at two different places is not in itself surprising, and calls for no special explanation.

Turning now to comparative counts on islands and mainlands, much of the recent interest in density compensation comes from Crowell's (1962) work on the birds of Bermuda, in the North Atlantic (Fig. 2.1). Counting singing males in plots of a few hectares, in scrub, brush, farmland, woods, and myrtle swamp, he found densities varying from 270 to 560 per 100 acres (0.4 km^2), with 7–10 species present. He compared these with counts recorded in the Audobon Field Notes for 158 censuses in North America, which he classified into the seven habitat types of brush, scrub, wet scrub, deciduous forest, floodplain forest, mixed forest, and edge. The average density per habitat in the mainland censuses varied from 144 to 423, and the number of species from 17 to 38 on areas much larger than the Bermuda plots. There seems nothing in these data to suggest phenomena not caused by the species–area relationship. The similarity and range of the densities recorded match the European data quite well.

A study in which the area was controlled was that undertaken by Grant (1966) on the Tres Marias islands (Fig. 6.6) and on the neighbouring mainland of west Mexico. There was one plot on the islands and one on the mainland, each of 4 ha, or one quarter the size of Eastern Wood. The island plot had fewer species (29 against 34) but more males singing or apparently holding territories (137 against 103). The larger total population on the islands comes largely from two species, *Parula pitiayumi* (olive-backed warbler) with 32 males and *Vireo flavoviridis* (yellow-green vireo) with 19. The difference, although formally significant, is no more than one would expect between any two such surveys, and so cannot be taken to show any peculiarity of island communities.

In tropical habitats Diamond (1970), MacArthur, Diamond, and Karr (1972) and MacArthur, MacArthur, MacArthur, and MacArthur (1973) report mist-net studies in and near New Guinea (Fig. 11.2) and on the Pearl archipelago off the coast of Panama (Fig. 9.1). The New Guinea results are shown in Table 11.1. The communities on the smaller islands seem to show density stasis; all the figures for these islands are well below the New Guinea figure in the penultimate column, but near the New Guinea rain-forest figure in the final column. The three figures for New Guinea, though, are more alike in the

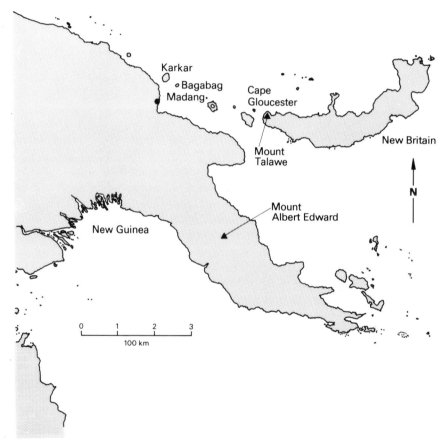

F IG. 11.2. Map showing the locations of Diamond's mist-netting sites in New Guinea and New Britain. Lowland samples were taken on the islands of Karkar and Bagabag, near Madang on New Guinea and near Cape Glouces-ter on New Britain. Montane samples were taken on the island of Karkar, near Mount Albert Edward on New Guinea and near Mount Talawe on New Britain.

Table 11.1. Population densities of birds estimated by mist netting (each net 22.5 m²)

Vegetation type	Island	Number of species of birds on the whole island	Number of local species	Number of birds per net per day	Average number of birds per species per net per day, × 100
Rain forest	New Guinea	512	132	0.82	0.62
	New Britain	126	88	0.48	0.55
	Karkar	52	48	0.30	0.63
	Bagabag	29	31	0.19	0.62
Montane forest	New Guinea	512	59	1.41	2.39
	New Britain	126	31	0.21	0.68
	Karkar	52	27	0.15	0.56
Subalpine mossy forest	New Guinea	512	31	0.71	2.29
	New Britain	126	17	0.15	0.88

Modified from Diamond 1970.

penultimate column than in the final column, indicating density compensation. However, it could be argued that none of the differences in the table is larger than would be expected in any set of censuses in the same general region. There is also an indication of density stasis, though probably not stastically significant, on the islands of Canas and Puercos in the Pearl archipelago. The counts were 0.23 and 0.20 birds net^{-1} h^{-1} from communities of 21 and 18 species.

If density stasis occurs on isolated islands, then it is perhaps another aspect of the impoverishment of small islands. In the limit, when there are no land birds, as on Easter Island, Trindade, or St. Paul (p. 66), then there can be no density compensation. It is unfortunate that information on island population densities is almost entirely lacking except for birds. The important exception is Janzen's (1973) study of insects in Costa Rica, in middle America, and on islands in the Caribbean. His samples were taken by sweep-netting secondary vegetation. The island sites usually had fewer plant species, and many of them recently introduced. In the wet season, the numbers of species and of individuals of insects on the islands are only about a third of those on the mainland. In the dry season the difference is smaller. The taxonomic composition of the island faunas also differs. Homoptera are dominant, while Coleoptera and Heteroptera are relatively scarce. The proportion of predators, particularly lady-birds (Coccinellidae) in the Coleoptera increases. How much of this density stasis and taxonomic change can be ascribed to sampling secondary, introduced, vegetation, how much to the differences between the seasonal climatic cycle on islands and mainland, and how much to different community structure on islands is not clear. Comparable work in native vegetation on other islands is clearly needed.

To clarify the nature of population density changes in different communities a series of population species counts is needed in areas of the same size in directly comparable habitats. The only such data appear to come from plants and are shown in Fig. 11.3. These are yield, in cropped weight, of herbage in the Park Grass plots at Rothamsted Experimental Station in the south of England. The plot has been divided along the species axis at the median number of points and regressions calculated for the two halves. This distinctly heterodox statistical procedure is adopted because it would appear in the left-hand half that there is no relationship between species number and total yield. In the right-hand half there is a rapid fall-off of yield with increasing species number, and, *a fortiori*, an even faster fall-off in the average yield per species. Fitting a curvilinear regression through the whole set of points would imply a change in the left-hand side of the graph, at least with any simple function, which would be unjustified.

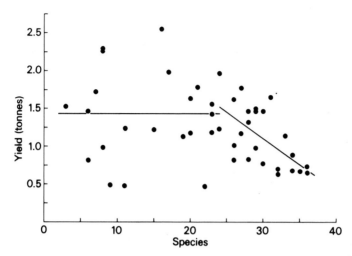

Fɪɢ. 11.3. Yield in the season 1948–9 on the Park Grass plots at Rotham-sted. Separate regressions are shown on each side of the median number of species. Yields are standardized per unit area, as the plots vary somewhat in size. (Data from Warington 1958.)

The experiments at Park Grass are not as widely known as they should be. Park Grass was a field which was divided up into plots in the nineteenth century. Thereafter, each plot had its own individually-determined fertilizer treatment, which in many cases has been main-tained every year from 1856. The data plotted in Fig. 11.3 are those for the season 1948/9, taken from Warington (1958). The experimental design has not been absolutely constant. In some plots, fertilizer treat-ment was changed in the 1860s and, in three cases, was also changed in 1904. The detailed variations in yield can be related to quite a large extent to the particular fertilizer treatments given. The effect that we are concerned with here, the decrease in yield with a high number of species, is in fact an effect the other way round. The plots with inad-equate fertilization give a poor yield, and this appears to allow the establishment of more species. So it is the number of species that go up as the yield goes down rather than the other way round. In natural habitats, the effects seen at Rothamsted could act so that in marginal habitats some competitively weak species would persist.

The Park Grass data, from plots in one field, show a range of yield of slightly more than five times. In the bird data, when a variety of habitats in the same geographical region is considered, a range of population densities of up to ten times, sometimes more, is found. There are two consequences for the study of islands. The first is that it will be very difficult to establish density compensation or density stasis against such large background variation. The second is that theories based on assumptions of constant total density should be treated cautiously. Nevertheless, the impoverished communities of isolated islands must surely remain excellent places to study the functioning of communities.

Finale

To conclude then, what are the major features of island populations, and what are their causes? The answer to the first part is essentially that given by Sir Joseph Hooker a century ago (p. 31): isolated islands have a distinctive biota, and the number of species per unit area is less than on an equivalent area of the mainland, or of less isolated islands. The simplest demonstration of the reduction in the number of species is in Fig. 2.4 (p. 38). In this figure there are two main points to explain: the monotonic relationship within each group within each archipelago, and the difference between the archipelagos and the different groups. That is, the slope and the intercepts of the curves both need to be explained.

Explanations for the slope were summarized in Chapter 10, and include habitat diversity, the extinction of small populations by normal variation in time, evolutionary effects, and the effects of trophic interactions. The proper weighting of these effects is now an important task for population biology, but all play some part.

The differences between intercepts of species–area relationships are a consequence of many things (Haas 1975) such as the general climate, from tropical to arctic and in other dimensions, the biology and evolutionary history of the group concerned, and so on. However, the differences between the intercepts of one group on an oceanic archipelago and on a continental archipelago seem to demonstrate the importance of variation in dispersal ability. In Fig. 2.4 there are data for three taxonomic groups: pteridophytes, vascular plants, and birds. The intercepts for pteridophytes do not differ significantly between the Azores and the Channel Islands, and this may well mean that the range of habitats and climates on the two archipelagos is not greatly different, allowing for island size, and that there are no impediments to dispersal. With vascular plants, the intercept for the Channel Islands comes at about two and a half times the number of species seen for the intercept on the Azores. The simplest explanation is that many species are unable to disperse to the Azores. This is a difficult proposition to prove, but is certainly consistent with the impoverished flora of Hawaii (Chapter 9).

The birds, that is the land and freshwater birds, are only a quarter as common on the Azores as on the Channel Islands, again measuring this by intercepts. It is clear from Norfolk Island (Fig. 2.6), Hawaii (Chapter 9) and other oceanic islands that, contrary to Lack's often stated opinion, birds do not get to all possible breeding places within the evolutionary time span of a typical species. This is also shown by the success of introduced birds in New Zealand, especially the redpoll (p. 29), and indeed by the existence of biogeographic regions for birds. So part of the explanation may be the lack of dispersal ability of some birds.

However, on the same sets of evidence, birds disperse as well in general as plants, yet in the comparison between the Azores and the Channel Islands, the intercepts of the plant curves are closer than those of the bird curves. Table 11.2 gives an indication of the shift in taxonomic composition for plants from the British Isles to the Azores. This is a very rough indication of the loss of diversity that must accompany the selection of a flora by dispersal ability. It is at least reasonable to suggest that the lack of birds comes to some extent from the lack of plants and so of suitable habitats on the Azores. There is a spiral of deprivation here. Few plants lead to few birds which lead to a lack of dispersal opportunities for plants.

Table 11.2. Percentages of angiosperm species in various families

Commoner on the Azores			
	Gramineae	Compositae	Leguminosae	Polygonaceae
Azores	13.3	10.5	8.1	2.9
British Isles	8.5	7.6	4.4	1.9
Rarer on the Azores			
	Cyperaceae	Scrophulariaceae	Caryophyllaceae	Rosaceae
Azores	4.6	3.8	2.5	1.9
British Isles	7.0	4.6	4.4	4.2

Data from Eriksson, Hansen, and Sunding 1974 and Turrill 1948.

The interactions between the diversities of different taxonomic groups on islands must be an essential part of the study of island populations. A proper understanding of island ecosystems cannot come from the study only of plants or only of birds or of any other group. All need to be considered to some extent, and the data for this is mostly lacking.

There is still a great deal to be learnt, not only of details but also of principles, of population dynamics, and evolution. What islands undoubtedly show is that variations in dispersal ability, environmental heterogeneity, and processes with widely different time scales have all been involved in the building of the ecosystems that can be seen today. The study of island ecosystems may well be a useful step to understanding the structure and function of other ecosystems.

Bibliography

Abbott, I. (1974). Numbers of plant, insect and land bird species on nineteen remote islands in the Southern Hemisphere. *Biol. J. Linnean Soc. Lond.* **6**, 143–52.

—— and Grant, P. R. (1976). Nonequilibrial bird faunas on islands. *Am. Nat.* **110**, 507–28.

Adsersen, A. (1976). A botanist's notes on Pinta. *Not. Galapagos* **24**, 26–8.

Amadon, D. (1950). The Hawaiian honeycreepers (Aves, Drepaniidae). *Bull. Am. Mus. nat. Hist.* **95**, 155–253.

Armstrong, E. A. (1955). *The wren.* Collins, London.

Armstrong, R. A. (1978). A note on the demography of colonization. *Am. Nat.* **112**, 243–5.

Arnold, E. N. (1979). Indian Ocean giant tortoises: their systematics and island adaptations. *Phil. Trans. R. Soc.* **B286**, 127–45.

Arnold, H. H. (ed.) (1978). *Provisional atlas of the mammals of the British Isles.* Natural Environment Research Council Institute of Terrestrial Ecology. Monks Wood Experimental Station, Huntingdon.

Arrhenius, O. (1921). Species and area. *J. Ecol.* **9**, 95–9.

Baird, D. E., Dickson, J. H., Holdgate, M. W., and Wace, N. M. (1965). The biological report of the Royal Society expedition to Tristan da Cunha, 1962. *Phil. Trans. R. Soc.* **B249**, 257–434.

Banfield, A. W. F. (1977). *The mammals of Canada.* (Corrected edn.) University of Toronto Press, Toronto.

Bannerman, D. A. and Bannerman, W. M. (1966). *Birds of the Atlantic Islands.* Vol. 3, *A history of the birds of the Azores.* Oliver and Boyd, Edinburgh.

—— and —— (1968). *Birds of the Atlantic Islands.* Vol. 4, *A history of the birds of the Cape Verde Islands.* Oliver and Boyd, Edinburgh.

Bartlett, M. S. (1957). Measles periodicity and community size. *J. R. statist. Soc.* **A120**, 48–70.

—— (1973). Equations and models of population change. In *The mathematical theory of the dynamics of biological populations* (ed. M. S. Bartlett and R. W. Hiorns), pp. 5–21. Academic Press, London.

Batten, L. A. and Marchant, J. H. (1976). Bird population changes for the years 1973–4. *Bird Study* **23**, 11–20.

Bellwood, P. (1978). *The Polynesians.* Thames and Hudson, London.

Bergerud, A. T. (1967). The distribution and abundance of arctic hares in Newfoundland. *Can. Fld Nat.* **81**, 242–8.

Berry, R. J. (1964). The evolution of an island population of the house mouse. *Evolution* **18**, 468–83.

—— (1975). On the nature of genetical distance and island races of *Apodemus sylvaticus. J. Zool. Lond.* **176**, 292–5.

—— (1977). *Inheritance and natural history*. Collins, London.

—— (1979). The Outer Hebrides: where genes and geography meet. *Proc. R. Soc. Edinb.* **B77**, 21–43.

—— and Murphy, H. M. (1970). The biochemical genetics of an island population of the house mouse. *Proc. R. Soc.* **B176**, 87–103.

—— and Searle, A. G. (1963). Epigenetic polymorphism of the rodent skeleton. *Proc. zool. soc. Lond.* **140**, 577–615.

—— and Tricker, B. J. K. (1969). Competition and extinction: the mice of Foula, with notes on those of Fair Isle and St. Kilda. *J. Zool. Lond.* **158**, 247–65.

Beven, G. (1976). Changes in breeding bird populations of an oak-wood on Bookham Common, Surrey, over twenty-seven years. *Lond. Nat.* **55**, 23–42.

Black, F. L. (1966). Measles endemicity in insular populations: critical community size and its evolutionary implications. *J. Theoret. Biol.* **11**, 207–11.

Bookstein, F. L., Gingerich, P. D. and Kluge, A. G. (1978). Hierarchical linear modeling of the tempo and mode of evolution. *Paleobiology* **4**, 120–34.

Brown, J. H. (1971). Mammals on mountain tops: nonequilibrium insular biogeography. *Am. Nat.* **105**, 467–78.

—— and Kodric-Brown, A. (1977). Turnover rates in insular biogeography: effect of immigration on extinction. *Ecology* **58**, 445–9.

Cameron, A. W. (1964). Competitive exclusion between the rodent genera *Microtus* and *Clethrionomys*. *Evolution* **18**, 630–4.

Carlquist, S. (1965). *Island life*, Natural History Press, Garden City, N.Y.

—— (1970). *Hawaii, a natural history*. Natural History Press, Garden City, N.Y.

—— (1974). *Island biology*. Columbia University Press, New York.

Carson, H. L. (1973). Ancient chromosomal polymorphism in Hawaiian *Drosophila*. *Nature, Lond.* **241**, 200–2.

—— (1976). The unit of genetic change in adaptation and speciation. *Ann. Mo. bot. Gdn* **63**, 210–23.

——, Hardy, D. E., Spieth, H. T., and Stone, W. S. (1970). The evolutionary biology of the Hawaiian Drosophilidae. *Evol. Biol., suppl.* 437–543.

—— and Kaneshiro, K. Y. (1976). *Drosophila* of Hawaii: systematics and ecological genetics. *Annu. Rev. Ecol. Syst.* **7**, 311–45.

Case, T. J. (1975). Species numbers, density compensation, and colonizing ability of lizards on islands in the Gulf of California. *Ecology* **56**, 3–18.

Casey, T. L. and Jacobi, J. D. (1974). A new genus and species of bird from the island of Maui, Hawaii (Passeriformes: Drepanididae). *Occ. Pap. Bernice P. Bishop Mus.* **24**, 215–26.

Clague, D. A. and Jarrard, R. D. (1973). Tertiary Pacific plate motion deduced from the Hawaiian-Emperor chain. *Bull. geol. Soc. Am.* **84**, 1135–54.

Clarke, C. A. and Sheppard, P. M. (1955). The breeding in captivity of the hybrid swallowtail *Pipilio machaon gorganus* Fruhstorfer ♀ × *Papilio hospiton* Gene ♂. *Entomologist* **88**, 1–6.

Clarke, J. F. G. (1971). The Lepidoptera of Rapa Island. *Smithson. Contr. Zool.* **56**, 1–282.

Colinvaux, P. A. (1972). Climate and the Galapagos Islands. *Nature, Lond.* **240**, 17–20.

Connell, J. H. (1975). Some mechanisms producing structure in natural communities. In *Ecology and evolution of communities* (eds. M. L. Cody and J. M. Diamond), pp. 460–90. Belknap Press of Harvard University Press, Cambridge, Ma.

Connor, E. F. and McCoy, E. D. (1979). The statistics and biology of the species–area relationship. *Am. Nat.* **113**, 791–833.

—— and Simberloff, D. (1978). Species number and compositional similarity of the Galapagos flora and avifauna. *Ecol. Monogr.* **48**, 219–48.

Cook. R. E. (1969). Variation in species density of North American birds. *Syst. Zool.* **18**, 63–84.

Corbet, G. B. (1961). Origin of the British insular races of small mammals and of the 'lusitanian' fauna. *Nature, Lond.* **191**, 1037–40.

—— (1978). *The mammals of the palaearctic region: a taxonomic review.* British Museum (Natural History), London.

—— and Southern, H. N. (ed.) (1977). *The handbook of British mammals* (2nd edn). Blackwell Scientific Publications, Oxford.

Cramp, S., Bourne, W. R. P., and Saunders, D. (1974). *The seabirds of Britain and Ireland.* Collins, London.

Crichton, M. (1974). *Provisional distribution maps of amphibians, reptiles and mammals in Ireland.* Folens, Dublin.

Critchfield, W. B. and Little, E. L. Jr. (1966). *Geographic distribution of the pines of the world.* US Department of Agriculture, Forest Service, Miscellaneous Publication 991, Washington, DC.

Crowell, K. L. (1962). Reduced interspecific competition among the birds of Bermuda. *Ecology* **43**, 75–88.

—— (1973). Experimental zoogeography: introductions of mice to small islands. *Am. Nat.* **107**, 535–58.

—— and Pimm, S. L. (1976). Competition and niche shifts of mice introduced on to small islands. *Oikos* **27**, 251–8.

Darlington, P. J. (1957). *Zoogeography.* Wiley, New York.

Darwin, C. (1842). *The structure and distribution of coral reefs. Being the first part of the geology of the voyage of the Beagle, under the command of Capt. Fitzroy, R.N., during the years 1832–36.* Smith, Elder, and Company, London.

—— (1859). *On the origin of species.* Murray, London.

Delany, M. J. and Healy, M. J. R. (1966). Variation in the white-toothed shrews (*Crocidura* spp.) in the British Isles. *Proc. R. Soc.* **B164**, 63–74.

Diamond, J. M. (1970). Ecological consequences of island colonization by south-west Pacific birds, I. Types of niche shifts. II. The effect of species diversity on total population density. *Proc. natn. Acad. Sci., U.S.A.* **67**, 529–36, 1715–21.

—— (1972). Biogeographic kinetics: estimation of relaxation times for avifaunas of southwest Pacific islands. *Proc. nat. Acad. Sci., U.S.A.* **69**, 3199–203.

—— (1974). Colonization of exploded volcanic islands by birds: the supertramp strategy. *Science, N.Y.* **184**, 803–6.

—— (1975). Assembly of species communities. In *Ecology and evolution of communities* (ed. M. L. Cody and J. M. Diamond), pp. 342–444. Belknap Press of Harvard University Press, Cambridge, Ma.

—— (1977). Continental and insular speciation in Pacific land birds. *Syst. Zool.* **26**, 263–8.

—— and May, R. M. (1976). Island biogeography and the design of natural reserves. In *Theoretical ecology* (ed. R. M. May), pp. 163–86. Blackwell Scientific Publications, Oxford.

—— and Mayr, E. (1976). Species–area relation for birds of the Solomon archipelago. *Proc. natn. Acad. Sci., U.S.A.* **73**, 262–6.

Dony, J. G. (1970). *Species–area relationships.* Unpublished. Report to the Natural Environment Research Council, London.

Douglas, G. (1969). Draft check list of Pacific Oceanic islands. (Foreword by E. M. Nicholson) *Micronesica* **5**, 327–463.

Eason, E. H. (1964). *Centipedes of the British Isles.* Warne, London.

Eliot, J. L. and Blair, J. (1978). Hawaii's far-flung wildlife paradise. *Nat. geogr. Mag.* **153**, 670–91.

Elton, C. (1942). *Voles, mice, and lemmings.* Clarendon Press, Oxford.

—— (1958). *The ecology of invasions by animals and plants.* Chapman and Hall, London.

Emlen, J. T. (1978). Density anomalies and regulatory mechanisms in land bird populations on the Florida peninsula. *Am. Nat.* **112**, 265–86.

Engen, S. (1977). Exponential and logarithmic species–area curves. *Am. Nat.* **111**, 591–4.

—— (1978). *Stochastic abundance models.* Chapman and Hall, London.

—— (1979). Stochastic abundance models in ecology. *Biometrics* **35**, 331–8.

Eriksson, O., Hansen, A., and Sunding, P. (1974). *Flora of Macaronesia. Check-list of vascular plants.* University of Umeå, Sweden.

Erskine, A. J. (1978). *The first ten years of the cooperative breeding bird survey in Canada.* Canadian Wildlife Service report series. No. 42, 61 pp.

Falconer, D. S. (1960). *Introduction to quantitative genetics.* Oliver and Boyd, Edinburgh.

Falla, R. A. (1960). Oceanic birds as dispersal agents. *Proc. R. Soc.* **B152**, 655–9.

Ferguson-Lees, I. J. (1978). The European atlas: pipits. *Br. Birds* **71**, 245–254.

Firth, R. and Davidson, J. W. (1945). *Pacific islands.* Vol. 1. *General survey.* Naval Intelligence Division, London.

Fisher, J. (1948). St. Kilda, a natural experiment. *New Nat.* **1**, 91–109.

Fisher, R. A., Corbet, A. S., and Williams, C. B. (1943). The relation between the number of species and the number of individuals in a random sample of an animal population. *J. Anim. Ecol.* **12**, 42–58.

Fitter, A. (1977). *An atlas of the wild flowers of Britain and Northern Europe.* Collins, London.

Flessa, K. W. and Sepkoski, J. J. Jr. (1978). On the relationship between phanerozoic diversity and changes in habitable area. *Paleobiology* **4**, 359–66.

Fosberg, F. R. (1976). Coral island vegetation. In *Biology and geology of coral reefs* (ed. O. A. Jones and R. Endean), Vol. 3, pp. 255–77. Academic Press, New York.

Fosberg, R. and Klawe, W. L. (1966). Preliminary list of plants from Cocos

Island. In *The Galapagos* (ed. R. I. Bowman), pp. 187–9. University of California Press, Berkeley, Ca.

Foster, J. B. (1964). Evolution of mammals on islands. *Nature, Lond.* **202**, 234–5.

Fridriksson, S. (1975). *Surtsey*. Butterworth, London. .

Gause, G. F. (1934). *The struggle for existence*. Williams and Wilkins, Baltimore. (Reprinted 1964, Hafner, New York.)

Geyh, M. A., Kudrass, H.-R., and Streif, H. (1979). Sea-level changes during the late Pleistocene and Holocene in the Strait of Malacca. *Nature, Lond.* **278**, 441–3.

Gillham, M. E. (1953*a*). An annotated list of the flowering plants and ferns of Skokholm Island, Pembrokeshire. *N. West. Nat.* **1953**, 539–57.

—— (1953*b*). An ecological account of the vegetation of Grassholm Island, Pembrokeshire. *J. Ecol.* **41**, 84–99.

Gilpin, M. E. and Diamond, J. M. (1976). Calculation of immigration and extinction curves from the species–area–distance relation. *Proc. natn. Acad. Sci., U.S.A.* **73**, 4130–4.

Gleason, H. A. (1922). On the relation between species and area. *Ecology* **3**, 158–62.

Good, R. (1974). *The geography of the flowering plants* (4th edn). Longman, London.

Goodman, G. T. and Gillham, M. E. (1954). Ecology of the Pembrokeshire islands. II. Skokholm, environment and vegetation. *J. Ecol.* **42**, 296–327.

Gorman, G. G. and Kim, Y. J. (1976). *Anolis* lizards of the eastern Caribbean: a case study in evolution. II. Genetic relationships and genetic variation of the *bimaculatus* group. *Syst. Zool.* **26**, 62–77.

Gould, S. J. (1979). An allometric interpretation of species–area curves: the meaning of the coefficient. *Am. Nat.* **114**, 335–43.

Grant, P. R. (1966). Density of land birds on the Tres Marias islands, Mexico. I. Numbers and biomass. *Can. J. Zool.* **44**, 391–400.

—— (1968). Bill size, body size, and the ecological adaptations of bird species to the competition situation on islands. *Syst. Zool.* **17**, 319–33.

—— (1970). Colonization of islands by ecologically dissimilar species of mammals. *Can. J. Zool.* **48**, 545–55.

—— (1971). Bill dimensions of the three species of *Zosterops* on Norfolk Island. *Syst. Zool.* **21**, 289–91.

—— (1972). Interspecific competition among rodents. *Annu. Rev. Ecol. Syst.* **3**, 79–106.

—— (1974). Reproductive compatability of voles from separate continents (Mammalia: *Clethrionomys*). *J. Zool.* **174**, 245–54.

—— (1975). Four Galapagos Islands. *Geogrl. J.* **141**, 76–87.

—— (1977). Review of 'Island Biology' by David Lack. *Bird-Banding* **48**, 296–300.

Green, R. (1966). Linguistic subgroupings within Polynesia: The implications for prehistoric settlement. *J. Polynes. Soc.* **75**, 6–38.

Greenslade, P. J. M. (1968). Island patterns in the Solomon Islands bird fauna. *Evolution* **22**, 751–61.

Gressitt, J. L. (1961). Problems in the zoogeography of Pacific and Antarctic insects. *Pac. insects Monogr.* **2**, 1–94.

Gross, G. F. (1975). The land invertebrates of the New Hebrides and their relationships. *Phil. Trans. R. Soc.* **B272**, 391–421.

Haas, P. H. (1975). Some comments on use of the species–area curve. *Am. Nat.* **109**, 371–3.

Hackman, W. (1959). On the genus *Scaptomyza* Hardy. *Acta zool. fenn.* **97**, 1–72.

Hall, B. P. and Moreau, R. E. (1970). *An atlas of speciation in African passerine birds*. British Museum (Natural History), London.

Hamilton, T. H. and Rubinoff, I. (1967). On predicting insular variation in endemism and sympatry for the Darwin finches in the Galapagos archipelago. *Am. Nat.* **101**, 161–71.

Handford, P. T. and Pernetta, J. C. (1974). The origin of island races of *Apodemus sylvaticus*: an alternative hypothesis. *J. zool. Lond.* **174,** 534–7.

Hardy, D. E. (1965). *Insects of Hawaii*. Vol. 12. *Drosophilidae*. University of Hawaii Press, Honolulu.

—— (1974). Evolution in the Hawaiian Drosophilidae: I. Introduction and background information. In *Genetic mechanisms of speciation in insects* (ed. M. J. D. White), pp. 71–80. Australia and N.Z. Book Co., Sydney.

Harris, M. P. (1973*a*). The Galapagos avifauna. *Condor* **75**, 265–78.

—— (1973*b*). *Coreba flaveola* and the Geospizinae. *Bull. Br. Orn. Club* **92**, 164–8.

Hasselmann, K. (1976). Stochastic climate models. Part I. Theory. *Tellus* **28**, 473–85.

Hawaii Audobon Society (1975). *Hawaii's birds*. Hawaii Audobon Society, Honolulu.

Heatwole, H. and Levins, R. (1972). Trophic structure stability and faunal change during recolonization. *Ecology* **53**, 531–4.

Heed, W. B. (1971). Host plant specificity and speciation in Hawaiian *Drosophila*. *Taxon* **20**, 115–21.

Hespenheide, H. A. (1979). Are there fewer parasitoids in the tropics? *Am. Nat.* **113**, 766–9.

Hocking, R. R. (1976). The analysis and selection of variables in linear regression. *Biometrics* **32**, 1–49.

Holdgate, M. W. (1960*a*). The fauna of the mid-Atlantic islands *Proc. R. Soc.* **B152**, 550–67.

——(1960*b*). Contribution to a discussion on the biology of the southern cold temperate zone. *Proc. R. Soc.* **B152**, 674–5.

Holloway, J. D. (1970). The biogeographical analysis of a transect sample of the moth fauna of Mt. Kinabalu, Sabah, using numerical methods. *Biol. J. Linnean Soc. Lond.* **2**, 259–86.

—— (1977). *The Lepidoptera of Norfolk Island, their biogeography and ecology*. Junk, The Hague.

Holt, R. D. (1977). Predation, apparent competition, and the structure of prey communities. *Theoret. populat. Biol.* **12**, 197–229.

Holyoak, D. T. (1974). Undescribed land birds from the Cook Islands, Pacific Ocean. *Bull. Br. Orn. Club* **94**, 145–50.

Hooijer, D. A. (1970). Pleistocene south-east Asiatic pygmy stegodonts. *Nature, Lond.* **225**, 474–5.

Huffaker, C. B. and Messenger, P. B. (1964). The concept and significance of natural control. In *Biological control of insect pests and weeds* (ed. P. DeBach), pp. 74–117. Chapman and Hall, London.

Hultén, E. (1974). *Flora of Alaska and neighbouring territories* (revised edn). Stanford University Press, California.

Imbrie, J. and Imbrie, K. P. (1979). *Ice ages.* Macmillan, London.

Jalas, J. and Suominen, J. (1972). *Atlas flora europaeae*. 1. *Pteridophyta.* The Committee for Mapping the Flora of Europe and Societas Biologica Fennica Vanamo, Helsinki.

James, F. C. (1970). Geographic size variation in birds and its relationship to climate. *Ecology* **51**, 365–90.

Janzen, D. H. (1973). Sweep samples of tropical foliage insects: effects of seasons, vegetation types, elevation, time of day, and insularity. *Ecology* **54**, 687–701.

Järvinen, O. (1979). Geographical gradients of stability in European land bird communities. *Oecologia* **38**, 51–69.

Johnson, M. P. and Raven, P. H. (1970). Natural regulation of plant species diversity. *Evol. Biol.* **4**, 127–162.

Johnson, M. S., Clarke, B., and Murray, J. (1977). Genetic variation and reproductive isolation in *Partula. Evolution* **31**, 116–26.

Johnson, N. K. (1972). Origin and differentiation of the avifauna of the Channel Islands, California. *Condor* **74**, 295–315.

—— (1975). Controls of number of bird species on montane islands in the Great Basin. *Evolution* **29**, 545–67.

Johnson, W. E., Carson, H. L., Kaneshiro, K. Y., Steiner, W. W. M., and Cooper, M. M. (1975). Genetic variation in Hawaiian *Drosophila.* II. Allozymic differentiation in the *D. planitibia* subgroup. In *Isozymes.* Vol. IV. *Genetics and evolution* (ed. C. L. Markert), pp. 563–84. Academic Press, New York.

Jones, H. L. and Diamond, J. M. (1976). Short-time-base studies of turnover in breeding bird populations on the California Channel Islands. *Condor* **78**, 526–49.

Jordan, P. A., Shelton, P. C., and Allen, D. L. (1967). Numbers, turnover, and social structure of the Isle Royale wolf population. *Am. Zool.* **7**, 233–52.

Kaneshiro, K. Y. (1976). Ethological isolation and phylogeny in the *planitibia* sub-group of Hawaiian *Drosophila. Evolution* **30**, 740–5.

——, Carson, H. L., Clayton, F. E., and Heed, W. B. (1973). Niche separation in a pair of homosequential *Drosophila* species from the island of Hawaii. *Am. Nat.* **107**, 766–74.

Keast, A. (1972*a*). Adaptive evolution and shifts in niche occupation in island birds. *Biotropica* **2**, 61–75.

—— (1972*b*). Faunal elements and evolutionary patterns: some comparisons between the continental avifaunas of Africa, South America, and Australia. *Proc. XVth Int. Orn. Congr.*, pp. 594–622.

Kempton, R. A. and Taylor, L. R. (1974). Log-series and log-normal parameters as diversity discriminants for the Lepidoptera. *J. Anim. Ecol.* **43**, 381–99.

—— and —— (1978). The Q-statistic and the diversity of floras. *Nature, Lond.* **275**, 252–3.

—— and Wedderburn, R. W. M. (1978). A comparison of three measures of species diversity. *Biometrics* **34**, 25–37.

Klein, D. R. (1968). The introduction, increase and crash of reindeer on St. Matthew Island. *J. wildl. Mgmt.* **32**, 350–67.

Kloet, G. S. and Hincks, W. D. (1964–78). A check list of British insects (2nd edn). *Handbooks for the identification of British insects*, Vol. 11. Royal Entomological Society, London.

Kuschel, G. (1962). The Curculionidae of Gough Island and the relationships of the weevil fauna of the Tristan da Cunha group. *Proc. Linnean Soc. Lond.* **173**, 69–78.

—— (ed.) (1975). *Biogeography and ecology in New Zealand*. Junk, The Hague.

Lack, D. (1935). The breeding bird population of British heaths and moorlands. *J. Anim. Ecol.* **4**, 43–51.

—— (1942). Ecological features of the bird faunas of British small islands. *J. Anim. Ecol.* **11**, 9–36.

—— (1942–3). The breeding birds of Orkney. *Ibis* **84**, 461–84 and **85**, 1–27.

—— (1947). *Darwin's finches*. Cambridge University Press, Cambridge.

—— (1968a). *Ecological adaptations for breeding in birds*. Methuen, London.

—— (1968b). *Preface to the Torchbook edition of Darwin's Finches*. Smith, Gloucester, Ma.

—— (1969a). The numbers of bird species on islands. *Bird study* **16**, 193–209.

—— (1969b). Population changes in the land birds of a small island. *J. Anim. Ecol.* **38**, 211–18.

—— (1969c). Subspecies and sympatry in Darwin's finches. *Evolution* **23**, 252–63.

—— (1970). The endemic ducks of remote islands. *Wildfowl* **21**, 5–10.

—— (1971). *Ecological isolation in birds*. Blackwell Scientific Publications, Oxford.

—— (1974). *Evolution illustrated by waterfowl*. Blackwell Scientific Publications, Oxford.

—— (1976). *Island biology illustrated by the land birds of Jamaica*. Blackwell Scientific Publications, Oxford.

Lazell, J. D. (1972). The Anoles (Sauria, Iguanidae) of the Lesser Antilles. *Bull. Mus. Comp. Zool. Harv.* **143**, 1–108.

Le Sueur, F. (1976). *A natural history of Jersey*. Phillimore, London.

Leader-Williams, N. (1978). Reindeer in the Antarctic. *Nat. Environ. Res. Coun. news J.* **2**, 4–6.

Legg, G. A. (1978). A note on the diversity of World Lepidoptera. *Biol. J. Linnean Soc.* **10**, 343–7.

Leslie, P. H. (1958). A stochastic model for studying the properties of certain biological systems by numerical methods. *Biometrika* **45**, 16–31.

Lighty, R. G., Macintyre, I. G., and Stuckenrath, R. (1979). Holocene reef growth on the edge of the Florida shelf. *Nature, Lond.* **278**, 281–2.

Lister, B. C. and McMurtrie, R. E. (1976). On size variation in anoline lizards. *Am. Nat.* **110**, 311–14.

Lockley, R. M. (1947). *Letters from Skokholm*. Dent, London.

Lorence, D. H. (1978). The pteridophytes of Mauritius (Indian Ocean): ecology and distribution. *Bot. J. Linnean Soc.* **76**, 207–47.

Lussenhop, J. (1977). Urban cemeteries as bird refuges. *Condor* **79**, 456–61.

Lynch, J. F. and Johnson, N. K. (1974). Turnover and equilibria in insular avifaunas, with special reference to the California Channel Islands. *Condor* **76**, 370–84.

MacArthur, R. H. (1972). *Geographical ecology*. Harper and Row, New York.

——, Diamond, J. M., and Karr, J. R. (1972). Density compensation in island faunas. *Ecology* **53**, 330–42.

——, MacArthur, J., MacArthur, D., and MacArthur, A. (1973). The effect of island area on population densities. *Ecology* **54**, 657–8.

—— and Wilson, E. O. (1963). An equilibrium theory of insular zoogeography. *Evolution* **17**, 373–87.

—— and Wilson, E. O. (1967). *The theory of island biogeography*. Princeton University Press, Princeton.

Marshall, L. G. and Hecht, M. K. (1978). Faunal equilibrium? Mammalian faunal dynamics of the great American interchange: an alternative explanation (with a reply to an alternative interpretation by S. D. Webb). *Paleobiology* **4**, 203–9.

Martin, P. S. (1973). The discovery of America. *Science, N.Y.* **179**, 969–974.

—— and Wright, H. E. Jr. (ed.) (1967). *Pleistocene extinctions*. Yale University Press, New Haven, Conn.

May, R. M. (1974). General introduction. In *Ecological stability* (ed. M. B. Usher and M. H. Williamson), pp. 1–14. Chapman and Hall, London.

—— (1975). Patterns of species abundance and diversity. In *Ecology and evolution of communities* (ed. M. L. Cody and J. M. Diamond), pp. 81–120. Belknap Press of Harvard University Press, Cambridge, Ma.

Mayr, E. (1942). *Systematics and the origin of species*. Columbia University Press, New York.

—— (1954). Change of genetic environment and evolution. In *Evolution as a process* (ed. J. S. Huxley, A. C. Hardy, and E. B. Ford), pp. 157–80. Allen and Unwin, London.

—— (1963). *Animal species and evolution*. Belknap Press of Harvard University Press, Cambridge, Ma.

—— (1969). Bird speciation in the tropics. *Biol. J. Linnean Soc.* **1**, 1–17.

—— (1976). *Evolution and the diversity of life*. Belknap Press of the Harvard University Press, Cambridge, Ma.

—— and Short, L. L. (1970). Species taxa of North American birds. *Publs. Nuttall Orn. Club* **9**, 1–127.

Mech, L. D. (1966). *The wolves of Isle Royale*. United States National Park Service, Fauna series, 7.

—— (1970). *The wolf*. Natural History Press, Garden City, N.Y.

Meggers, B. J., Ayensu, E. S., and Duckworth, W. D. (ed.) (1973). *Tropical forest ecosystems in Africa and South America: a comparative review.* Smithsonian Institution Press, Washington.

Mitchell, F. (1976). *The Irish landscape.* Collins, London.

Mitchell, G. F. (1977). Raised beaches and sea-levels. In *British quaternary studies* (ed. F. W. Shotton), pp. 169–86. Clarendon Press, Oxford.

Molnar, P., Atwater, T., Mammerickx, J., and Smith, S. M. (1975). Magnetic anomalies, bathymetry and the tectonic evolution of the South Pacific since the late Cretaceous. *Geophys. J. R. Astr. Soc.* **40**, 383–420.

Montgomery, S. L. (1975). Comparative breeding site ecology and the adaptive radiation of picture-winged *Drosophila* (Diptera: Drosophilidae) in Hawaii. *Proc. Hawaii ent. Soc.* **22**, 65–102.

Moore, N. W. and Hooper, M. D. (1975). On the number of bird species in British woods. *Biol. Conserv.* **8**, 239–50.

Moreau, R. E. (1966). *The bird faunas of Africa and its islands.* Academic Press, New York.

Murton, R. K. (1971). *Man and birds.* Collins, London.

Nei, M. (1972). Genetic distance between populations. *Am. Nat.* **196**, 283–292.

Nicoll, M. J. (1909). *Three voyages of a naturalist.* Witherby, London.

Niering, W. A. (1963). Terrestrial ecology of Kapingamaringi atoll, Caroline islands. *Ecol. Monogr.* **33**, 131–60.

Olson, S. L. (1973*a*). Evolution of the rails of the South Atlantic islands (Aves: Rallidae). *Smithson. Contr. Zool.* **152**, 1–53.

—— (1973*b*). A classification of the Rallidae. *Wilson Bull.* **85**, 381–416.

—— (1975). Paleornithology of St. Helena Island, South Atlantic Ocean. *Smithson. Contr. Paleobiol.* **23**, 1–43.

—— (1977). Additional notes on subfossil remains from Ascension Island. *Ibis* **119**, 37–43.

Parsons, P. A. (1977). Lek behaviour in *Drosophila* (*Hirtodrosophila*) *polypori* Malloch—an Australian rainforest species. *Evolution* **31**, 223–5.

Perring, F. H. and Walters, S. M. (1962). *Atlas of the British flora.* Nelson, London.

Philbrick, R. N. (ed.) (1967). *Proceedings of the symposium on the biology of the California Islands.* Santa Barbara Botanic Garden, Ca.

Pielou, E. C. (1975). *Ecological diversity.* Wiley, New York.

Power, D. M. (1972). Numbers of bird species on the California islands. *Evolution* **26**, 451–63.

—— (1975). Similarity among avifaunas of the Galapagos islands. *Ecology* **56**, 616–26.

Preston, F. W. (1948). The commonness, and rarity, of species. *Ecology* **29**, 254–83.

—— (1962). The canonical distribution of commonness and rarity. *Ecology* **43**, 185–215, 410–32.

Rand, A. S. (1969). Competitive exclusion among Anoles (Sauria: Iguanidae) on small islands in the West Indies. *Breviora* **319**, 1–16.

Raup, D. M. and Stanley, S. M. (1978). *Principles of paleontology* (2nd edn). Freeman, San Francisco.

Raven, P. H. and Axelrod, D. I. (1972). Plate tectonics and Australasian paleobiogeography. *Science, N.Y.* **176**, 1379–85.

Richardson, R. H. (1974). Effects of dispersal, habitat selection and competition on a speciation pattern of *Drosophila* endemic to Hawaii. In *Genetic mechanisms of speciation in insects* (ed. M. J. D. White), pp. 140–64. Australia and N.Z. Book Co., Sydney.

Richter-Dyn, N. and Goel, N. S. (1972). On the extinction of a colonizing species. *Theor. populat. Biol.* **3**, 406–33.

Ricklefs, R. F. and Cox, G. W. (1972). Taxon cycles in the West Indian avifauna. *Am. Nat.* **106**, 195–219.

—— and —— (1978). Stage of taxon cycle, habitat distribution, and population density in the avifauna of the West Indies. *Am. Nat.* **112**, 875–95.

Ripley, S. D. and Bond, G. M. (1966). The birds of Socotra and Abd-el-Kuri. *Smithson. misc. Collns* **151**, 1–37.

Rogers, J. S. (1972). *Measures of genetic similarity and genetic distance.* University of Texas publications **7213**, 145–53.

Rothstein, S. I. (1973). The niche-variation model—is it valid? *Am. Nat.* **107**, 598–620.

Roughgarden, J. (1972). Evolution of niche width. *Am. Nat.* **106**, 683–718.

Rusterholz, K. A. and Howe, R. W. (1979). Species–area relations of birds on small islands in a Minnesota lake. *Evolution* **33**, 468–77.

Scheffer, V. B. (1951). The rise and fall of a reindeer herd. *Scient. mon.* **73**, 356–62.

Schlanger, S. O. and Gillett, G. W. (1976). A geological perspective of the upland biota of Laysan atoll (Hawaiian Islands). *Biol. J. Linnean Soc.* **8**, 205–16.

Schoener, T. W. (1968). Sizes of feeding territories among birds. *Ecology* **49**, 123–41.

—— (1976). The species–area relation within archipelagos: models and evidence from island land birds. *Proc. 16th Int. Ornithol. Congr.* 629–42.

Scott, J. A. (1972). Biogeography of Antillean butterflies. *Biotropica* **4**, 32–45.

Selander, R. K. (1966). Sexual dimorphism and differential niche utilization in birds. *Condor* **68**, 113–51.

Sepkoski, J. J. Jr. (1978). A kinetic model of phanerozoic taxonomic diversity. I. Analysis of marine orders. *Paleobiology* **4**, 223–51.

Sharrock, J. T. R. (1976). *The atlas of breeding birds in Britain and Ireland.* Poyser, Berkhamsted.

—— (1979). Did the tree pipit formerly nest in Ireland? *Br. birds* **72**, 41–42.

Shepard, F. P. (1977). *Geological oceanography.* Heinemann, London.

Sibley, C. G. (1970). A comparative study of the egg-white proteins of passerine birds. *Bull. Peabody Mus. nat. Hist.* **32**, 1–131.

Simberloff, D. S. (1969). Experimental zoogeography of islands: a model for insular colonization. *Ecology* **50**, 296–314.

—— (1970). Taxonomic diversity of island biotas. *Evolution* **24**, 23–47.

—— (1976a). Trophic structure determination and equilibrium in an arthropod community. *Ecology* **57**, 398–8.

—— (1976*b*). Experimental zoogeography of islands: effects of island size. *Ecology* **57**, 629–48.

—— (1976*c*). Species turnover and equilibrium island biogeography. *Science, N.Y.* **194**, 572–8.

—— (1978). Using island biogeographic distributions to determine if colonization is stochastic. *Am. Nat.* **112**, 713–26.

Simpson, G. G. (1940). Mammals and land bridges. *J. Wash. Acad. Sci.* **30**, 137–63.

—— (1944). *Tempo and mode in evolution.* Columbia University Press, New York.

—— (1950). History of the fauna of Latin America. *Am. Scient.* **38**, 361–89.

—— (1964). Species density of North American recent mammals. *Syst. Zool.* **13**, 57–73.

—— (1969). The first three billion years of community evolution. *Brookhaven symp. Biol.* **22**, 162–77.

Slud, P. (1967). The birds of Cocos Island (Costa Rica). *Bull. Am. Mus. nat. Hist.* **134**, 261–96.

—— (1976). Geographic and climatic relationships of avifaunas with special reference to comparative distribution in the Neotropics. *Smithson. Contr. zool.* **212**, 1–149.

Smith, C. A. B. (1977). A note on genetic distance. *Ann. hum. Genet.* **40**, 463–479.

Smith, H. G., Hardy, P., Leith, I. M. Spaull, V. W., and Twelves, E. L. (1974). A biological survey of St. Paul's rocks in the equatorial Atlantic Ocean. *Biol. J. Linnean Soc.* **6**, 89–96.

Snow, D. W. (ed.), (1978). *An atlas of speciation in African non-passerine birds.* British Museum (Natural History), London.

Sondaar, P. Y. (1976). Insularity and its effect on mammal evolution. In *Major patterns in vertebrate evolution* (ed. M. K. Hecht, P. C. Goody, and B. M. Hecht), pp. 671–707. Plenum, New York.

Soulé, M. (1970). A comment on the letter by Van Valen and Grant. *Am. Nat.* **104**, 590–1.

—— (1971). The variation problem: the gene flow-variation hypothesis. *Taxon* **20**, 37–50.

Southwood, T. R. E. (1978). *Ecological methods* (2nd edn). Chapman and Hall, London.

Spieth, H. T. (1966). *Courtship behaviour of endemic Hawaiian Drosophila.* University of Texas publication **6615**, 245–313.

—— (1968). Evolutionary implications of sexual behaviour in *Drosophila*. *Evol. Biol.* **2**, 157–93.

—— (1974). Mating behaviour and evolution of Hawaiian *Drosophila*. In *Genetic mechanisms of speciation in insects* (ed. M. J. D. White), pp. 94–101. Australia and N.Z. Book Co., Sydney.

Stalker, H. D. (1972). Intergroup phylogenies in *Drosophila* as determined by comparisons of salivary banding patterns. *Genetics* **70**, 457–74.

Stearns, S. C. (1977). The evolution of life history traits: a critique of the theory and a review of the data. *Annu. Rev. Ecol. Syst.* **8**, 145–71.

Steers, J. A. and Stoddart, D. R. (1977). The origin of fringing reefs, barrier reefs, and atolls. In *Biology and geology of coral reefs* (ed. O. A. Jones and R. Endean), Vol. 4, pp. 21–57. Academic Press, New York.

Stehli, F. G. and Wells, J. W. (1971). Diversity and age patterns in hermatypic corals. *Syst. Zool.* **20**, 115–26.

Stone, A., Sabrosky, C. W., Wirth, W. W., Foote, R. H., and Coulson, J. R. (1965). *A catalog of the Diptera of America north of Mexico.* U.S. Department of Agriculture, Washington, D.C.

Stonehouse, B. (1960). *Wideawake island.* Hutchinson, London.

Synge, F. M. (1977). Records of sea levels during the late Devensian. *Phil. Trans. R. Soc.* **B280**, 211–28.

Taylor, L. R. (1978). Bates, Williams, Hutchinson—a variety of diversities. *Symp. R. Entomol. Soc. Lond.* **9**, 1–18.

Taylor, R. J. and Regal, P. J. (1978). The peninsular effect on species diversity and the biogeography of Baja California. *Am. Nat.* **112**, 583–93.

Terborgh, J. (1973). Chance, habitat and dispersal in the distribution of birds in the West Indies. *Evolution* **27**, 338–49.

—— (1977). Bird species diversity on an Andean elevational gradient. *Ecology* **58**, 1007–19.

Thomas, W. L. (1963). The variety of physical environments among Pacific islands. In *Man's place in the island ecosystem* (ed. F. R. Fosberg), pp. 7–37. Bishop Museum Press, Honolulu.

Thomson, A. L. (ed.) (1964). *A new dictionary of birds.* Nelson, London for British Ornithologists' Union.

Thornton, I. (1971). *Darwin's islands: a natural history of the Galapagos.* Natural History Press, Garden City, N.Y.

Throckmorton, L. H. (1966). *The relationship of the endemic Hawaiian Drosophilidae.* University of Texas publication **6615**, 335–96.

—— (1975). The phylogeny, ecology and geography of *Drosophila.* In R. C. King (ed.) *Handbook of genetics,* Vol. 3, pp. 421–69. Plenum Press, New York.

—— (1977). *Drosophila* systematics and biochemical evolution. *Annu. Rev. Ecol. Syst.* **8**, 235–54.

Timofeeff-Ressovsky, N.V., Vorontsov, N. N., and Yablokov, A. V. (1977). *An outline of evolutionary theory.* Academy of Sciences, Moscow (in Russian).

Tordoff, H. B. (1954). Relationships in the New World nine-primaried oscines. *Auk* **71**, 273–84.

Tsacas, L. and Cogan, B. H. (1976). Drosophilidae. La Faune Terrestre de l'Île de Sainte-Hélène. *Ann. Musée r. Afr. cent. Sér 8vo* **215**, 82–95.

Turrill, W. B. (1948). *British plant life.* Collins, London.

—— (1964). *Joseph Dalton Hooker.* Nelson, London.

Udvardy, M. D. F. (1975). A classification of the biogeographical provinces of the world. International Union for Conservation of Nature and Natural Resources occasional paper 18.

U.S. Committee for the Global Atmospheric Research Program (1975). *Understanding climatic change.* National Academy of Sciences, Washington, D.C.

Uyeda, S. (1978). *The new view of the Earth.* Freeman, San Francisco.

Vagvolgyi, J. (1975). Body size, aerial dispersal, and origin of the Pacific land snail fauna. *Syst. Zool.* **24**, 465–88.

Val, F. C. (1977). Genetic analysis of the morphological differences between two interfertile species of Hawaiian *Drosophila*. *Evolution* **31**, 611–29.

van Balgooy, M. M. J. (1969). A study on the diversity of island floras. *Blumea* **17**, 139–78.

—— (1971). Plant geography of the Pacific. *Blumea suppl.* **6**, 1–217.

Van Valen, L. (1965). Morphological variation and width of ecological niche. *Am. Nat.* **99**, 377–90.

Vaurie, C. (1972). *Tibet and its birds*. Witherby, London.

Venables, L. S. V. and Venables, U. M. (1955). *Birds and mammals of Shetland*. Oliver and Boyd, Edinburgh.

Vevers, H. G. (1948). The natural history of Ailsa Craig. *New Nat.* **1**, 115–21.

Voous, K. H. (1960). *Atlas of European birds*. Nelson, Edinburgh.

Walters, S. M. (1978). British endemics. In *Essays in plant taxonomy* (ed. H. E. Street), pp. 263–74. Academic Press, London.

Warington, K. (1958). *The Park Grass plots at Rothamsted* 1856–1949. Rothamsted Experimental Station, Harpenden.

Watson, G. E. (1964). Ecology and evolution of passerine birds on the islands of the Aegean Sea. Yale University, Ph.D. dissertation. (Dissertation microfilm 65-1956).

—— (1975). *Birds of the Antarctic and Sub-Antarctic*. American Geophysical Union, Washington, D.C.

Wheeler, M. and Takada, H. (1966). *The nearctic and neotropical species of* Scaptomyza *Hardy (Diptera: Drosophilidae)*. University of Texas publication **6615**, 37–78.

Whittaker, R. H. (1969). Evolution of diversity in plant communities. *Brookhaven Symp. Biol.* **22**, 178–96.

Whittaker, R. H. and Goodman, D. (1979). Classifying species according to their demographic strategy. 1. Population fluctuations and environmental heterogeneity. *Am. Nat.* **113**, 185–200.

White, M. J. D. (1978). *Modes of speciation*. Freeman, San Francisco.

Whitehead, D. R. and Jones, C. E. (1969). Small islands and the equilibrium theory of insular biogeography. *Evolution* **23**, 171–9.

Wickens, G. E. (1979). Speculations on seed dispersal and the flora of the Aldabran archipelago. *Phil. Trans. R. Soc.* **B286**, 85–97.

Williams, C. B. (1964). *Patterns in the balance of nature*. Academic Press, New York.

Williams, E. E. (1969). The ecology of colonization as seen in the zoogeography of anoline lizards on small islands. *Q. Rev. Biol.* **44**, 345–89.

—— (1972). The origin of faunas. Evolution of lizard congeners in a complex island fauna: a trial analysis. *Evol. Biol.* **6**, 47–89.

Williamson, G. B. (1978). A comment on equilibrium turnover rates for islands. *Am. Nat.* **112**, 241–3.

Williamson, K. and Boyd, J. M. (1960). *St. Kilda summer*. Hutchinson, London.

Williamson, M. (1972). *The analysis of biological populations*. Edward Arnold, London.

—— (1973). Species diversity in ecological communities. In *The mathematical theory of the dynamics of biological populations* (ed. M. S. Bartlett and R. W. Hiorns), pp. 325–35. Academic Press, London.

Wilson, E. O. (1959). Adaptive shift and dispersal in a tropical ant fauna. *Evolution* **13**, 122–44.

—— (1961). The nature of the taxon cycle in the Melanesian ant fauna. *Am. Nat.* **95**, 169–93.

—— (1969). The species equilibrium. *Brookhaven symp. Biol.* **22**, 38–47.

—— (1975). *Sociobiology*. The Belknap Press of Harvard University Press, Cambridge, Ma.

——, Eisner, T., Briggs, W. R., Dickerson, R. E., Metzenberg, R. L., O'Brien, R. D., Susman, M., and Boggs, W. E. (1973). *Life on earth*. Sinauer Associates, Stamford, Conn.

Wyatt-Smith, J. (1953). The vegetation of Jarak Island, Straits of Malacca. *J. Ecol.* **41**, 207–25.

Yang, S. Y., Soulé, M., and Gorman, G. C. (1974). *Anolis* lizards of the eastern Caribbean: a case study in evolution. I. Genetic relationships, Phylogeny, and colonization sequence of the *roquet* group. *Syst. Zool.* **23**, 387–99.

Yoon, J. S., Resch, K., Wheeler, M. R., and Richardson, R. H. (1975). Evolution in Hawaiian Drosophilidae: Chromosomal phylogeny of the *Drosophila crassifemur* complex. *Evolution* **29**, 249–56.

Zimmerman, E. C. (1948). *Insects of Hawaii*. Vol. 1. *Introduction*. University of Hawaii Press, Honolulu.

—— (1958). Three hundred species of *Drosophila* in Hawaii? A challenge to geneticists and evolutionists. *Evolution* **12**, 557–8.

—— (1972). Adaptive radiation in Hawaii with special reference to insects. *Biotropica* **2**, 32–8.

Author index

Subject index

Taxonomic index

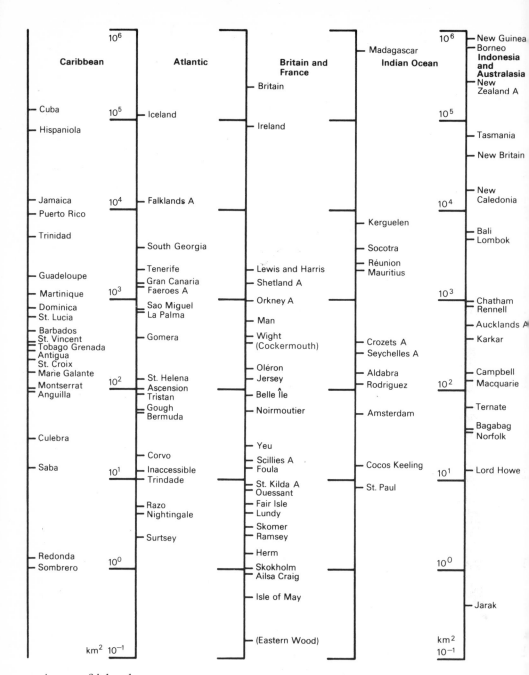

Caribbean	Atlantic	Britain and France	Indian Ocean	Indonesia and Australasia
			10^6	10^6 New Guinea / Borneo
			Madagascar	Indonesia and Australasia
		Britain		New Zealand A
Cuba — 10^5	Iceland			10^5
Hispaniola	Ireland			Tasmania
				New Britain
Jamaica — 10^4	Falklands A			New Caledonia 10^4
Puerto Rico			Kerguelen	Bali
Trinidad	South Georgia		Socotra	Lombok
	Tenerife	Lewis and Harris	Réunion	
Guadeloupe	Gran Canaria	Shetland A	Mauritius	
Martinique — 10^3	Faeroes A	Orkney A		10^3 Chatham
Dominica	Sao Miguel			Rennell
St. Lucia	La Palma	Man		Aucklands A
Barbados	Gomera	Wight (Cockermouth)	Crozets A	Karkar
St. Vincent			Seychelles A	
Tobago Grenada		Oléron		
Antigua		Jersey	Aldabra	Campbell
St. Croix	St. Helena — 10^2		Rodriguez — 10^2	Macquarie
Marie Galante	Ascension	Belle Île		
Montserrat	Tristan	Noirmoutier	Amsterdam	Ternate
Anguilla	Gough			Bagabag
	Bermuda			Norfolk
Culebra		Yeu		
	Corvo	Scillies A	Cocos Keeling	Lord Howe
Saba — 10^1	Inaccessible	Foula		10^1
	Trindade	St. Kilda A	St. Paul	
		Ouessant		
	Razo	Fair Isle		
	Nightingale	Lundy		
		Skomer		
	Surtsey	Ramsey		
		Herm		
Redonda — 10^0		Skokholm		10^0
Sombrero		Ailsa Craig		
		Isle of May		Jarak
km^2 10^{-1}		(Eastern Wood)	km^2 10^{-1}	

Areas of islands

The sizes of islands and archipelagos (marked A) shown on a logarithmic scale. Most of the islands discussed in the text are included, but many of those appearing just as dots in figures, as in Fig. 3.3, are excluded. Some largish islands round Britain and North America which are not mentioned in the text are included for comparison. In the Atlantic set, Sao Miguel is the largest of the Azores, Corvo the smallest,